THE MGM EFFECT

THE MGM EFFECT

HOW A HOLLYWOOD STUDIO CHANGED THE WORLD

STEVEN BINGEN

WITH MARC WANAMAKER, BISON ARCHIVES

Essex, Connecticut

An imprint of Globe Pequot, the trade division of The Rowman & Littlefield Publishing Group, Inc.
4501 Forbes Blvd., Ste. 200
Lanham, MD 20706
www.rowman.com

86-90 Paul Street, London EC2A 4NE

Distributed by NATIONAL BOOK NETWORK

British Library Cataloguing in Publication Information available

Library of Congress Cataloging-in-Publication Data

Names: Bingen, Steven, author.
Title: The MGM effect : how a Hollywood studio changed the world / Steven
    Bingen.
Description: Guilford, Connecticut : Lyons Press, [2022] | Includes
    bibliographical references and index.
Identifiers: LCCN 2021060035 (print) | LCCN 2021060036 (ebook) | ISBN
    9781493060542 (cloth) | ISBN 9781493067961 (epub)
Subjects: LCSH: Metro-Goldwyn-Mayer—Influence. | Motion picture
    studios—California—Los Angeles. | Motion picture industry—United
    States.
Classification: LCC PN1999.M4 B563 2022 (print) | LCC PN1999.M4 (ebook) |
    DDC 384/.80979494—dc23/eng/20220310
LC record available at https://lccn.loc.gov/2021060035
LC ebook record available at https://lccn.loc.gov/2021060036

∞™ The paper used in this publication meets the minimum requirements of American National Standard for Information Sciences—Permanence of Paper for Printed Library Materials, ANSI/ NISO Z39.48-1992.

Contents

CONTENTS

Introduction

Arguably, that roaring lion, that Metro Goldwyn Mayer (MGM) emblem that has opened thousands of movies since 1924, is the most recognized corporate symbol in the world—not just in the entertainment industry it should be noted, but of any industry, anywhere, in the history of human civilization.

This is all particularly surprising since MGM has been a competitively insignificant force in the motion picture industry for nearly as long as it, colossus-like, once completely dominated that industry. In recent years MGM's market share among US film studios has been less than 2 percent. The Walt Disney Company, a mere irritant during MGM's heyday, by contrast, has controlled around 20 percent of this same market during that same period!

These numbers make it even more astonishing that in a 2005 market survey, when asked to name one US film studio, a whopping 45 percent of the public picked MGM first, making it by far the most recognized single brand in

Bison Archives

entertainment. Disney by contrast, in the same survey, was identified by less than 15 percent of those polled.

Most consumers are thought to have a comparatively short collective memory regarding the brands they buy. Does anyone remember, for example, the name of the type of paper towels they consumed last year? Or the company that manufactures their mouthwash or multivitamins? And yet, paradoxically, like a sci-fi telescope that operates in reverse, MGM seems to loom ever larger in popular culture the further away from its long-ago heyday we happen to recede.

This is all particularly surprising because much of MGM's cinematic legacy grows less accessible, and quainter, to modern audiences as the decades tick by. Time and cancel culture have now eroded much of the once nearly universal public adoration long lavished on the previously unassailable *Gone with the Wind*. Even *The Wizard of Oz*, the studios other once-believed ageless gift to the world is no longer broadcast on network television.

Undoubtably part of this odd affection many still feel for the studio is nostalgia, a longing for a long-gone, perhaps even largely mythical Hollywood Shangri-La among rapidly graying baby boomers. But it certainly goes beyond that. For example, in 1987, Disney, which remember, now controls almost a quarter of the entire motion picture industry, instead of using only their own name, paid MGM to license their logo for an amusement park in Orlando, Florida. Surely, middle-aged film buffs were not the target demographic for that venture?

Likewise, Leo, the omnipotent and ageless MGM lion, now presides not only over movies alone but also over thirty world-class resorts and is, or has been, a recognized leader in the fields of real estate, theme parks, casinos, consumer products, and even airlines all around the world!

But how did this happen? How did MGM evolve from a film company, which, it should be mentioned originally was Frankensteined together through a most uneasy and contentious merger, to the inexplicable creation of a business model still relevant today for the entire US film industry—and as one of the world's most recognizable and resilient brands?

In his chapter on MGM in his book *50 Companies That Changed the World*, Howard Rothman sites that during its heyday "MGM ruled Hollywood and Hollywood ruled the world." But Rothman is also astute enough to note that what makes a company outstanding is that it also somehow changes us. This is an important part of our story as well. Therefore, although the studio's tempestuous corporate history will be dealt with, the studio's cultural history, meaning its ultimate impact on its fans and detractors and employees and audiences and obsessives, and how that impact has been reflected onto our lives and into other art forms, will also be scrutinized between these covers in some depth.

This examination of MGM from beyond its gates, from the outside looking in, if you will, has never really been attempted before. Actually, as far as I can ascertain, this tact has not been grappled with in any depth for any other individual company ever.

A few more words are in order about the shape and form that this book has taken. The truth is everything about MGM is fraught with quicksand. Fans and critics and historians and survivors and victims of the studio all still argue about virtually everything relating to it. For example, many modern writers now consider much of the company's early product to be dated and less "interesting"—whatever that means—than comparable films made by less commercially successful studios like Warner Bros., which after all, had its gangsters, and Universal, which had its monsters. Consequently, many who readily admit to MGM's being Hollywood's premiere studio during its golden age still don't happen think much of that studio's actual product.

Actually, the truth is that MGM made its *own* horror films and its *own* crime dramas. And many of these films, in their time, found broad favor with audiences too. If current taste, and political correctness, doesn't concur with these audience's opinions and with these film's successes, that only proves that MGM's product was perfectly designed to suit public taste at that time. What more could anyone want of a provider of "popular" entertainment? Debating quality or artistic merit then, and by today's standards yet, is not really the point. Although many a so-called film historian would wish it to be so.

Another issue is the vast and often contradictory amount that has already been written about the studio and its stars. There has been so much ink and broadband space devoted to the subject that it could now be debated whether MGM's continuing presence in popular culture is actually a cause or an effect of all of this attention. But for good or ill, any book about the MGM effect does have to deal with all this material in some sort of reasonably comprehensive way. The solution, for me, has been to go with a few representative offshoots of MGM-centric literature rather than to try to document, for example, every bloody blow ever recorded in the fan magazines regarding MGM stars Debbie Reynolds and Elizabeth Taylor in their fight over Eddie Fisher (although, note to you completists out there, Liz and Debbie both lost).

Therefore, the figure I have thus chosen to represent the studio's eventful gallop through popular culture, in most cases at least, has been Louis B. Mayer, the studio's mercurial leader for the company's phenomenally successful first quarter century.

Mayer and, by definition, MGM have, after all, taken on an entire second life in popular culture. Mayer has been portrayed in movies, for example, probably more times than Jesus Christ or Adolf Hitler. From a 1925 studio promotional short, in which the producer played himself, to 2019's *Judy*, where Oscar-winner Renée Zellweger's Judy Garland grapples with both L.B. and with her own demons and beyond, the notorious Louie B. has been used as a tool to illustrate the glories and the evils of classic Hollywood. In the #MeToo era, Mayer's name has even been evoked (unfairly, it turns out) alongside that of Harvey Weinstein, as the sort of powerful, predatory male our culture now needs to rid itself of. So, he will here serve as our primary avatar and tour guide through MGM's cultural history.

Some fans, of course, will probably insist that this cultural history only reference "classic MGM," meaning product made by, and preferably at, the Culver City studio, circa 1924–1959. I get that. The romantic tug of glamour and nostalgia for this era is a big part of our story, and it's been a big part of my life. But the story I want to tell needs to be, and is, much bigger than that. I do hope that all of my "classic MGM" friends will still follow along with me for the rest of the story. You might just learn something about that story you didn't know.

There has also been a great deal of largely unnecessary contention and debate among fans as to what exactly constitutes an MGM movie at all. For the purpose of this discussion, I've chosen to include anything and everything that the studio has ever produced, released, acquired, or foreclosed on. Therefore, films that the studio made but no longer controls the rights to, like *The Wizard of Oz*, or that they distributed but no longer control the rights to, like *Gone with the Wind,* or acquired the rights to through mergers or library acquisitions, like the James Bond, *Rocky*, and *Pink Panther* titles all play a part in the company's history, and so will play a part in our story too.

For heaven's sake, the name Metro Goldwyn Mayer itself can be contentious. Many fans of classic MGM now insist that the name should only be abbreviated in print as "M-G-M," with a smaller faction contentiously preferring the alternate "M.G.M." I've got a friend in the pro-hyphen camp who wrote an MGM-heavy volume recently and, to his horror, discovered that he could whittle down the page count dramatically just by taking out these hyphens. I've taken them out too, in both the company's entire name and its abbreviation, except when it's quoted or referenced as such, but my reasons are less practical in that the name is not hyphenated, and seldom has been, in the opening logo *on-screen*. It's also worth noting that the current, contemporary iteration of the company does not use them, except legally. They should know, shouldn't they?

Bison Archives

To understand the studio's effect on our overall cultural history, the history of MGM itself needs to be studied, at least to a certain degree. Therefore, the first part of the book is a chronological look at the company's romantic and rocky first (hopefully) one-hundred-odd years. What this part of the book is not, though, is yet another study of the films and the stars who dominated the studio and its times. That is ground that has been microscopically well-covered before and by those better able to do so than I. Although those works *about* those films and their makers and their romantic pull are going to be accounted for later in these pages themselves.

What this section of this book is, rather, is a *corporate* history of MGM and those who influenced, for better or worse, its growth and decline. Please note that if the musical chairs parade of sometimes clueless and sometimes devious executives trying to steer the ship in the company's later decades is confusing, there is an appendix included at the end of the book listing all of the studio CEOs and production heads for your convenience and incredulity.

Some of this has been covered before as well but almost always the emphasis has been exclusively on the "golden years," with little attention paid to what came after. This is odd because this dramatic era of decline and desecration, all largely unchronicled, has now lasted longer than the studio's salad days did. The decline and fall of the Roman Empire after all, received a six-volume literary summation. MGM's somewhat similar topple from Mount Olympus does not warrant that, at least not here—if only because that ultimately is not the primary goal of this book. But it should be noted that in this section, for good or ill, Kirk Kerkorian warrants as much ink as Mayer, although Mayer certainly does cast the longer shadow over our culture, which will be examined in part II.

Part II? Here I will attempt to grapple with MGM's place in the larger world, at how the studio has been portrayed on film (by itself and by other studios), on television, in books, comics, song, parody, and prose. Likewise, MGM's branding outside Hollywood will be examined for the first time—with comparative and quizzical visits to Las Vegas casinos, odd theme park attractions, into the lairs of Italian Mafiosos, through interactive worlds, and even through a most decadent flight aboard MGM Grand Airlines, all scheduled here as part of the agenda. All of this, as well as the company's perhaps unique-in-all-the-world ripple effect through the twentieth century and beyond, and on its ever-fervent fan base is fair game. All of these properties and all of us, after all, are now part of the MGM effect.

So, hang on tight, because with MGM, one quickly realizes that the product, as romantic as it is, is perhaps less pertinent than the effect that product has had on us.

Despite what you may think, it was never just about the movies.

Steven Bingen
Hollywood, California, 2022

PART 1

1
Dedications and Dedication

The corkscrew origins of what would become Metro Goldwyn Mayer (MGM) began with Marcus Loew, an enterprising son of Viennese emigrants. Born in New York in 1870, Loew was making a decent enough living selling fur coats when, in 1904, he met Adolph Zukor. Zukor, a future founder of Paramount Studios, for some reason enlisted Loew as a partner in a hardscrabble penny arcade company. Even before their contentious partnership would come to a close, both Loew and Zukor discovered that the short films that their audiences could view in these arcades—by bending over

uncomfortably and looking into a wooden cabinet, could also be seen by more people, and with significantly more profit, if projected on a wall in a theater or lecture hall.

At the time, Joseph and Nicholas Schenck were operating an amusement park across the river in New Jersey, which they had hopefully titled Paradise Park, and where they had built what was reportedly the largest Ferris wheel in the Northeast. The brothers had originally immigrated from Russia in 1892; Joseph, the older by four years, had been born in 1876. It's often been claimed in print that Loew, largely divested of Zukor by this time, met the Schencks in 1909 while

Marcus Loew (previous page) and Joseph Schenck represented two divergent types of studio executives in the 1920s. Loew preferred the hands-off approach, wielding power from boardrooms on the East Coast, while Joseph (quite unlike his younger brother Nicholas) advocated for a more hands-on approach. Here those hands are seen on that of his wife, actress Norma Talmadge in 1926. *Photofest*

projecting his movies at their fairgrounds. But author Scott Eyman tells us that Loew and the brothers had some sort of business connection going back to 1906 at least. So, we'll go with that version.

However, the three of them aligned, together the trio quickly realized that ownership of actual theaters, which were still mixing little movies with vaudeville acts then, could itself be lucrative, especially because immigrants and lower-income families, aside from church and sports, had virtually no other entertainment options to swallow up their free time and disposable income.

Joseph Schenck was originally the partner responsible for creating these movies to amuse the audiences in these theaters. Some of their earliest films, made in a New York warehouse, starred future star Norma Talmadge, whom he married in 1916. Joseph, however, took his wife and his fledgling operation, independently, to Los Angeles in 1921. Left largely without a means of production again, the situation made it obvious to Loew and to Nicholas that a more consistent and mechanized way of producing product internally would be required if the Loews Theater chain, as it was being called, were to prosper.

Metro, or Metropolitan Pictures, had itself been founded as a film booking agency at the end of 1914 in Jacksonville, Florida, although, as a production company, the operation also had facilities on Cahuenga Boulevard in Hollywood, California, which even then was where the production end of the business seemed to be migrating to. This little factory, which would later be where series like *I Love Lucy* would be shot, is still there and is now known as Red Studios. Loew bought the company and this studio in 1920 for $3.1 million, presumably ensuring a way to keep what had happened with independent brother Joseph from ever happening again.

It is one of those only in the movies, or only of the movies, little ironies that one of the executives who had formally been associated with Metro Pictures was named Louis B. Mayer.

But was that even his name? Although he would soon be the highest paid executive in the US, the name and the person sporting that name is a complete and completely American invention. None of his biographers can tell us exactly what this man's name really was, when his birthday occurred, or what soil exactly he had sprung from.

Let's start with that moniker. "Lazar Meir" or a variation is usually given as the man's actual name, although that surname, as one of his daughters admitted, also "could well have been Baer . . . or Meir." So, she concludes by admitting that "only God knows."[1]

What is known is that shortly after the family emigrated from the Russian empire, now Ukraine, that family did, apparently, and randomly, start to call themselves

"Mayer," first, perhaps, in England (1886), then in New York (1887), and finally, Canada (circa 1891), by which time Louis, whatever his name really was, was already calling himself Louis. Likewise mysterious is this Louis's seemingly always present middle initial; that letter "B" is sometimes referred to as standing for "Burt," although, again, no one, not even the family, maybe especially not the family, has any idea why that should be the case. Maybe Mayer just liked the sound of "L.B." because those oft-used initials would soon become a second first name for him.

Somewhat endearingly, Mayer also liked brag that, like showman George M. Cohan, he was born on July 4. But like Cohan (who, sadly, was born on July 3, 1878), even this is apparently apocryphal. Although, again, who can say? It is known that in the 1901 Canadian census, his father gave his son's birthdate as July 12, 1884, although the July 4 date, but now pushed ahead to 1885, has also been suggested, occasionally, by other family members.

Oh, and there are also, just to add to the confusion, at least three different Ukrainian/Russian villages with entirely different and, of course, confusingly conflicting names in each language that have been suggested as the spot where that birth actually occurred, whenever it may have actually occurred. And whatever the resultant child was then so named.

The "Mayers" became naturalized Canadian citizens in 1892, and Louis's father Jacob, (accept that name too, at your own peril) became a hardscrabble scrap metal dealer and peddler. But like Loew and the Schencks, the younger Mayer sought opportunity and success, not in hauling lead and old clothes up and down the dirty streets but, improbably enough, in the theater.

In 1907 Mayer, now married and living in Boston, opened his first theater, a run-down former burlesque house in nearby Haverhill, Massachusetts. To attract families familiar with his venue's sordid past, he first had to book religious films. The relative success of this venture led to a successful partnership with Nathan Gordon, another early exhibitor, and to more theaters. In 1915 Mayer successfully played D. W. Griffith's *The Birth of a Nation* across New England, which led him to Metro Pictures, and in 1918, to the Louis B. Mayer Pictures Corporation.

Like his future partners, the new impresario eventually gravitated into production. He based his first tiny studio at the Selig lot in East Los Angeles, which also contained a small zoo, the tenants of which were also available for filming purposes. Fatefully, one of these animals, a lion named Jackie would later play Leo, the MGM figurehead. Florence Browning, Mayer's secretary during this period endearingly remembered her boss as "a funny little man riding around in a Ford telling everybody confidentially he was going to be the greatest man in the picture-making-business." One can almost see Browning shaking her head as she continues on by saying that "he seemed to have absolutely no reticence, no inhibitions, no sense of embarrassment at his evident manifestations of conceit."[2]

Mayer's filmed product during this period lived up to his bluster. His first movies were melodramatic and well made, but unlike the hearth-and-home-themed tales he would personally favor later, these films also addressed current issues like class consciousness (*A Midnight Romance* [1919]), attempted suicide (*Her Mad Bargain* [1921]), divorce (*Why Men Leave Home* [1924]), and even, contrary to what *The Birth of a Nation* had assured audiences, the evils of the Ku Klux Klan (*One Clear Call* [1922]). Mayer however, whatever his ambitions, was still an independent producer, scrambling for bookings in theaters that he had sometimes once owned and then releasing his films through larger companies, like First National, through deals that favored those larger companies.

In 1922, Mayer met Irving Thalberg, who, although only twenty-three, was already the head of production at Universal Studios. Like everyone who encountered him, Mayer was impressed with the frail, almost ethereal young executive. Thalberg had been born in Brooklyn in 1899 with a congenital heart defect and, consequently, spent his life haunted by the certainty that he would die young. With this certainty always in mind, he therefore realized that he would need to make his probably limited time on earth count. As a secretary at Universal's New York offices, the young man impressed the studio's founder, Carl Laemmle, so much that Thalberg quickly found himself whisked out to Hollywood supervising the studio's entire output.

Mayer and Thalberg met in November 1922 at Mayer's studio/office/zoo, which of course was much smaller and shabbier than Universal's already vast complex. It was quickly arranged that Thalberg would take over all aspects of Mayer's physical production for $500 a week—a hundred dollars more than Laemmle had been paying him but still a seeming demotion because Mayer's productions, like his studio, were considerably smaller than Universal's, and at least at first, there would be less of them.

One wonders, if when Mayer and Thalberg sealed the deal and shook hands in Mayer's tiny office, Jackie the Lion thought to roar from outside the window?

Mayer and Thalberg's partnership was very much a Mutt and Jeff one. But the two shared similar ambitions. Both had a cost-conscious nature, both regarding when to spend money on production value and when not to. They also agreed on what type of

Louis B. Mayer and Irving Thalberg, seen at work in 1930, represented the greatest collaboration of commerce (Mayer) and art (Thalberg) in modern theatrical history. Although by the mid-1930s both were chaffing under the weight of that perception. *Author's collection*

pictures the new studio would produce. "Both believed movies to be primarily escapism-type entertainment," recalled their studio's longtime story editor Samuel Marx:

> Throughout his life—even in later years when he tossed aside the moral principles so deeply ingrained in him since childhood—Mayer looked on himself as the saintliest of humans. He strove to prove it by devotion to wholesome films picturing men and women in heroic terms, and even those characters tarnished by sin reached ultimate perfection through love. He wanted all his movies to fade out with bells pealing, rose petals softening the path of lovers until the camera gazed mistily on a handsome and triumphant groom embracing a beautiful blushing bride in the inevitable happy ending. Thalberg had a natural instinct for creating rainbows in the dark, manufacturing dreams for the disadvantaged, illustrating that life could be lived for a joyous hour or two in an evanescent world. Throughout their careers, Mayer and Thalberg concentrated on movies intended to bathe the earth in rays of romance, optimism and well-being, to make people forget these were temporary things and reality was waiting outside when the show was over.[3]

This shared vision, still cherished by Mayer even after Thalberg was gone, would permeate the studio for more than thirty years—raising it to unparalleled heights but, eventually, with changing times, helping bring about its destruction.

Across town, in Culver City, another lion besides Jackie was already roaring, or at least scowling silently at the camera as the mascot for Goldwyn Pictures. Goldwyn had been founded in 1916 by Samuel Goldfish—another Americanization of what was

Samuel Goldwyn both took his name from, and gave that name to, the company, although he would play no part in its management or its operation, circa 1930s. *Photofest*

this time a Polish moniker, whose owner had been born in Warsaw in 1879; Goldfish, along with Zukor and Jesse Lasky, had previously been involved in the formation of what would become Paramount Pictures. But Goldfish's rather combative nature had forced him to strike out on his own in 1916.

His partners in this new venture were two brothers, Edgar and Archie Selwyn. Decades later, Goldfish enjoyed telling the tale of the company's name to friends like Garson Kanin. "We decided to take half of each name. Half of my name, Goldfish, and half of their name, Selwyn, and so we called it the Goldwyn Pictures Corporation. It came out Goldwyn because we wanted to put our names together—and listen, it was the only way to do it. Archie—he was the jolly brother—I remember he said, 'Another way to do it is to call it *Selfish* Pictures, Incorporated.'"[4]

Goldfish, of course, took that name, Goldwyn, not Selfish, as his own in 1918, although he faced legal actions from the Selwyns for doing so. Once again, however, his personality and some outside investors would force him out of a company that this time bore his own, now legally changed name. In 1923, he established yet another company, Samuel Goldwyn Productions. This time, without partners to argue with, Goldwyn would successfully manage it for the rest of his life.

The result of all of this wrangling and name changing was that Samuel Goldwyn would play no further part in the operations of a company, which, again, his name is still a part of. Although it should be noted that in 1955, MGM would release the Goldwyn-produced *Guys and Dolls*. Today, much of the Goldwyn library, perhaps fittingly, also belongs to MGM!

According to Goldwyn there was also talk of a Goldwyn and MGM merger in the 1950s after Mayer, whom Goldwyn disliked, was gone. Reportedly the combined companies were then to be called Metro-Goldwyn-Mayer and Goldwyn. Goldwyn also had an odd habit of forgetting L.B.'s name whenever he mentioned his bastard stepchild. To the end of his life, the mogul referred to the studio as the "Metro-Goldwyn Company."

The Goldwyn Pictures lot in Culver City, located at 10202 West Washington Boulevard, and several miles south and west of Hollywood proper, had been built in 1916 for the Triangle Film Company, which had sold the twelve-acre property to Goldwyn for $325,000 in October 1918. Goldwyn added another twenty-three acres to the complex and additional stages and support departments as well. By 1924, the studio was already one of the best equipped in the world.

All, however, was not well behind the property's white walls and ornate colonnade. Like Metro and Louis B. Mayer Productions, the Goldwyn-less Goldwyn company was being squeezed by the majors, although it did possess that state-of-the-art studio, and a contract with William Randolph Hearst's Cosmopolitan Pictures to distribute their product and also to advertise that product in the Heart Press.

Loew saw the innate value in the entity and purchased Goldwyn, in 1924 for $4.7 million, which effectively merged Goldwyn's production facilities with Metro/Loews theater chain. In the same marble-grabbing fell swoop he also snatched up Louis B. Mayer Productions—for a modest $76,500.

What was the attraction of Louis B. Mayer Productions? Certainly, Goldwyn and Loews/Metro had the theaters and the assembly line, but Mayer was in possession of the management skills and of the innate understanding of the process that, perhaps, could make these three independent and rather impotent failures, hopefully, into one shining success. Loew, for his part knew that he was an exhibitor, and not a filmmaker, a discipline that he was not particularly interested in anyway. It is certainly to Loew's credit that he realized this. "I don't sell tickets to movies," he is quoted as saying, "I sell tickets to theaters."

And it is to Mayer's credit that he insisted that Thalberg be included in the buyout as head of production for the combined companies.

On April 18, 1924, the formal papers for the merging of Metro, Goldwyn, and Mayer were signed. The new conglomerate, however, was unsure about even what to call the new company. Mayer, or rather his company's name, as very much the junior partner was sometimes named on early letterhead, and on-screen, and sometimes not, which must have pleased Goldwyn immensely. Eventually a hyphenated Metro-Goldwyn-Mayer became the legal name of the entity, although, again, the hyphens, to this day, are usually omitted on-screen and even in (most) legal documents. Loews, as the parent company, was occasionally included as part of the legal boilerplate as well, making the company name almost as long running as some of its films.

On April 26, 1924, a full week after the legal merger, an official opening day ceremony was held on the lot. Inside of that impressively gated colonnade, a small crowd—movie fans, local residents, and those probably looking for extra work—watched curiously. Although such crowds, impressed for years by the Corinthian columns and wrought-iron gates, were probably surprised to discover how plain the row of factory-like studio buildings inside really were.

Those invited to that Saturday morning ceremony, like any Hollywood event, then or today, included both civic leaders and celebrities. They passed through the crowd, through the gate, made an immediate left past a lone fig tree, which was standing like a sentinel just inside the property, past a row of small wooden offices and dressing

Production executive Harry Rapf, Mayer, and Thalberg take the stage, and an oversize prop key, on opening day, April 26, 1924. *Bison Archives*

rooms built up against Washington Boulevard, and gathered around a stage built on a confetti-strewn lawn. This central lawn, unlike the buildings round it, was scented by magnolia trees and lovely gardens, commissioned by Goldwyn. Pathways crisscrossed to the glass-walled soundstages nearby.

Admiral Samuel Robinson, commander-in-chief of the Pacific fleet, Major George Ruhlen Jr., of Fort MacArthur, and Culver City Mayor C. V. Loop were among the guests. The studio's new managers, with typical chutzpah, had invited President Calvin Coolidge, who, not surprisingly, was a no-show. But congratulatory telegrams did arrive from Coolidge and from then Secretary of Commerce Herbert Hoover.

But the company's stars were well-represented. There that day could be found the entire cast of *Tess of the D'Urbervilles* (Blanche Sweet, Conrad Nagel, Stuart Holmes, and George Fawcett) and their director, Marshall Neilan, who were in the midst of shooting. Matinee idols such as John Gilbert, and Goldwyn stars Lon Chaney and Will Rogers were also there. Rogers characteristically quipped that he enjoyed Mayor Loop's speech, particularly because he had heard it a few weeks before at the opening of a racetrack that had subsequently gone broke.

On the stage, watched by a photograph of (the absent) Loew, Mayer accepted an oversized prop key with the word "Success" on its spine. "MGM will reach a point of perfection never approached by any other company," he said, hands on lapels and like Lincoln at Gettysburg. "If there is one thing I insist upon, it is quality. . . . I hope that it is given me to live up to this great trust. This is a great moment for me. I accept this solemn trust and pledge the best that I have to give,"[5] he intoned.

It would be only the first of many such impassioned speeches he would give there.

Immediately after the ceremony everyone from stars to janitors scurried back to their respective places on the new, Detroit-inspired assembly line, which the ever-organized Mayer and the ever-creative Thalberg had just wired together, a necessity, because Loews Theaters would be owed fifteen feature-length films in the company's first two years.

It should be noted that nothing like this had ever been attempted before. Even the largest studios in the 1920s were still run somewhat haphazardly, with everyone from every department randomly pitching in, or not, to achieve a common goal—a scatter-

In 1925, life at the studio was relatively relaxed, with well-landscaped lawns and Greta Garbo's favored fig tree helping to contribute to the lot's oddly genteel ambiance, which was quickly about to change. *Bison Archives*

MGM was justifiably renowned for possessing "more stars than there are in heaven." But unlike at any other studio, producers there were afforded nearly equal prestige and prominence, as these pages from a 1929 exhibitor's guide illustrate. *Bison Archives*

shot practice that would be rendered inconceivable in a few years as unionization and a widespread acceptance of filmmaking as a factory effort become commonplace.

But Mayer and Thalberg achieved their then impossible-sounding goal right out of the gate, delivering their contracted fifteen films to theaters, a full *eighteen months* ahead of deadline. The films they delivered were all quality productions which usually garnered critical, as well as and more importantly, audience approval.

The Greatest Producers

IRVING THALBERG: While the world showers him with plaudits he goes forward, the modest Lieutenant of Chief Mayer, the Genius to whom all the industry makes its bow.

HARRY RAPF: A product is known by the men who make it. Tireless, practical, dependable—Harry Rapf is the Showman First, Last and Always. M-G-M is proud of his presence as an Associate Producer.

HUNT STROMBERG: Young blood behind the M-G-M product. He was producing hits on his own, but preferred to join the only real showman outfit in film business. Hunt Stromberg typifies the M-G-M idea!

The largest Studio in the world. Forty-three acres, more stages, more facilities, greater resources than any company. And developing all the time. Only with such a Studio can a program of many Big Productions be carried on. Not only in personnel, but in equipment does M-G-M lead the field.

M-G-M wishes that each exhibitor could visit its Studios at Culver City, California. When you see its acres of activity, its fabulous resources, and talk with the practical men who are back of the product you'll agree that M-G-M is the logical producer for all real showmen.

EDDIE MANNIX: The production executives of M-G-M are experienced in all lines of show business. Eddie Mannix brings to picture making experience right in the theatre that M-G-M considers essential in its studios.

BERNIE HYMAN: (Middle). He has what money cannot buy, the outlook of youth, understanding what the millions of fans love on the screen. M-G-M has the production personnel that reflects its product — new ideas, pep, the modern spirit!

LOUIS D. JACOBS (Right). Other companies are trying to institute M-G-M's idea of Associate Producers at their studios. It takes smart showmen of the Jacobs type to make that plan work out into great product.

Mayer and Thalberg's rather revolutionary model of creating these movies on an automobile-style assembly line was immediately copied by other studios and by businesses far afield of the entertainment industry as well. Brothers Maurice and Richard McDonald, for example, after working briefly in Hollywood, would apply the same system to the fast-food industry, and the result was the McDonald's hamburger empire. A movie about the creation of McDonald's, *The Founder* (2016), even paid this debt forward by describing the opening of the first McDonald's as "a gala premiere that will put Louie B. Mayer to shame."

The factory continued to ramp up as well. Soon the studio would be setting, if not always attaining, goals approaching a film a week, although it would eventually take distribution deals with outside producers like Hal Roach to make this number approachable. During the Thalberg era, the closest the MGM assembly line itself ever came to this was the 1927–1928 season when the studio produced fifty-one pictures.

More importantly, in its first year of operation, MGM celebrated a profit of $4,708,631. By its second full year, 1926, those profits had well-surpassed $6 million, making the formerly fledgling company the indisputable leader of the entire industry.

And those numbers, astonishingly, continued to rise. In 1929 the Great Depression left millions jobless and even homeless and eventually caused rival studios Fox, Paramount, and RKO to topple into receivership. But the trend of escalating, doubling or even tripling of, profits at MGM astonishingly continued. The studio's best year until after World War II, which would bring soldiers and profits back into theater in record numbers, would be 1930, when MGM would post then astonishing profits of $15 million.

2
Players and Their Plays

MGM was so influential that almost immediately the Motion Picture Academy of Arts and Sciences was founded in 1927, largely because Louis B. Mayer asked that it be done. Mayer's unstated motive was that unionization in the motion picture industry would be less likely to occur, or less likely to occur so soon, if there was an avenue for technicians to bargain directly, if not collectively, with their employees. So, the Academy was initially intended to be a not-so-well-veiled mediation tactic between producers and labor.

Mayer insisted, of course and unsurprisingly, that this new association also wrap itself in verbiage about advancing the art form and rewarding those who distinguished themselves or their industry—whatever that meant. Years later, writer David Thomson wryly commented that "the 'Arts and Sciences' touch was genius, because it made you think the Academy had always been there, arranged by God and Harvard and Albert Einstein."[1]

To this end, the distribution of a trophy, designed by the studio's art director Cedric Gibbons, was, almost as an afterthought, added to the Academy's lofty-seeming agenda the following year. The first "Academy Award," was presented to a film named *Wings*, although the category it won in was then, rather breathlessly, called "The Academy Award for Outstanding Picture."

Wings, significantly, was a Paramount release. Largely because the wily Mayer had no desire that his shiny new organization be perceived as merely an appendage to MGM, which was to the detriment of his own studio's sublime *The Crowd*. Of course,

The Academy Awards were established largely because Louis B. Mayer requested that they be. Douglas Fairbanks is shown here presenting the Best Actress Award to Janet Gaynor at the first Academy Awards ceremony in May, 1929.

Photofest

this reticence to pat his own back would not long last, and to no one's surprise, the studio would take home that same prize, slightly renamed as "Best Picture," the following year. In the next decade, MGM would go on to win that award in 1931/1932, 1935, 1936, and 1939. Whatever it was officially being called, the shiny trophy would soon be nicknamed, for largely undetermined reasons, the Oscar, although Gibbons's bald little man statue would not be officially sanctioned as such by the Academy until 1939.

The popular dictum about MGM during this era was "more stars than there are in heaven." MGM, luckily, had acquired much of their ready-made stables of contract players and directors through the merger. Those directors, with a few exceptions, were relatively anonymous to the general public, but their collective body of stars together then represented the pinnacle of the studio's prestige and profitability.

Unfortunately, many of these stars were, at the time of the merger, already aging out of many of the roles that they had previously specialized in. MGM's contract lists were always rich with character actors or with those who had formerly been leads. So, finding new, younger talent would always prove to be a problem—especially with the coming of sound, when even many young matinee idols found their popularity on the wane with the changes in technology and fashion that the talkies would bring on. Many MGM stars also were beset with personal problems, addictions, or insecurities, which eventually overshadowed their desirability to the front office.

The resultant search for new talent in the early 1930s would result in the almost magical appearances of many of the most legendary of MGM movie stars during this Halcomb era. Jean Harlow had received a measure of notoriety in Howard Hughes's independently produced *Hells Angels* (1930). But it was at MGM where she would become a legendary siren and comedienne, although the highbrow nature of the studio's output, and the stricter enforcement of the production code in 1934, would make it hard for the studio to find vehicles suitable to her talents.

Likewise, Spencer Tracy first came onto the lot as a character actor, whose everyman looks seemingly precluded him from leading man roles. But MGM instead developed him into one of Hollywood's most enduring and beloved leading men. Like Tracy, Luise Rainer would win back-to-back Oscars in the 1930s, but unlike him, however, she was unable, or possibly unwilling, to try to parlay her prestige into long-term viability.

Even more prestigious than Rainer, and much more enduring, was the exotic and imperious Greta Garbo, who despite her thick Swedish accent, easily became a major talking star. Garbo's allure and impact on audiences was legendary, even during a time

JEAN HARLOW, que figura en las constelaciones de Columbia y que, con Loretta Young y Robert Williams, acaba de terminar una excelente producción: "Platinum Blonde".

Jean Harlow's earthy sexuality made it hard for the rather puritanical MGM to find vehicles suitable to her talents. Which is probably the same reason this 1932 publicity shot only made it into the Spanish-language version of *Moving Picture World. Author's collection* when stars really did cast bigger-than-life shadows over their fans. But even on the lot, Garbo was a mysterious, largely unapproachable figure. Several employees have remarked that she seemed to enjoy the company of the lot's lonely fig tree and its fruit more than that of her fellow humans.

Garbo's career was relatively short. She retired from the screen in 1941 with her allure intact, and so her mystique survived that career by decades. Remarkably, her appeal has continued to straddle all facets of both high art and popular culture. Ernest Hemingway, for example, mentioned Garbo by name in *For Whom the Bell Tolls*. Anne Frank kept a photograph of the star on her wall in the room where she hid from the Nazis. The Garbo mystique has also been evoked in popular songs, including Cole Porter's "You're the Top," Kim Carnes's "Bette Davis Eyes," the Kinks' "Celluloid Heroes," and Madonna's "Vogue." The lady has been pictured on both US postage stamps and on Swedish currency. Closer to home, Garbo's name and image would be evoked by her old studio in pictures like 1952's *Strictly Dishonorable*. And as late as 1984, that studio could still make a movie called *Garbo Talks*, about that star's ever-mesmerizing effect on her fans. And those aging fans could still empathize.

Like Garbo, Joan Crawford had been toiling at the studio during the silent era. But unlike Garbo, the slightly younger, much more middle-class Crawford was usually cast as ingenues or flappers during this era. The roles of shopgirls and showgirls, which would make Crawford a screen legend, would all come later, in the 1930s. Crawford would prove to be so popular in these roles, and so durable as a star that even after MGM, perhaps unwisely, cut her loose in the 1940s, she managed to parlay her continuing popularity, and a 1945 Oscar win, into a legendary and long-lasting career.

But the biggest triumph of the entire star system was of course, Clark Gable, who the company quickly and most expertly transformed from an awkward bit player into the biggest star in the world. In 1931, his first year at the studio, Gable made a dozen films. These roles were designed to make audiences discover the young man, and for the studio to discover if this young man really was a star and then what sort of a star persona he would then assume. In his first film for the studio, *The Easiest Way*, Gable had a small part as a lowly deliveryman, but by the end of the same year, he was costarring, and co-billed with Garbo, no less. Gable's durability with audiences, however, must have surprised even the studio. He left that studio to serve in World War II, returned, and after a few postwar hiccups, he continued his career with little diminishment in his appeal. Gable was still successfully playing leading roles, but not for MGM, at the time of his death in 1960.

As the decade ended, new stars, like Lana Turner and Hedy Lamarr would replace the now-themselves aging first-generation of MGM talking stars, although many of those earliest stars, mostly male, would remain and would go on to successfully costar with these younger actresses, almost as a studio rite of passage and for that studio to see if these youngsters could hold their own opposite the charisma of a Gable or a Tracy, for example.

In 1940, Hedy Lamarr, a definite standout among her generation of MGM stars, held her own even when pitted against an "old-timer" like Spencer Tracy, in *Boom Town*. *Photofest*

Through the merger, MGM had also acquired several important but problematic pictures already in production, or nearly so. Notably, Goldwyn brought to the table prestige projects like *Ben-Hur* and *Greed*; Metro contributed Buster Keaton's *The Navigator* and Rex Ingram's *The Arab*. Louis B. Mayer productions, in contrast, was presumably the weak link because they brought the least amount of promising material into the mix. But that company, of course, did offer the incalculable asset of Mayer himself, with Thalberg ever at his side, to manage the company.

And manage they did. As they increased the size and prestige of the company, Mayer and Thalberg were careful to not allow autocrats like Ingram and Erich von Stroheim to run unchecked. They knew full well that they were the only autocrats allowed on the lot. They made sure that everyone on that lot realized that the studio, with them as its representatives, was the boss. It must be said though, that Mayer and Thalberg also effectively destroyed the careers of artists like von Stroheim and Keaton, who were unable to subvert their individuality to the wills of the assembly line.

Despite the company's outward success, all was not well internally, however. Mayer's relationship with Nicholas Schenck had never been particularly cordial. But with the death of Marcus Loew in 1927 Schenck officially became Mayer's boss.

And Mayer's boss was unlike Mayer, not personally invested in MGM as a company. Schenck's name was neither on the screen nor painted on the studio water tower. What Schenck was invested in was money. And L.B. was undoubtedly aware of the rumors that Schenck had wanted to replace him—despite his and Thalberg's success—with Schenck's ever-lurking brother, Joseph.

This didn't happen. But in the late 1920s another rumor started to circulate throughout the industry regarding a projected sale of MGM to Warner Bros. or to Fox. And this time it was not a rumor.

Of these two contenders for MGM, Fox quickly emerged as a likely candidate. William Fox had founded the Fox Film Corporation in 1915. His studio complex was only a short distance from MGM's. Actually, Motor Avenue, which began at the Fox gate, then terminated almost in front of the MGM colonnade, physically and literally chaining the two properties together. So, that MGM water tower, with Mayer's name proudly painted on it was nearly visible from William Fox's office window.

It's unclear who instigated the deal, but it is known that Schenck, armed with his own stock and with that of Loew's widow, worked out a deal to sell that stock to Fox in 1929. Fox's purchase of these assets and other apparently open-market acquisitions of Loews' stock eventually totaled up to more than $70 million in 1920s dollars. But to Mayer's relief, the deal quickly unraveled with both the 1929 stock market crash and a potential antitrust suite. To Mayer's probable delight, Fox also suffered an auto accident that year, which left the mogul watching from his hospital bed as the prices of the stock he had so expensively purchased plummeted.

In 1930, Fox would lose his own studio as well, as part of a hostile takeover that had been instigated by his house-of-cards grab at MGM. In 1935, the outfoxed Fox-less Fox Film Corporation would merge with 20th Century Pictures. That company, it should be noted, had been founded in 1933 by ex-pat Warner Bros. producer Darryl F. Zanuck, and by the seemingly ever-present, Joseph Schenck.

Mayer and Thalberg had survived, seemingly by divine intervention, an attempt to take MGM from their control. But it was now more than evident that Schenck could not be trusted. And the incident also proved that the power at the studio truly rested in the boardroom rather than in the front office.

Further proof of this, if it was needed, came from a 1934 effort by screenwriters to unionize. Sol Rosenblatt, a former attorney for the Democratic National Committee, surveyed the industry from the outside. "It is only an illusion that Mayer controls the industry. Nick Schenck [chair of the board of MGM] and Harry Warner [chair of the board of Warner Bros.] really control the industry," he affirmed.[2]

In March 1933, Mayer delivered an infamous speech to his employees asking them to take a temporary pay cut as a Depression-era belt-tightening measure. This address has since been widely derided, discussed, and even dramatized in movies. No one who was there can quite agree what exactly Mayer said, but all concede that it was one of the greatest performances ever given at MGM because after watching their boss on the stage shedding tears, wiping his eyes with a handkerchief, and prophesizing that the studio and that the entire industry might otherwise disappear forever, his army of technicians and stars thunderously agreed to their own pay cut. And not only did they agree, but when L.B. stepped away from the podium, it was to rapturous applause. "How did I do?" he reportedly then asked executive Ben "Benny" Thau. Thau must have told him that he had done well indeed.

Mayer's many detractors have used this admittedly self-serving speech to point out how manipulative and selfish Mayer could be, which is undoubtedly true. Usually, it is also then trotted out that MGM, despite Mayer's prophesies of impending doom, still was the undoubted colossus of the industry, eventually posting a not inconsiderable $4 million profit for the 1933–1934 season. It's also been much noted that Mayer took no such equivalent pay cut for himself.

This last, however, is not the truth because he, Thalberg, and other top executives had already been operating under 35 percent pay cuts since July. And at the meeting he pledged to again cut his own salary, this time by 85 percent, while only asking his employees to (briefly) halve theirs.

Despite this apparent show of financial solidarity between Mayer and Thalberg, by this time it was obvious to those who spent any time around them that the once nearly paternal relationship between the two executives was rapidly shredding. Mayer's always delicate ego, for example, had been reportedly wounded by an article in *Fortune* magazine in December 1932 about MGM, which reverently, almost rapturously, praised Thalberg, while barely mentioning Mayer at all. Mayer was particularly irked by this because Thalberg had recently told Mayer and Schenck that he wanted to take a year off. This did not immediately happen, but it did result in Thalberg's being given more stock options and a larger piece of the company, which Mayer had reportedly been opposed to, in return for Thalberg's staying at his desk.

This obviously posed, mid-1930s study of matinee idol Maurice Chevalier, flanked by his bosses, offers public smiles and congeniality. Behind the scenes, however, the relationship between Irving Thalberg and Louis B. Mayer was by this point much more ... complicated. *Photofest*

About the same time that the contentious *Fortune* magazine article came out, Thalberg suffered a heart attack, which kept him away from that desk for several months anyway. During this period, Mayer divided Thalberg's responsibilities among a group of producers and executives, including his own son-in-law, David O. Selznick, which could not have pleased the bedridden Thalberg. When the producer finally did return, later in 1933, Mayer's so-called college of cardinals remained in place, as it would for the rest of Mayer's tenure at the studio. Thalberg would now effectively just be another producer on the lot.

With Thalberg largely marginalized, Mayer should have been content that his powers, in Culver City, if not in New York, were now unchallenged. But the legend of Thalberg only continued to grow. Mayer was unhappy in that he felt like he was widely being dismissed as a bureaucrat throughout the industry, while Thalberg was regarded as the creative genius actually responsible for the studio's success. Whether this was the case apparently didn't matter. Selznick left MGM in 1935 to start his own company, and it was widely suspected that Thalberg was planning on doing the same thing soon, although Mayer and even Schenck still tended to defer to the "boy wonder's" every whim at MGM.

The only thing lacking in the coronation of Thalberg as Hollywood godhead during this contentious period was of course a finale, which arrived on September 14, 1936, when the producer died at the age of thirty-seven.

Thalberg's canonization began immediately. For the first time in its history, every studio in Hollywood observed five minutes of silence in his honor; MGM even remained closed for the entire day. Accolades singing Thalberg's praises came from all over the industry and around the world. President Franklin D. Roosevelt sent his condolences. Even von Stroheim, whom Thalberg had fired, and more than once, attended his funeral.

In 1937, the Irving G. Thalberg Award was established by the Academy to honor "creative producers, whose bodies of work reflect a consistently high quality of motion picture production." The award is still given out irregularly and is widely considered to be the highest honor the industry can bestow on one of its own.

Thalberg, now as he was even before his death, is widely considered to be the most creative producer in Hollywood history. And the undebated consensus on this subject is as steadfast now as it was then. For example, in 2012, acclaimed essayist Joseph Epstein asserted that "the word 'filmmaker' has been much bandied around in recent decades, usually applied to directors sufficiently modest to eschew the more pretentious 'auteur.' But in the history of American movies, there may have been only one true filmmaker: a man whose hand and mind were there from inception through conception of hundreds of movies, seeing to each detail and without whose behind-the-scene participation the movie would fail to exist—and that man was Irving Thalberg."[3]

Throughout history, as the movies have dramatized for us, governments and religions and organizations have required a martyr, someone's blood is always needed to canonize and legitimize these groups' beliefs. Therefore, individuals from Jesus Christ to Joan of Arc to Abraham Lincoln have been enlisted for this purpose. Hollywood, needing its own such sacrificial goat, has thus conscripted Thalberg. Thalberg possessed the talent, drive, and creativity to embody this role, all certainly true, but, as this was Hollywood, it did not hurt a bit that he was also young, attractive, and wealthy and that he left behind a beautiful widow, actress Norma Shearer. Mayer's more shadowy and ambivalent persona could offer up none of these qualities save one. The movies had already profitably enacted this blood ritual before with Rudolph Valentino and would do so again with James Dean. But Thalberg, as a producer rather than an actor, added an intellectual component to this particular communion.

As with martyrs throughout history, Thalberg's tale has attracted the heady attention of literary types too. F. Scott Fitzgerald's *The Last Tycoon* was posthumously published in 1941. Monroe Stahr, the book's protagonist, is obviously a fictionalized Thalberg. Famously, Fitzgerald here said that "you can take Hollywood for granted like I did, or you can dismiss it with the contempt we reserve for what we don't understand. It can be understood too, but only dimly and in flashes. Not half a dozen men have ever been able to keep the whole equation of pictures in their heads."[4] The implication being that Stahr/Thalberg understood the whole equation, even if the Mayer surrogate, here named Pat Brady, does not.

What no one has noticed is that Fitzgerald's much-beloved-by-Hollywood, and often quoted words, were actually a paraphrasing and an obvious improvement on what Cecil B. DeMille had already told the *Los Angeles Times* at the time of Thalberg's passing. For comparison, the actual quote by DeMille (or his publicist) is, "there are hundreds of executives but only about six men with the genuine genius for making motion pictures and Mr. Thalberg was the greatest of those."[5]

Shorn of its myth, and of Hollywood's penchant for self-aggrandizement then, what are we to make of Irving Thalberg? Fitzgerald's *Last Tycoon*, unfinished and unpolished as it is, is certainly helpful as a case of a great artist in one discipline trying to grapple with and then appreciate a great artist in another. But Fitzgerald's passion for the written word is ultimately unsuitable as a study of an artist passionate about cinema—two art forms dependent on one another but hardly the same in aspiration or affect. So, as a Hollywood outsider desperately trying to be an insider, even Fitzgerald can only, sadly, give us a peak through a keyhole into a different, if not contradictory, discipline—a discipline that he himself had already proven to possess little understanding of.

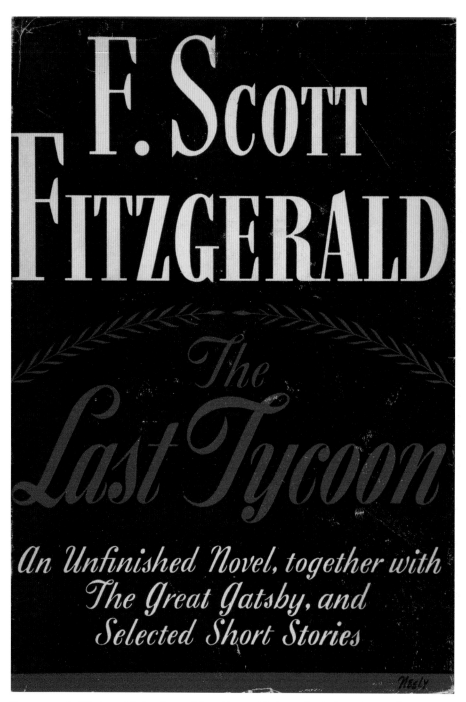

Sometimes titled *The Love of the Last Tycoon*, F. Scott Fitzgerald's, last, unfinished novel, as seen here in its 1941 first edition, has shaped the opinions of readers regarding Hollywood and specifically regarding MGM for generations. *Author's collection*

Yes, Stahr is most certainly Thalberg, but he is also Fitzgerald. Both of them are brilliant but ultimately are also frustrated, misunderstood, and held back by the weaknesses of inferiors. So, it is a sad irony that unlike Thalberg or Stahr, Fitzgerald himself actually possessed little understanding of Hollywood's "whole equation." Perhaps this explains why the author is so slavishly admiring of a character who would never have admired him back. One of Thalberg's biographers, Roland Flamini, once referred to Fitzgerald's novel as "a classic tale of a victim's identification with his torment[or]."[6]

And Flamini is right. This near-hero worship extends to his character's name, which, really, is just too damn spot-on. It's comparable to how, in early drafts of *Dracula*, author Bram Stoker reportedly named his title character "Count Wampyr" before wisely rechristening his monster into something (at least then) more subtly sinister. So, likewise, Fitzgerald too, might have eventually changed Monroe Stahr's name in rewrites had he lived just a little longer.

As hard as it is to now separate the man from the myth, one does have to admire Thalberg's body of work at MGM and, before that, at Universal to appreciate the man's genuine, extraordinary talent for finding properties and then for perfectly realizing those properties.

But according to actor Robert Montgomery, the real Thalberg was not the soft-spoken, intellectual inhabiting his myth at all. "Thalberg, not Mayer, was the toughest and most ruthless man in the industry," Montgomery said. "He was nothing of the dreamer. He was money-mad. He was a shrewd, tough, hard, cold operator, with a complete ruthlessness toward people."[7]

Longtime studio General Manager/fixer Eddie Mannix was even more bluntly succinct. "Thalberg was a sweet guy but he could piss ice water,"[8] he once said.

Thalberg was not quite the perfect juncture of art and craft that his legend paints him as either. He failed to see the coming of sound and then color films, and he fought alongside Mayer against the unionization of the studios. He could also be pompous about his own self-importance. One of Mayer's biographers, Scott Eyman put it well when he wrote that "there was a perceptible sense of Thalberg as a man having to cope with people he clearly regarded as his intellectual inferiors"[9]

One of those supposed "inferiors" whether or not Thalberg acted like that around him, was probably Mayer. Maybe that's why after the funeral Mayer reportedly remarked, "Isn't God good to me?"

Fortune magazine, the same contentious periodical which in 1932 had been responsible for stoking the jealousy by Mayer over Thalberg's status, was back to report on the funeral too. In this article, the uncredited author quoted an uncredited producer as

Constructed in 1937–1938, the Irving Thalberg Building remains a tangible monument to both a single life and to an art form that is much more ethereal. *Bison Archives*

stating about Thalberg that "they won't miss him today or tomorrow or six months from now or a year from now. But two years from now they'll begin to feel the squeeze."[10]

The article was certainly prescient. But it took longer than that. Under Mayer, and aided by his college of cardinals, MGM instead continued its long winning streak. In 1937 the profits for the company were $14.3 million. That year Mayer's personal salary was $1.3 million, making him the highest paid executive in the US for the first time. His salary was higher even than that of his own boss, Nicholas Schenck.

That same year, Mayer started construction of the Thalberg building on the eastern corner of the lot as a new corporate headquarters. Mayer's office, the largest of the 235 in the building, was on the third floor and included a private elevator and a huge white desk that director William Wellman recalled was "damn near as big as a pool table."[11]

It was from behind this white expanse that Mayer, seated on a raised platform, would scold, coerce, or praise his thousands of minions for the rest of his career.

L. B. Mayer at the big white desk about which not a single personage, be they dignitary, screenwriter, peasant, producer, or star, who ever saw it has ever failed to comment. *Bison Archives*

Everyone who ever stood in front of that desk and in that office seems to have vivid memories of doing so. Samuel Goldwyn, definitely neither an employee nor a fan of Mayer, told him that "you need an automobile just to reach your desk."[12]

Jane Powell and Debbie Reynolds, two of the many stars Mayer created, remembered the same vast white spectacle too. "The walk seemed endless. Mayer's office seemed huge,"[13] Powell said. Reynolds recalled that "Mr. Mayer must have had the biggest office in the history of Hollywood. You entered this enormous room, all white, for what some people called the 'quarter-mile walk' to a desk the size of a small helicopter pad, all highly polished and shining. Because Mr. Mayer was not very tall (about five feet), and rather roundish and portly, he had his desk built on a platform, lest some big temperamental star or director come in and forget who was boss."[14]

Reportedly, an unnamed (probably for a reason) actress once walked in and requested that Mayer stand up in the presence of a lady. "Madam, I am standing,"[15] Mayer then had to admit.

But let's give the last word on the subject of that office to William Randolph Hearst, who would have known a thing or two about big offices himself, and who visited Benito Mussolini before the war and remarked that the dictator's office was "almost as big as Louis B. Mayer's at MGM."[16]

From movie stars to moguls to mortals, whoever they were, it was from behind this white behemoth that Louis B. Mayer, finally shorn of the millstones of genius or art, would come into his own.

3
Old Men and New Blood

Despite the loss of the foreign market, which came before and during World War II, in the 1940s Louis B. Mayer's studio continued to outperform all others. In 1941 the company's profits were $11 million, $11.8 million in 1942, and $14.5 million in 1944, which was all the more remarkable because the company was now making less movies, only thirty that year, as opposed to forty-nine only two years earlier. But because the company was so top-heavy with producers by this time, there was always a struggle among them to get their own pictures made and seldom was one of these producers able to win this struggle more than once a year.

These producers, seeking an audience with Mayer, had to first get past his secretary, the formable Ida Koverman, who came to MGM in 1929 after having previously worked for President Herbert Hoover. A childless, stern-faced widow, Koverman, known as "Kay" to those brave enough to address her as such, literally held the keys to the kingdom, via access to the most powerful man in the movies, in her bony hands. She was one tough cookie, maybe even a tougher cookie than her boss, who, after all, did possess a well-documented sentimental side. In the novel, *Beautiful Invention*, author Margaret Porter has Mayer refer to her, with minor dramatic license, as "fiercer than Leo the Lion."

But Koverman was not without her softer side. For example, she championed and protected Judy Garland, who seemingly viewed Mayer's stern gatekeeper as a beneficent, even maternal, figure, a rarely seen side of Ida's usually stern character, which would eventually also surface in her biography and be dramatized in another novel, *Finding Dorothy*.

Other fixtures at the studio during this era, and in some cases through several eras, included studio manager J. J. Cohn, who made everything on the lot run like clockwork, and even had a section of the backlot, the formal garden, or "Cohn's Park," named in his honor. Cedric Gibbons was the head of the Art Department and so was for decades credited as such for every film made at the studio, eventually accruing more on-screen credits than anyone in screen history. Lillian Burns was the drama coach, and so every future star and would-be future star from 1937 until the early 1960s had only to impress her. Likewise, Mary McDonald, the studio's on-lot schoolteacher coached and cajoled child stars and future stars for decades. George Gibson ultimately ran the Scenic Arts Department for almost thirty-five years. Douglas Shearer (Norma Shearer's brother) ran the Sound Department until 1968. William Tuttle in the Makeup Department and A. Arnold "Buddy" Gillespie in Special Effects each first worked in and eventually headed those departments for more than forty years each.

A 1936 conference on the set of *Camille*, involving studio mainstays Cedric Gibbons (MGM's supervising art director), screenwriter/director Harry Beaumont, director George Cukor, and Gibbons's Art Department associate, Fredric Hope. Together, these four would eventually rack up 110 cumulative years working at MGM. *Photofest*

Howard Dietz, the studio's Director of Advertising and Publicity, a noted lyricist, and even an occasional on-screen talent, also survived at MGM for decades. Dietz even survived an encounter with Mayer in which he was reprimanded for leaving early. "Yes, Mr. Mayer," he responded, "but you have to realize that I also get to work very late!"[1]

Dietz and the almost five thousand others who worked on the lot every day, many for decades, were important components that made up and infused MGM with a corporate memory that would serve it well decade after decade.

In 1944, the studio's twentieth anniversary, Lot One, which the nerve center of the studio had come to be called, alone could boast of 177 standing buildings across its forty-four acres, with 170 arts, crafts, and technical departments represented inside. The twenty-four-hour private police department alone boasted a staff of seventy-five, the on-lot electrical plant reportedly had the capacity to power a city of twenty-five thousand people. The makeup department could process as many as twenty-seven hundred extras in an hour, and the costume department could then dress them at the rate of five thousand a day. The commissary was open twenty-four hours a day and averaged three thousand diners per shift, and the telephone exchange had more than twelve hundred stations. A call to the research department on one of them, and there were reportedly then five hundred such calls made to that department every day, ensured historic and geographic authenticity for the product being shot on the twenty-seven soundstages and out on the backlots on that day. The property department boasted of more than a million items. The music department that year housed more than four million individual selections, making it, along with the Library of Congress and the New York Public Library, one of the three largest depositories of musical selections in the world. The story department had half a million synopses on file based on the seven hundred books, stories, and plays that were submitted to them annually. The trailer department made not just promotional commercials for its upcoming releases but also specially themed promos for those same movies for particular regions or holiday-themed ones to run during the Christmas season. The studio was also then equipped with its own sawmill, lumberyard, blacksmith shop, upholstery shop, foundry, film lab, camera department, dozens of postproduction suites, forty screening rooms, an employee railroad tram system, a zoo, and its own twenty-four-hour-a-day on-lot fire department.

MGM was indeed a factory, a massive, humming industrial site. Yet, it was also a bizarre and wonderous and sometimes terrifying amalgamation of gossamer fantasy and heavy industry. Erté, the studio's first, and short-lived, production designer (although that term had yet to be coined during the brief period when he was employed there),

STAGE Nº	W	L	H	STAGE Nº	W	L	H	STAGE Nº	W	L	H
						M G M CULVER CITY					
1	66	93	27	10	87	149	30	22	102	152	29
2	64	93	26	11	104	189	35	23	102	157	35
3	77	97	29	12	101	177	37	24	102	157	35
4	79	99	29	14	89	179	35	25	116	196	40
5	79	125	44	15	133	310	40	26	116	195	40
6	79	73	80	16	103	196	20	27	132	235	59/80
7	76	102	26	18	106	141	28	28	116	195	40
8	74	102	26	19	105	158	28	29	116	195	40
9	73	152	33	21	102	152	29	30	130	235	50

Culver Boulevard in the 1940s was a relatively typical suburban street, distinguished by billboards, gas stations, liquor stores, and a large and rather prominent movie studio (top). Lot One stage chart, although some of those buildings identified here as "stages," were not usually used as such (bottom). *Bison Archives* once both mocked and marveled at the sublime oddness of the whole crazy endeavor by specifically noting and then wryly calling out the "royal façades without palaces; stupendous interiors without walls; kings and queens in full regalia eating sandwiches in a cafeteria with beggars in rags."[2]

That said, the truth about the studio lot itself was that most of it was surprisingly nonglamorous and workaday. Yes, the Colonnade on Washington Boulevard was impressive enough, but that had been there before the merger, and so it doesn't count. And yes, Goldwyn-era, the place also did originally boast of those expansive rolling lawns and of Garbo's beloved fig tree. But much of that had been bulldozed away with the advent of Mayer and Thalberg's frantic push toward first industrialization and then sound. So, at MGM, most of the perceived glamour was, always and astonishingly, strictly to be found in front of the cameras and on the screen.

Sodom and Gomorrah: The Story of Hollywood, a 1935 book warning readers of the evils of movieland, describes a Midwest beauty contest winner venturing out to California and being surprised at MGM. "The lobby, if that's what it may be called, in the big Culver City studio is neither large nor pleasant. A few hard benches, an ugly desk and scratched, dark woodwork are the outstanding features. There is nothing about the room to encourage the visitor. Surely the executives at this studio cannot be accused of undue extravagance,"[3] it warned its readers, who might otherwise have been tempted to follow this poor, misguided girl's ultimately tragic trek West.

Proudly presiding over all of this, like the mayor of his own private principality, was Louis B. Mayer. Mayor Mayer was, among many other things, a master showman. He could intimidate a star, browbeat an agent, or even cry on command as he reportedly had to do to put over that largely and legendarily self-serving Depression-era pay cut to his employees. "By God he could act in an office. Put on the damnedest performances you ever saw," marveled Buster Keaton once, who then went on to comically impersonate Mayer in the documentary *Buster Keaton Rides Again* (1965) as a "hysterical-cry-moan-heartbroken-beaten-down old man!"

The "old gray Mayer" also possessed, or perhaps pretended to possess, a volcanic, even violent temper. The list of those whom L.B. reportedly struck or physically assaulted included John Gilbert, Ted Healy, Charlie Chaplin, and Eric von Stroheim. Those who faced Mayer from the other side of his white desk, knowing of these stories—which after all, *might* have been true—inevitably tended to force those many opponents to agree to almost anything just to avoid the same alleged pummeling, at the very least giving Mayer/MGM a decided physical and psychological advantage in their negotiations.

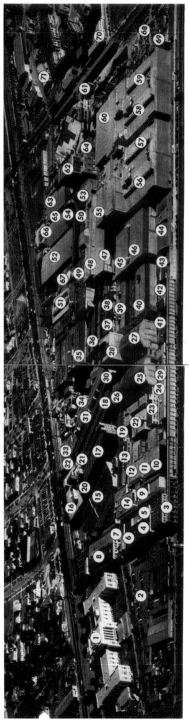

THE M-G-M STUDIOS

In contrast to the six tiny glass stages on the lot in 1924, when the company was founded, the M-G-M Studio today has 30 massive, modern stages equipped with every improvement known to the industry. From its original 40 acres, the studio has grown to 187 acres. In today's studio 117 arts and crafts are represented in the various departments, with 263 different technical jobs requiring specialized skill.

BUILDING IDENTIFICATION AND THE TALENTS THEY HOUSE

1—IRVING THALBERG BUILDING . . . executives, producers, writers, legal, story, radio, stenographic, projection, medical.

2—PARKING LOT

3—PUBLICITY, POLICE AND CASTING BUILDING

4—PURCHASING

5—WARDROBE . . . designers, tailors, seamstresses.

6—ACCOUNTING . . . comptroller, accountants, cashiers, studio club, insurance.

7—OLD SCENARIO BUILDING . . . international, script, new talent, dramatic coach, fan mail, projection, safety engineers.

8—MUSIC BUILDINGS . . . music library, composers, arrangers, conductors.

9—ADVERTISING AND CUTTING . . . ad creators, trailer producers, exploitation, cutting.

10—STAGE 1, 1A . . . recording and sound experts.

11—STAGE 2 . . . sound effect recording stage.

12—STAGE 2A . . . converted into Todd-AO theatre.

13—PRODUCTION DEPARTMENT . . . studio, production and unit production managers, assistant directors, location and dialogue directors, estimators, labor relations, barber shop, newsstand.

14—COMMISSARY AND DRAFTING . . . architects, sketch artists, estimators.

15—STAGE 16

16—MOTION PICTURE LABORATORY . . . negative developers, positive developers, printers, color experts, negative cutters, technical engineers, chemists, color control, color engineers, assemblers, inspectors, waxers, timers, shipping clerks.

17—PROPERTY . . . set dressers, drapers, property men, interior and floral decorators.

18—CAMERAS . . . cinematographers, cameramen and assistants, still photographers, technicians.

19—RESEARCH . . . history and custome experts.

20—ENGINEERING . . . engineers, lathe operators, mechanics.

21—MAINTENANCE . . . window washers, janitors, laborers

22—SOUND . . . scientists, engineers, optical authorities, sound recorders, mixers, cutters.

23—DIRECTOR AND MAKE-UP BUILDING . . . directors, make-up men, hair stylists, hairdressers, facial sculptors, secretaries.

24—STAR DRESSING ROOMS

25—STAGE 3

26—STAGE 4

27—STAGE 5

28—STAGE 6

29—STAR DRESSING ROOM SUITES

30—STAGE 18

31—STAGE 19

32—PORTRAIT GALLERY . . . portrait artists, electricians.

33—DANCE REHEARSAL HALL

34—STILL LABORATORY . . . black-and-white negative and color developers, printers, enlargers, retouchers, air brush artists, silk screen technicians, clerical workers.

36—STAGE 9

37—STAGE 7

38—STAGE 8

39—STAGE 22

40—STAGE 21

41—HOSPITAL . . . Doctors, nurses, receptionist.

42—SCHOOL HOUSE . . . Accredited teachers.

43—SHORT SUBJECT BUILDING . . . Also headquarters Rogers & Hammerstein and Todd-AO organization.

44—REHEARSAL HALLS 1, 2, and 3 . . . Choreographers, dancers.

45—STAGE 23

46—STAGE 24

47—MEN'S CHARACTER WARDROBE . . . Fitters tailors, wardrobe men.

48—STAGE 16

49—STAGE 11

50—STAGE 12

51—INDUSTRIAL CENTER . . . Carpenters, cabinet makers, upholsterers, plastic workers, sculptors, painters, metal workers, lathe operators, draftsmen, plumbers, laborers.

52—SCENE DOCK . . . Grips, laborers.

53—GRIP BUILDING . . . Grips, office workers.

54—TRANSPORTATION . . . Automotive mechanics, truck drivers, bulldozer operators, chauffeurs.

55—STAGE 27

56—STAGE 25

57—STAGE 26

58—STAGE 28

59—STAGE 29

60—STAGE 30

61—SCENE DOCK 3

63—SCENIC DEPARTMENT . . . Scenic painters, designers, sketch artists, canvas workers.

63—SCENE DOCK 4

64—SCENE DOCK 5

65—PAINT SHOP . . . Sign painters, sketch artists, house painters, mixers.

66—GARAGE MAINTENANCE . . . Body and fender workers, mechanics, grease and oil men.

67—PLASTER SHOP . . . Sculptors, mould makers, plaster workers.

68—STORAGE YARD.

69—SPECIAL EFFECTS . . . Artists, glass experts, trick cameramen, optical printers, Newcomb specialists.

70—CARTOON DEPARTMENT . . . Producer, directors, writers, animators, composers, arrangers, musicians, layout men, background artists, cameraman, sound men, film editors, painters and inkers, production manager, checkers.

71—LOT 2 . . . Green men (handling shrubbery) florists, outdoor set maintenance workers.

A 1950s aerial look at Lot One, with a few of its myriad amenities helpfully highlighted. *Bison Archives*

MGM
STUDIOS

METRO-GOLDWYN-MAYER INC

CONFIDENTIAL DIRECTORY

CALL:
M-G-M STUDIOS   VE 8-2161
            EX 7-2101
CR 6-1039   UP 0-3311
      EMERGENCY NUMBER
EAST GATE   262-3131

NEW YORK OFFICE
    1350 Avenue of the Americas
    New York, N.Y. 10019
            (212) 262-3131

CABLE ADDRESS:
    Metrofilms
    (Used throughout the world)
EFFECTIVE JUNE 1, 1967

Even into the 1960s the studio maintained its own private phone directory, listing thousands of on-lot personal extensions, offices, and departments. *Author's collection*

With the end of the war, profits continued to rise as movie-starved solders came home and foreign markets opened back up. Although the studio's overall market share and gross income also started to decrease during this period.

At first no one was particularly worried by this. With the benefit of hindsight, however, it becomes obvious that the vast overhead accrued by the operation itself, the plethora of executives, and the choking, expensive, roster of sometimes aging, sometimes troubled stars that the studio was saddled with were already playing a part in this almost imperceptible, at first, slide into the red.

None of this was lost on Nicholas Schenck in New York, however. The old man in his own big office knew that if he waited long enough, Mayer would become complacent and start to falter. And this seemed, by the later 1940s, to finally be happening.

In 1947, Mayer finally divorced his wife Margaret, who he had long been estranged from. The payout his lawyers agreed to ultimately amounted to more than $3 million, reportedly the highest divorce settlement in US history to that time. Mayer would wed Lorena Danker, a widow, in 1948.

But the bad news continued. Shortly after his divorce, Mayer's brother Jerry (whose first name was actually, maybe, Gershon?) died of cancer. At about the same time, the House Un-American Activities Committee began an exploration of potential communist influences in Hollywood. And during these same weary months, overall movie attendance started to fall, from eighty million admissions in 1946 to only sixty-seven million in 1948.

More bad news came to the white office. Television, long only a blurry black-and-white rumor, was finally and loudly crashing into US homes, giving the people who lived in these homes the option of *not* going to the movies for their entertainment at all.

During this era, unfortunately, Mayer was not spending as much time in that white office either, having become preoccupied with horse racing. And so, he spent increasingly greater amounts of time over on "Lot Eight," which was the internal code name for his various stables and for the local racetrack.

Perhaps worst of all, after a decade of wrangling between the courts and the studios, by the late 1940s it was becoming obvious that those studies would be forced, and soon, to sell off their theaters. The final decree would come in May 1948. Although it would not be until 1954 that MGM would fully comply with the court's ruling by splitting Loews into two companies, Loews Theaters (for exhibition) and Loews Inc. (MGM) for production and distribution. Fortunately, this landmark decree, widely credited with ultimately destroying the US studio system, would itself eventually be struck down by the Department of Justice—but this would not happen until August 7, 2020.

Because of all of this, and because of his weakened position, when Schenck told Mayer that he wanted a younger man to assist him in the running of the studio, Mayer found himself to be in no particular position to argue.

At first, Columbia Pictures' Sidney Buchman would have seemed to have been just the right guy for the job too. Buchman had risen through the ranks there as a writer and producer, was good at working with talent, and even possessed an affinity for musicals, which MGM specialized in. And most importantly, he got along as well with Mayer as he had with Columbia's even more prickly Harry Cohn. Unfortunately for Mayer, Buchman received a last-minute offer from Cohn to start his own independent production company there, and so ultimately, he remained at Columbia. Another man, another heir apparent, would therefore have to be found.

That man turned out to be forty-three-year-old Dore Schary. On August 19, 1948, Schary, who had worked at Metro as a writer in the 1930s and who had recently successfully run RKO, signed an Irving Thalberg–type contract as vice president in charge of production at MGM.

Dore Schary: A new Thalberg? *Bison Archives*

As he had with Thalberg, Mayer initially got along with his new protégé/heir apparent. Never a hands-on and hanging-out-on-the-set sort of a producer, Mayer appreciated that Schary enjoyed working with his directors and that the younger man seemingly possessed the aptitude to punch-up screenplays with the writers or to work in the editing bays with the cutters, none of which Mayer had ever even pretended to have an interest in doing.

In Schary's first year on the job, the studio made a small if not spectacular profit of $4.2 million. Even though the profits the year before had been more than double this ($10.5 million), this seemingly still validated the younger man's value on the lot and with New York.

On February 10, 1949, MGM celebrated its twenty-fifth anniversary. Mayer was presented a silver commemoration key by actress Greer Garson for the occasion, which must have reminded him of the much larger key given to him at the incorporation ceremony. This time, however, it was Schary, rather than Thalberg, who was standing at his side. At a banquet on Stage 15, the world's largest soundstage, virtually all the studio's stars were trotted out for the accompanying, and probably uncomfortable, meal and for a historic photograph, which was taken of them all to celebrate the event.

Within a few years Mayer, Schary, and most of the participants would be gone.

In 1951, Mayer was given an honorary Academy Award to commemorate his lifetime in the industry, which is never a good sign.

Back at the studio, Dore Schary's insistence on being a hands-on producer, unfortunately was now more often than not resulting in rampant micromanagement on his part as he dithered, backtracked, and interfered with his producers and his productions. It also quickly became apparent that although Schary had an innate sense for intimate little dramas set in foxholes or kitchens, he turned out to have no affinity whatsoever for musicals or epics, which was what the studio was best at creating, and he tended to get lost in the thousands of production problems, which these films forced on him when he tried to make them, even though there were hundreds on payroll who could have helped him with these problems had he let them do so. Schary was also, according to actress Esther Williams and others, a bit of an elitist, who preferred character actors like James Whitmore to stars like she and Clark Gable, both of whom would soon be gone. Schenck, of course, in his carpeted New York office, didn't see any of this. He only saw the critical and financial praise for Schary's *Battleground* and for other MGM hits of the era like *Adam's Rib* and *Mogambo*.

For certain anniversaries and special events, the studio occasionally summoned all of its stars, or at least most of them, under one roof to partake in what can only be called the world's ultimate self-aggrandizing photo op. The 1944 version (top) was for the twentieth anniversary gala and the 1949 version for its twenty-fifth. But by 1974, for the fiftieth anniversary, time had thinned the ranks considerably. *Bison Archives*

Mayer, of course, realized that Schary was being groomed as a younger, cheaper replacement for himself. But what could he do? He was after all, even though his name was still painted on that water tower, only a salaried employee, working at the pleasure of Loews Incorporated.

What Mayer did in May 1951 was to reportedly send Nicholas Schenck a letter asking to him choose between he and Schary. This supposed correspondence apparently no longer survives, but if L.B. did send this letter, it represented a serious miscalculation on his part to force an ultimatum on his old enemy and to expect Schenck to do anything but choose his rival, which he did. In August 1951, Loews/Schenck and Mayer each released impersonal statements announcing their separation and with each mechanically wishing the other success.

Shorn of his kingdom after twenty-seven years, Mayer left the studio on his last day via a red carpet thoughtfully placed there only because Howard Strickling, the studio's longtime publicity director, insisted that it be done in his honor. Likewise, a handful of stenographers working in the Thalberg building were pulled from their desks, along with some of the braver executives, to applaud the old man as he departed the studio. His name would remain on the water tower and as part of the logo, but otherwise, at MGM, it was then as if that old man had never existed.

Outside of MGM, it was almost as if he never had. Mayer had subverted and cocooned his identity inside his studio for so long that he apparently found it hard to establish a persona beyond that of the company. Therefore, with nothing else to do, he went to the racetrack, developed properties that everyone knew he would never film, and plotted corporate takeovers of his old studio that everyone knew he would never be able to pull off. "I am lonely for Leo the Lion,"[4] he was quoted as saying in 1956.

He also talked about starting his own production company, which caused Schary to publicly intone years later that "the fact is Mayer was an entrepreneur; bold, reckless, tough, rough, and mean as a polecat, but he had never made a film, nor could he have. However, he did draw the basic pattern for a big studio, and all of those that followed were imitations of MGM. Mayer's unique gifts were his vision and the verve to bring his dreams into reality."[5]

Without a studio, Mayer's "vision" quickly floundered. His former son-in-law, David O. Selznick, who undoubtedly saw a lot of himself in the old lion, reluctantly even had to refuse to give L.B. an office on his own lot, which he too was about to lose.

The man who may have once been, decades ago, someone named Lazar Meir died on October 29, 1957. His last words, to Strickling, were reported to be "nothing matters."

Years later, and with the benefit of hindsight, one of his stars, June Allyson said that "I think when he went, he took the studio with him."[6]

At that studio it suddenly seemed that everything was different with Mayer gone. Child star Claude Jarman Jr., who had worked on the lot in its heyday, came back in 1951, right after Mayer's outing, and was shocked to find how much the place had changed within a matter of months. "Around every corner new faces peered at me, most of them cold and unfriendly," he recalled. "Seemingly overnight the family atmosphere became a hostile unfamiliar setting. The fun was draining away."[7]

The profits were draining away as well. Schary ultimately proved himself to be a surprisingly ineffectual studio head. Although it is hard to imagine who at that point could have successfully changed the course that the company then seemed to be headed down. On his ascension to the throne, cynics had remarked that Schary had become the mayor of Rome while it was burning. Although it must be said that many of the studio's most beloved films would come out under his watch. And most of these iconic pictures were musicals, a genre that Schary had little interest in or understanding of, and so, wisely, mostly allowed and mostly ignored, even though they were expensive, hard to release overseas, and even then, commercially risky.

Scott Eyman, author of what is perhaps the best overall biography of Mayer, has stated that it had quickly become "clear just how much of a second-rater [Schary] had been . . . and how weakened Mayer had been to be picked off by someone like that."[8]

Schary would himself be picked off in 1956. *Gun Glory* (1957), a western with British-born, and sounding-like-it, Stewart Granger in the lead, would be the last film Schary would release during his reign. It lost $265,000.

Benny Thau inherited Mayer's office in 1956. Thau had been with the company since 1927, initially as a booker with the Loews theater chain. And it had been he to whom Mayer had addressed his infamous "How'd I do?" comment in 1933, so he was, to his credit, personally invested in the company. But he only lasted two years in the hotseat, despite successfully avoiding a potential, if ultimately toothless, hostile takeover by Mayer, and despite his capable shepherding of *Jailhouse Rock* (1957) and *Some Came Running* (1958) into hits for the studio.

In 1955, that studio had belatedly, and unhappily, ventured into television with *The MGM Parade*, although the division itself, originally and bluntly called "MGM-TV" (with a hyphen), would not launch until 1956. Unfortunately, most of that division's early offerings were simply old movies culled from the studio's vast library. And original programming, when it came, largely consisted of unimaginative, low-budget remakes of those old movies or self-serving promotions for their new ones.

One of the better of these TV retreads, *Dr. Kildare* (1961–1966), brought actor Richard Chamberlain onto the lot. Chamberlain reflected about that time that "you had the feeling even though that MGM was very vital, a lot of features, a lot of television being done there, that somehow there was a downward motion, there was a certain anxiety, you could feel a little bit of fear lurking in the corners of the management."[9]

Some of this fear was lurking in New York as well as in Culver City. Nicholas Schenck would resign as president of Loews, Inc. in 1955, although he lingered, wraith-like on the board of directors until 1957; he would die in 1969. Schenck's brother Joseph, who had eventually ended up as one of the founders of what became 20th Century Fox, would unhappily take time out from his duties there to serve time in prison for income tax evasion, but like his brother, he retired in 1957. Joe would live until 1961.

In 1955, Arthur M. Loew, the son of Marcus Loew, would become president of the company, although he himself would only last for a year, meaning that there would no longer be a Loew involved in Loews, Inc. The name "Loews" would be purged from MGM's letterhead on February 25, 1960, when Loews, Inc. would officially be

In the 1950s, the name "Loews" was finally retired and Metro-Goldwyn-Mayer belatedly became its own parent company, as reflected by this 1960s stationery and by its early twenty-first-century equivalent. *Author's collection*

renamed Metro-Goldwyn-Mayer Inc., resulting in, for the first time and after thirty-five years, MGM's finally becoming its own parent company.

In January 1958, under new CEO Joseph Vogel, Sol C. Siegel was awarded, if that could still be considered the proper word, the approximation of Mayer's old title at MGM. Seigel had been at the studio since 1956, which, by that point, was a long time indeed. He held on to that title for a little more than three years; although hits like *North by Northwest* (1959), *Ben-Hur* (1959), and *How the West Was Won* (1962) would be greenlit under his watch, the studio posted losses of $17.5 million in 1963.

"When I got to MGM," actor George Hamilton, who worked under Siegel, wrote in his memoirs, "you'd never know that the decline and fall of a celluloid empire was at hand. Its *Gigi* broke all records for a musical, its *Cat on a Hot Tin Roof* was the biggest moneymaker of 1958. Its *Ben-Hur* came out the year I arrived, as did its Hitchcock masterpiece *North by Northwest*. If this was failure, I wanted a big piece of it, with an Oscar on top."[10]

Unfortunately, Hamilton fails to inform us that these notable films were followed by the expensive failures of less-liked widescreen epics like *Mutiny on the Bounty* (1962) and *The Wonderful World of the Brothers Grimm* (1962), which would help lead to Siegel's replacement that year.

Robert M. Weitman followed Seigel. Under the thumb of company president Robert H. O'Brien, who had replaced Vogel, Weitman successfully expanded the studio's perpetually moribund TV division and shepherded theatrical hits like *Doctor Zhivago* and *The Dirty Dozen*. But in 1967, Weitman was replaced by G. Clark Ramsay, who lasted until 1969. By this time, two years in power at MGM was considered quite an accomplishment.

In 1969, Edgar Bronfman Sr., of the Seagram beverage firm, gained control of MGM after a brutal boardroom battle. Bronfman handpicked Louis F. "Bo" Polk Jr. as president of the company. Polk had no entertainment industry experience, although he did hire Herbert Solow, who had previously managed the studio's television division, as his head of production. Solow saved the company an estimated $800,000 a year by shifting the company's headquarters, which from 1966 on had been based in an expensive eleven-floor suite in New York, to the Thalberg building in Culver City in 1970. Although it was then ominously announced that a staff of ninety would remain in Gotham—for the moment.

But the Bronfman/Polk era was itself fated to last less than a year. A year in which the studio would lose a reported $36 million, and Bronfman would lose his hard-fought seat in the boardroom. MGM would lose something else during this regime too.

As two of the biggest hits of their era, *Doctor Zhivago* (1965) and *The Dirty Dozen* (1967) each returned their studio to profitability, if only briefly. *Author's collection*

Roger Mayer, the studio's vice president of administration at the time, later recalled that "this is what set the studio on its path to destruction. Bronfman tended to scale back rather than expand. It became about the quick buck. Something MGM had never done before"[11]

In 1969, sharpster Las Vegas lawyer Gregson Bautzer called on behalf of his employer to inquire as to purchasing the company from Bronfman. Bronfman. and Polk initially assumed that Bautzer must have been working for mysterious Vegas billionaire Howard Hughes, who years earlier had previously bought and then decimated RKO.

They were wrong.

4

Gamblers and Their Games

Kirk Kerkorian, for good or ill, is the most important person in the history of MGM. Movie buffs, writers, fans, and even serious historians tend to forget, or dismiss, the inarguable fact that Kerkorian bought and sold that company three times between 1969 and 2005, over thirty-six years in all, and each time with remarkable tenacity. This is a longer chronological span than any single movie star, or lurking behind the stars, even than Mayer, Thalberg, or Schenck were ever involved with the studio. Actor Robert Taylor, whose partnership with the company lasted thirty-four years, does come close, however. Perhaps the only significant individual, and this is perhaps regrettably ignoring "below-the-line" technicians or department heads who were associated with MGM longer (if often nonexclusively) than Kerkorian, was director tor George Cukor, who first worked at the studio for *Dinner at Eight* in 1933 and directed *Rich and Famous* there in 1981—forty-eight years later!

Kirk Kerkorian, inarguably, for good or bad, remains the single-most significant individual in the corporate history of MGM. *Bison Archives*

Not to take anything away from Taylor's or Cukor's achievements, it was, indisputably Kerkorian—corporately, if not creatively or chronologically—who had the bigger effect on the studio's past, present, and future.

Little-noted before is that Kerkorian, like all of those mentioned previously, was himself romantically, almost cosmically, tied to the studio's destiny. The child of poor Armenian immigrants from Fresno, his family immigrated to Los Angeles in the 1920s. Between bouts as an amateur boxer he used to pick up extra cash working as a day laborer moving scenery around on the MGM backlot. No one else mentioned already ever started at the studio so low, nor would ever rise so high.

Like Howard Hughes, Kerkorian romantically gravitated toward aviation first and movies afterward. After distinguishing himself as a flier in World War II, he invested in commercial aviation, ironically using money loaned to him by the Seagram family, among others. The TransAmerica Company, which was first known as the Bank of Italy, and later as the Bank of America, initially funded many early Hollywood studios and was also a major backer in Kerkorian's early ventures—at least until he sold his interests to them outright in 1968.

Kerkorian, like Hughes, eventually set his sights on Las Vegas, understandably, because Vegas was, even then, a 3D, interactive, and potentially more expensive version of what Hollywood had been offering to Kerkorian and his greatest-generation-era colleagues for decades. In 1962 he wisely started buying land adjacent to the Vegas Strip in Nevada, anticipating that this previously undervalued real estate would quickly become fabulously desirable as the casinos on the Strip expanded and other, less well-

Although Kerkorian coveted Leo the Lion, he briefly allowed the live cat to be replaced with this unsatisfactory, corporate, and very 1960s version, a variation of which can still be found at MGM resorts around the world. *Bison Archives* positioned hotels then tried to horn in. He also snatched up prestigious already-there hotels inside the existing definition of the Strip, including infamous gangster Bugsy Siegel's blood-stained-but-romantic Flamingo Hotel in 1967, which, of course, had been Las Vegas's first major hotel casino ever, leading to the birth of the Strip and of modern Las Vegas.

Why Kerkorian then set his eyes toward Culver City is difficult to ascertain. Although TransAmerica, among its many holdings, already owned United Artists, which might have drawn his attention to Hollywood, although his association with that company eventually became a potential monopoly or conflict of interest for him when he tried to acquire MGM.

The truth is, probably, that Kerkorian wasn't particularly interested in the entertainment industry in and of itself. And he certainly wasn't interested in the then debt- and ghost-ridden MGM in particular, although he did perceive of the studio as being a valuable and undervalued commodity with which to enrich his empire.

What it seems that he actually really wanted was Leo the Lion.

Kerkorian coveted that lion. Like millions of others, he had sat in theaters his whole life through his metamorphosis from laborer to warrior to millionaire transfixed by this visual and aural image of the king of beasts. That lion had perhaps struck the ambitious hustler as representative of something classical and classy and refined of which to aspire to. He also liked the idea that this lion, for all of its strength and power, was here subservient both to art and, especially, to its keepers. To Kerkorian then, being that lion's keeper, being literally the lord that made that lion roar, would seem to be a transcendent, life-altering aspiration.

But his interests were not solely personal, of course. He also envisioned that logo lion adoring not just movies. In fact, according to his grand plan, he intended movies to be a relatively insignificant, if prestigious, appendage to an empire branded by Leo the Lion. He envisioned this empire, presided over by himself and by this lion as also including his hotels, airlines, rental car companies, financial services, casinos, resorts, theme parks, and television networks. Far from breaking the company up to sell its components as had been supposed, Kerkorian rather wanted to expand it, to diversify it, with the lion logo being more important than any single component that it represented.

But how does one set a value on an image? At the time, MGM stock had guttered out at twenty-five dollars a share. Kerkorian started buying it at ten dollars above that price to acquire the 30 percent of the company necessary to challenge Bronfman.

Eventually, to enact this coup he, upped his ante to forty-two dollars a share—nearly twice what it was then estimated to be worth. In October 1969, with 32 percent of the company in hand, he fired Louis F. "Bo" Polk and strongarmed Edgar Bronfman's resignation from the board.

Kerkorian had captured his lion.

Even then, his associates realized that their boss's dreams of global domination, as presided over by a lion, was somehow profoundly and deeply personal and not just a speculative cash grab. For example, Gregson Bautzer insightfully remarked right after the sale about Kerkorian that "Kirk felt he had bought a little immortality."[1]

With Polk gone, Kerkorian would need an executive with entertainment industry experience to try to turn the company around, and quickly he chose James T. Aubrey, a former television executive sometimes rather disturbingly referred to as the "smil-ing cobra." Aubrey and Kerkorian have taken blame from historians and hatred from fans for the desecrations that were perpetuated against MGM over the next four years. Some of this scorn is deserved, although in recent years Kerkorian has been absolved, at least somewhat, more so than Aubrey, because of the latter's heavy-handed insistence on making the company profitable, whatever the cost in livelihood or legacy to that company or its employees.

The truth is there is plenty of blame to go around. Like Louis B. Mayer, Kerkorian never intended, nor was he at all suited, to be a hands-on boss. He believed in hiring the presumed best men for the job and then leaving those men to largely navigate by their own lights to complete that job. So it is Aubrey who is responsible for the 3,500-plus worldwide layoffs during his

James Aubrey, the so-called Smiling Cobra, was hired by Kerkorian in 1969 to manage his studio at a salary of $4000 a week. *Author's collection*

tenure; the many expensive and unpopular movies from this era; the auctions of the company's heirlooms; the shortsighted sale of overseas theaters, of the British studio, and of much of the Culver City plant as well. It all needs to be laid at his feet. Herb

Solow, Douglas Netter, Jack Haley Jr., and Daniel Melnick, Aubrey's sometimes momentary heads of production during this period, bear responsibility as well. And finally, Kerkorian, although always regarded as the consummate businessman, is guilty of allowing all of these unfortunate business desecrations to happen on his watch and so still remains personally culpable for what happened as well.

Some of the changes inflicted on the company and its employees during this period seemed more psychological than financial. Roger Mayer remembered that

> they even took Thalberg's name off the Thalberg [b]uilding, saying that this was the "new MGM," and that the name was somehow now old fashioned, although I'm not sure I understand how the name in itself was old fashioned. I retrieved the plaque that used to be near the front door with that name on it and took it up to my office. A couple years later they changed their minds and decided to put Thalberg's name back up. So, I gave them back their sign. It's probably still there.[2]

The greatest single desecration ever self-perpetuated by the studio was the notorious auctions of its own heirlooms. Those asset sales came about when Aubrey, who seemingly couldn't comprehend there being any value associated with the acres of props and costumes the studio had accumulated over fifty years, allowed the David Weisz Company to take whatever they wanted for a flat $1.5 million. The subsequent auctions, which began on May 3, 1970, netted Weisz an estimated $10 million for selling off Garbo's gowns, Gable's trench coat, Tarzan's loincloth, and Dorothy's slippers.

The auctions also attracted wide and damning publicity that shamed even callous Hollywood and clueless MGM. Those auctions also sparked a seemingly insatiable and increasingly expensive appetite among collectors for screen-used movie props. For example, the Cowardly Lion skin from *The Wizard of Oz*, which in 1970 sold for $2,400, would be auctioned again in 2014, when the price surpassed $3 million.

Despite Kerkorian's stated penchant for not being involved with Metro's day-to-day operations, it was he, not Aubrey, who in 1973 sold off the studio's distribution apparatus, first overseas to a consortium and then domestically to United Artists, rendering MGM the only major in Hollywood that did not distribute its own product. In fact, the much-vilified Aubrey objected to this in a letter to his boss that reportedly made the tycoon furious. Disgusted, Aubrey then told a colleague that "if I was a regular stockholder, I'd sue us."[3]

It has been reported that Aubrey resigned after sending this letter because "the job I agreed to undertake has been accomplished."[4] This is untrue. Aubrey was fired. But Kerkorian allowed him to resign publicly and issue that terse statement to save face.

For his part, Aubrey, widely vilified in the industry, in the business community, and among the general public, deservingly or not, never toplined a studio or a TV network again. Although he did produce insipid, successful TV movies like *The Dallas Cowboy Cheerleaders* (1979). Sadly, that's more than Mayer, post MGM, was ever allowed to do.

Aubrey was replaced by Frank Rosenfelt. Daniel Melnick, the latest in the ever-spinning collage of production heads (as of 1972), was kept on by Rosenfelt, only because Kerkorian instructed him to do so. Although, par for the course, Richard Shepherd would replace him in 1977. Melnick himself moved on to Columbia Studios in 1978 to replace an executive named David Begelman. Begelman had been fired from Columbia for embezzling checks, including one intended for actor Cliff Robertson, who subsequently blew the whistle. And yet, despite this, the disgraced Begelman, in 1980, was *still* then hired by Rosenfelt and by Kerkorian to supervise MGM!

During this confusing, scandalized, low-water era, there truly seemed to be no muddy depth MGM was not capable of flailing into. A disgusted actor, Kirk Douglas, later mused, "This is the town where Cliff Robertson exposed David Begelman as a forger and a thief, with the net result that Begelman got a standing ovation at a Hollywood restaurant, while Robertson was blacklisted for four years."[5]

The controversial Begelman did not last long, but Rosenfelt himself, despite his perceived moral shortcomings, proved surprisingly durable, tenaciously hanging on at the studio until 1982. After that, he moved over to its sister company, United Artists, with Frank Rothman replacing him as CEO.

During this period, Kerkorian tried to appear unconcerned with the day-to-day (mis)management of his studio. Although, as he had done with Aubrey, he sometimes wrote letters admonishing his executives and privately seethed over some of those executives' confounding decisions. Unsurprisingly, he did take a personal interest, however, in transitioning the Leo the Lion brand onto his other businesses.

The first MGM Grand hotel in Las Vegas opened on December 4, 1973. It had twenty-six floors under an eleven-acre roof, making it, at the time, the largest hotel in the world. Originally Kerkorian had wanted to base the hotel on Cedric Gibbons's grand art deco sets from the movie *Grand Hotel*, although ultimately, despite some deco flourishes in the lobby probably suggested by the movie and, of course, the hotel's name, this did not really happen.

In every other way, however, the hotel was very much a Hollywood spectacle, and like every Hollywood spectacle, it had a glittering premiere. Kerkorian's ever-debonair friend, actor Cary Grant, hosted the event, which, along with the hotel's subsequent and continued success, validated Kerkorian's beliefs that the MGM brand could be

Kerkorian's original MGM Grand, as seen in this vintage postcard, was the largest hotel in the world when it opened in 1973. *Author's collection*

used on products other than motion pictures—and perhaps more successfully than it was then being used in motion pictures.

At the same time, Kerkorian briefly flirted with buying Columbia Pictures. When that didn't work out, he instead looked to United Artists, which he already had an interest in due to its distribution deal with MGM and his prior involvement with TransAmerica. At the time, MGM was a studio that had a library and a factory but no distribution operation. United Artists was a studio in possession of a library and distribution apparatus but no physical facilities. United Artists was also financially strapped at the time due to the crushing commercial and artistic failure of their $44 million epic *Heaven's Gate* (1980)—the fortuitous timing of which Kerkorian knew he could then take advantage of.

As he knew it would be, Kerkorian's offer of $380 million in cash and loan certificates was eventually accepted, leaving the combined company with, according to Kerkorian's biographer William C. Rempel, "about 35 percent of all movies ever made, twice to three times as many as any other single studio."[6] Consequently, the studio name and logo would be modified to read "MGM/UA," although, of course, Leo the Lion would continue to roar above those words.

Kerkorian's waltz with the studio, his pattern of tearing down and then building up the company, would continue for another five erratic years. But by summer 1985, he was perhaps tiring of the game. No matter who he handpicked for the board of directors or dropped into Mayer's chair in the Thalberg building, they inevitably disappointed him and his stockholders by delivering lackluster returns and bad films. A good year like 1982 would yield hits like *Poltergeist*, *Victor/Victoria*, and *Rocky III* but would also bring forth flops like *Cannery Row* (with an $11.5 million budget versus a $1.5 million return), *Yes, Giorgio*, and *Inchon*—the last of which by itself improbably managed to lose $40 million.

Morale on the lot was, as can be imagined, abysmal during this era. Nervous executives, worried that they would be fired at any minute, second-guessed every decision and expense that crossed their desks, ultimately resulting in expensive and embarrassing about-faces and recalculations that would then ripple from the front office to the backlot. Longtime below-the-line employees tried to hunker down beneath the executive musical chairs ever-shuffling above them, but layoffs and departmental closures were common. Employees who had been on the lot for decades were randomly sent home, sometimes with no notice or warning.

New staffers were also astonished at the toxic corporate culture that they found themselves suddenly a part of. Greg Gormick, a music researcher hired for the much-troubled flop *Pennies from Heaven* (1981) said that

> in 1974, I saw *That's Entertainment!* and it literally changed my life. I promised myself then that someday I would work at mighty MGM. So, when I was hired to work on the lot, and on an MGM musical yet, it was the most exciting thing that had ever happened to me in my life. But be careful what you wish for! My friends would call me from Canada every week to find out how I was doing in my dream job, and every week, I'd sound more disillusioned and depressed and miserable. My bosses kept getting fired. I kept getting fired. And then they'd bring us all back with different titles and more responsibilities and it'd just start all over again.[7]

Eventually it must have occurred to Kerkorian that there was no reason to continue to endure, and absorb, season after season, all of this embarrassing and expensive red ink. After all, despite his affection for movies, he was the only mogul ever who enjoyed seeing films, even his own films, in a regular theater and with the public, but he was never a showbiz-type person. He didn't fit in, in Hollywood. He didn't even try.

And why should he? He had bought the studio for its logo after all, and he was now using that logo successfully on his other business ventures. Why not sell the studio, with its endless drama and travails and red ink, keep the name for his hotels, and then just get the hell out of Hollywood?

There was even, as fate would have it, just then someone waiting in the wings who was interested in buying MGM. In 1985, Ted Turner, who had made a fortune as a cable TV mogul, and who had recently and unsuccessfully tried to acquire CBS, received a call from Kerkorian, who asked him if he would be interested in buying all, or part, of the MGM/UA conglomerate.

Turner was interested indeed—not only for the studio and for the film library, which he saw as fodder for his television networks, but because, well, it was MGM. And MGM had produced *Gone with the Wind*, the Atlanta-raised Turner's favorite movie. *Gone with the Wind*, in effect, represented to Turner what Leo the Lion had to Kerkorian.

Unfortunately, the price, $1.6 billion, was too much for Turner. Obligingly, Kerkorian eventually agreed that if Turner purchased the company, he in turn would then buy back UA for $480 million through a complicated sale-loan arrangement that Kerkorian then worked out with his investment bankers. Although Turner himself has

Media mogul Ted Turner is seen here in his Atlanta office, although some of the souvenirs on display indicate that his ambition and reach once extended into Hollywood as well. *Author's collection*

subsequently said that Kerkorian had intended to carve out UA for himself from the beginning.

But even with this slice severed from the pie, there was no avoiding the numbers on the table. Turner would still be responsible for finding more than a billion dollars! And if he could manage that, he would then also have to assume the responsibility for Metro's considerable debt load. Upon examination of the books, it didn't help that none of the movies then in the pipeline looked like potential cash cows either. As Turner struggled to come up with the financing, Kerkorian, who rather seemed to like the younger man, obligingly kept tinkering with the terms, price, and conditions of the sale in a sincere attempt to keep Turner in the game.

That game dragged on through most of the tenures of Kerkorian's newest studio saviors: Frank Yablans (1983–1984), Jay Kantor (1984), and Alan "Laddie" Ladd Jr. (1985–1988) and into March 1986, when Turner finally got his studio. But the debt Turner got with his studio, when combined with its then $1.4 billion price tag, now amounted to some $1.6 billion!

To pay down this debt, the new mogul was forced to sell off, piecemeal, what he had just purchased. Tragically, he immediately sold that studio, or at least the physical plant, or at least what was left of the physical plant, then reduced to some forty-four acres, to Lorimar-Telepictures, which had long been a major tenant there, for $190 million. Lorimar would subsequently be purchased by Warner Bros., who in 1990 sold the lot to Sony Electronics, as a home for their recently purchased Columbia Pictures.

It was too little too late. Two months after the sale closed, Kerkorian bought back the MGM production and home-video units for $300 million. Turner, however, still got to keep all the non-UA library titles, including *Gone with the Wind*. Blistering from his short, expensive waltz with Hollywood, Ted Turner wryly wisecracked that "I never even had a chance to use a casting couch."[8]

Variety, however, was blunter still. Turner, it said, "came to Hollywood fully clothed and left in a barrel."[9]

The divided library caused some definite irregularities. Although the older films would keep the MGM logo, newer MGM films, and Kerkorian's hotel casinos, would be able to use it as well. In fact, Kerkorian had unsurprisingly and specifically made sure that Turner would not be able to use any other lion-related imagery going forward.

The cutoff between the two libraries was determined to be May 1986. Therefore, *Killer Party*, a dire horror film released that month, was determined to be the last film in a library that officially went all the way back to 1924's *He Who Gets Slapped* and

A Lorimar publicity still from 1990 emphasizing their new signage atop Stage 6, which would not be there for long. *Bison Archives*

so would go to Turner. On the other side of the divide, *Poltergeist II: The Other Side*, another horror movie released later the same month, would be the first "new MGM" library title. But because of this release, MGM was able to preserve the remake rights to this franchise, leading to *Poltergeist III* in 1988 and a 2015 remake. Although the first *Poltergeist*, made in 1982, would now belong to Turner.

The irregularities from this divorce were endless and confounding. MGM's successful musical *Fame* (1980) went to Turner. But the same-named TV series, which ran from 1982 to 1987 and so was still on the air at the time, was deemed to stay at MGM as a special swap so that Turner could own the TV series *Gilligan's Island* (1964–1967) and future rights to the *Fame* franchise. MGM also was left with one of the largest library catalogs in the world, some two-thousand-plus feature films then, although many of these titles, at least until 1986, had come from United Artists.

Turner received some of this library as well. Most of his UA titles were cartoons or television releases, but he also pocketed thousands of choice releases from other studios, including nearly RKO's entire catalog and most Warner Bros. films dating

Originally the newest owner of the property renamed that property "Columbia Studios." But in 1992, "corporate synergy" dictated that the parent company's name instead be placed above the gates. *Bison Archives*

to before midcentury, which collectively and inarguably gave Turner another of the largest and most valuable media libraries in the world. Turner would keep this library until 1996 when his company would merge with Warner Bros.

Kerkorian, having again caged his lion, now realized that Leo needed a new home. In 1987, he first moved across the street from the old studio to 1000 Washington Boulevard, a Mayan-influenced ziggurat-shaped glass building, which he had briefly flirted with turning into a Vegas-style hotel. However, according to *Variety* columnist and former MGM executive Peter Bart, the industry joke about the building was that "it looked like a place where human sacrifices would be taken, not movies made."[10]

To run this fiefdom, Kerkorian poached Lee Rich from, ironically, Lorimar, as his CEO and head of production. In addition to the usual flops, Rich and his successors Stephen Silbert (1988) and Jeffrey Barbakow (1988–1990) managed to oversee some

Building of the Year

Filmland Corporate Center is proud to have won the BOMA of Greater Los Angeles "1989 Building of the Year" award in the 100,000 to 500,000-square-foot category. This 360,000-square-foot structure, which is home of MGM/UA and other entertainment industry firms, features a dramatic eight-story glass atrium with horseshoe-shaped architecture allowing for numerous corner offices, interior balconies, expansive outdoor terraces and spectacular,

unobstructed views of the Pacific Ocean, Santa Monica Mountains, San Gabriel Mountains and downtown Los Angeles skyline.

A magnificent Grande Atrium lobby, underground parking which can accommodate 1200 cars, individual air conditioning and lighting zones, and state-of-the-art amenities throughout were designed to meet the business needs of the most sophisticated tenants.

Divested of its longtime home, MGM moved across the street from their old lot and into this ziggurat-shaped office, which in 1989 was voted "Building of the Year" by someone. *Author's collection*

successes like *Moonstruck* (1987), *A Fish Called Wanda* (1988), and *Rain Man* (1988), the last of which, from the UA division, won the Best Picture Academy Award for that year.

Despite these occasional bright spots, Kerkorian continued to tinker with the company and to flirt with again selling it outright. For example, in 1988 he nearly sold a 25 percent interest to producers Jon Peters and Peter Guber, and in 1989, Qintex, an Australian conglomerate, almost picked up the whole bag of marbles. Both deals precariously fell through only at the last minute. All of this financial drama again made it hard to attract creative talent and angered Rich, who ultimately resigned in 1988, leaving the company, again, in a chaotic free fall.

For his part, Kerkorian bristled at the suggestion that his long years in the lion's den had only been some sort of cash grab. "I've operated eight different businesses in my career and MGM is the only one I couldn't turn into a profitable operation," he told to anyone willing to listen. "I kept trying but I couldn't come up with the right management team."[11]

But in 1990, Kerkorian did exactly what his employees, and Hollywood at-large, feared he would do and sold the company outright—and to the worst possible candidate.

Italian financier (and suspected mobster) Giancarlo Parretti was also the owner of Pathé Communications, which seemingly had roots going back to 1896 in France and 1914 in the US. Although Paretti's Pathé was actually a renaming of his own low-rent production company, the Cannon Group, which he had done in anticipation of buying the original Pathé.

This little detail alone should have given Kerkorian pause before proceeding, but it didn't. One seemingly odd consistency in Kerkorian's character, perhaps stemming from years spent dealing with Las Vegas gangsters, was his ability to consistently turn a blind eye to personal and even criminal character flaws in those with whom he dealt.

The price this time for the lion was $1.25 billion, and it took Parretti, like Turner before him, nearly a year to come up with the financing. Largely, the money came from sources no one was sure of the origins of. But despite any misgivings, which many appeared to have about Parretti's character and motivations, those at the studio at least tried to make the best of this transition. "I think the world of Parretti," said Jeffrey Barbakow, who had been fulfilling Silbert's duties since his immediate predecessor's departure. "He's extremely bright, and he's a global thinker."[12]

The rest of Hollywood, however, was not so certain about Parretti or about the recent influx of foreign companies and executives that were then buying their way

Giancarlo Paretti, somehow finding a few minutes to relax at the Chateau Marmont during his brief, spectacular Holly-wood adventure, reportedly had ties to organized crime, which the studio later fictionalized in 1995's *Get Shorty* (top), with John Travolta now doing the dirty work. *Author's collection*

into quintessentially US companies like film studios. The press was quick to cite Australian-born American Rupert Murdoch's acquisition of 20th Century Fox in 1985 and Columbia's 1989 sale to Japanese electronics giant Sony, as examples.

Parretti's MGM, officially launched in November 1990, was renamed again. This iteration of the company would be called MGM-Pathé Communications. For the launch, a live lion named Sudan was hired for the day from Cougar Hill Ranch, a respected supplier of trained animals, to pose with his new keepers at a party. But the only way to get to the event, scheduled to take place on the upper floor of an LA high-rise, was on a public elevator. "The elevator ride was interrupted two times. When the doors opened the looks on the people's faces were priceless,"[13] Sudan's trainer, Nicholas Toth, remembers. Once there, however, Parretti, in particular, seemed fascinated by the big cat and included him in multiple photos taken throughout the evening.

But chaos descended on the company almost from the moment the signage was changed. First off, the studio had to move again, this time to the existing Cannon Pictures/Pathé Communications offices located at 640 San Vicente in Beverly Hills.

Once they were there, almost immediately, Parretti displayed an off-putting sense of entitlement, which rubbed Hollywood's old guard the wrong way. Steven J. Ross, the well-respected chair of Time Warner (Warner Bros.), originally had intended to help finance MGM's purchase by Pathé in return for the home-video rights to the MGM, or rather the UA, catalog. But Parretti fumbled the deal by objecting to giving Ross a copy of the guest list for a breakfast they were both attending. Perhaps to make up for this perceived slight, Parretti later, and with much ceremony, gifted Ross a supposed Picasso drawing that—surprise—turned out to be a forgery. The resultant scandal was "a lot of hoo-ha over nothing that cost us $650 million,"[14] Giovanni Di Stefano, one of Parretti's partners in the deal grumbled.

And the grumbling continued. Parretti did not inspire confidence among his ever-shell-shocked employees when he "hired" his inexperienced twenty-one-year-old daughter Valentina as a chief financial officer for the company. Nor was his approval rating among his staff boosted by his oft-reported and oft-repeated habit of having sex with various "actresses" in his office suite and from his showering these conquests with lavish, company-funded gifts. Parretti also propositioned movie star Meryl Streep and producer Dino De Laurentiis's daughter Raffaella—both of whom, they undoubtedly would want here noted, rebuffed his advances. "Laddie make-a-the-deals, I (expletive) the girls," he publicly was quoted by *Variety* as saying.[15]

Not surprisingly, some tension eventually developed between Parretti and "Laddie," who had been brought back into the fold for another try as studio chair/CEO but who was abused and constantly second-guessed by Parretti, even though Ladd, like Barbakow, had originally supported him.

More publicly, in 1990, Sean Connery had to threaten to boycott the premiere of his own film, *The Russia House*, until he was issued a letter of credit he was owed. Furthermore, in 1991 a check to another star, Dustin Hoffman, bounced, the sound of which was heard ricocheting all over Hollywood.

At the Academy Awards that year, host Billy Crystal wisecracked that "from now on the lion is not going to roar, it will be taking the fifth." When asked to comment on the remark, however, the ever-placating Di Stefano only shrugged it off by saying that "in fairness we were told the joke before going to the Oscars and we all had a good laugh. *Thelma and Louise* won, so we really did not care."[16]

Much less of a laughing matter for everyone, especially to a particular former owner of MGM, was the fact that at about the same time, the studio started missing their promised payments to Kerkorian.

That MGM-Pathé could continue to stumble along at all during this dire period was largely due to dubious assurances from their chief financial backer, the French bank Crédit Lyonnais. And Crédit Lyonnais, as most Hollywood players and would-be players already knew, was then the cash withdrawal machine of choice for independent film companies in need of outside finance. The bank was then bleeding so much money in the US that the French press was starting to become openly critical. But in Hollywood, no one seemed to want to heed the flashing warning signs. What could go wrong?

In May 1991, even Crédit Lyonnais finally began to realize that they had been grossly lied to by Parretti, his family, and his enablers. To look out for their own interests, the bank sent their own man, lawyer Charles Meeker, to California to "co-manage" the company. Ultimately though, Meeker's most important duty ended up as acting as moderator in the ongoing blood-sport battles between Parretti and Ladd. Eventually, the lawyer's watchdog presence in the room itself seemed to be enough to enrage the volatile Parretti, who once memorably shouted at "Meekers" as he called him, that "I want you to understand, Meekers, that I am really crazy. . . . I want you to understand that I am really dangerous. I am very dangerous. Do you understand, Meekers? I'm very dangerous."[17]

Meeker's subsequent reports back home to the bank, as interesting as they must have been, probably did little to allay Crédit Lyonnais's fears. One unnamed and soon-to be former banker there memorably told Peter Bart that "I realized that . . . $3 billion of wasted money could have saved the Middle East peace process. What were we doing giving the money to Hollywood?"[18]

On Monday, June 17, the bank finally seized control of 98.5 percent of MGM, removed Parretti, removed his hangers on, removed his girls, his family, and his threats from the premises and formally instituted a lawsuit against him in the Chancery Court of Delaware, where MGM had been incorporated. Parretti promptly countersued in both Delaware and in California. The final net result of this legal wrangling was that Crédit Lyonnais became the unwilling owner of the most famous movie studio in the world.

Unfortunately, because of its expensive misadventures in La La Land, Crédit Lyonnais was now on the verge of financial ruin itself. Eventually the bank was saved only by a controversial and widely unpopular bailout by the French government. As part of their emergency restructuring, in September 1991, Crédit Lyonnais changed the name of Metro-Goldwyn-Mayer back to Metro-Goldwyn-Mayer. They also again moved the company from Beverly Hills back to their previous Culver City address at 1000 Washington Boulevard, although in 1993 they chaotically pulled up stakes yet again, this time landing at the corner of Colorado Avenue and 26th Street in Santa Monica.

The ten-year lease on the new complex was $25 million cheaper than the old digs had been. And the owner of the property, who was thrilled to have such a prestigious client, happily renamed the campus-like complex "Metro Goldwyn Mayer Plaza." Amenities there eventually would include screening rooms, editing suites, a fitness center, commissary, daycare center, and a "studio" store.

Alan Ladd Jr. was thrilled to finally be vacating Culver City for good, probably just as thrilled as he had been to get rid of Parretti. Just before the move he had wearily looked out his window into the shadows of the old studio while telling a reporter that "what I see now is what once was. I'm counting down the minutes until we leave here. We have been so snakebit. I feel like the move to Santa Monica means more than just fresh air. I feel like our luck may finally change."[19]

It hadn't. Not for Ladd, anyway. In July of that year, MGM replaced him with former Paramount executive Frank Mancuso Sr., probably because Ladd had, by now, been tainted by his not always harmonious relationship with Parretti, who himself eventually received (but due to extradition issues never served) a jail sentence for misuse of corporate funds.

Charles "Meekers," and many, many others, probably breathed easier knowing that Parretti was finally gone—perhaps with good reason. Significantly, in May 1996, the Crédit Lyonnais headquarters was gutted by a mysterious fire, the cause of which has never been determined.

Crédit Lyonnais would operate MGM until 1996. During their reluctant reign they perpetuated MGM's tradition of releasing many unsuccessful films and a few hits as well. One of the bright spots was 1995's *Get Shorty*. Although based on a 1990 Elmore Leonard novel, the story, which concerned itself with an Italian gangster's shady dealings in Hollywood, was curiously "meta" long before meta was a thing. In one scene, a scene that must have resonated in the halls of the studio's offices, hoodlum Chili Palmer (John Travolta) comments that it's a "rough business, this movie business. I'm gonna have to go back to loan-sharking just to take a rest."

The eventual buyer of MGM, to Crédit Lyonnais's undoubted relief, was again and for the third time, Kerkorian, who in 1996 paid $870 million this time. Again, Kerkorian followed his usual business pattern of initially building the company up. However, by this time, shorn of its studio lot, its distribution arm, and much of its original library, there was much less to build on.

Outside, of course, of that roaring lion.

Kerkorian realized that the company may not have owned *Gone with the Wind* or *Singin' in the Rain* anymore. After all, he was the reason why they didn't. But what remained in the library was still massive and, in the wake of the then current home-video boom, massively exploitable. To supplement this, in 1997, he purchased Metromedia, which, along with other, subsequent library grabs, eventually provided MGM with the collected libraries of Orion Pictures, American International, Filmways, the Motion Picture Corporation of America, PollyGram, and most aptly of all, the Samuel Goldwyn Company. Collectively, this film-buying spree ultimately reaffirmed MGM as one of the largest cinema rights libraries in the world with four thousand film titles and some seventeen thousand individual TV episodes, almost all of them (save for 297) made before 1948 but still narrowly second only to that of Warner Bros., which had acquired Turner's library in 1996 and so was slightly larger—due to its thousands of old MGM titles.

In 1999, Kerkorian also replaced Mancuso with Alex Yemenidjian and Chris McGurk. Although once again he frustrated his very well-paid executive team by constantly and publicly fishing about for a buyer, which made it hard for MGM to attract the best material and hard to placate creative individuals worried about their project's futures. Kerkorian's outrageous $7 billion asking price for the company kept many potential buyers at bay too.

In 2003, MGM moved again to a high-rise office tower, specifically, the newly constructed "MGM Tower," in Century City. The complex, with delicious but undoubtedly unintentional irony, had been specially built on the ruins of a studio backlot, not that of MGM but rather of 20th Century Fox, which had sold the property in the early 1960s for real estate development. The new building, at 10250 Constellation

MGM Tower in Century City was the company's opulent corporate home from 2003 to 2010. *Author's collection*

Boulevard, located on the newly named street "MGM Way" was opulent in the style of a Kerkorian Las Vegas hotel. Of course, those hotels had been originally designed to mimic the look of Hollywood movies, so the irony was two-fold, at the very least.

In fact, the complex had been the vision of Kerkorian's lieutenant, Yemenidjian. The *Los Angeles Times* described the building as containing

> such Las Vegas-style flourishes as towering marble pillars and a grand spiral staircase lined with a wall of awards. In the lobby of the 14th floor, which includes the executive suites, is a wall of floating Oscar statuettes for such Academy Award winners as *Silence of the Lambs*, *Rocky* and *West Side Story*. The bottom third of the tower was built with extra-large floors to oblige MGM, architect Scott Johnson said. That design allowed executives to have outdoor decks.[20]

In September 2004, Kerkorian's quest to again sell the company concluded when he found himself in the enviable position of being in the middle of a bidding war between

Sony (which then owned the studio's old lot) and Warner Bros. (which then owned the studio's old library). Warner Bros. blinked first, so the final winner was Sony. But the electronics giant was still uncomfortable with the reduced $4.8 billon price, so they ultimately formed a consortium of outside companies to help shoulder the bill. Unfortunately for Sony, however, although this did minimize their investment, it also minimized their control.

There was much talk at the time that MGM would be brought back to Culver City and that perhaps some of the original signage could be ceremonially returned to the lot. But this was not to be, even if Sony had agreed to it, because the new company, with Sony only a minority shareholder, instead ignored the Japanese giant and defiantly continued to operate as an independent studio, which it effectively now was because of the ineffectualness of that consortium.

Harry E. Sloan became MGM chair/CEO in 2005 and continued to assert the company's independence; he even rejected Sony's home-video distribution offer in favor of that of, yes, their neighbor, 20th Century Fox. The deal probably made Columbia Studios executives as livid as it would have once made Mayer.

In 2006, with a network of smaller studios, MGM again flaunted their independence, this time by defiantly returning to theatrically distributing their own product for the first time in decades. *Lucky Number Slevin* was the first film domestically distributed by MGM since *The Outfit* (1973). Sadly, this new division only lasted through *Hot Tub Time Machine* (2010), when due to bad films outnumbering good ones, and to a worldwide economic downturn, the studio again found itself facing bankruptcy. In the future, various production or finance partners would provide domestic, home video, and international distribution for MGM product.

Also in 2006, Sloan revived the then long-dormant United Artists brand as a production unit to operate from within MGM. Paula Wagner was named CEO of United Artists with her longtime partner, superstar Tom Cruise, as executive/star for the revived company. And *The Hollywood Reporter* noted in November:

> When CEO Harry Sloan gives visitors a tour of MGM's airy executive offices on the 14th floor of the MGM Tower in Century City, he enjoys pointing out an antique document in one of the display cases. The paper in question is the founding agreement that Charlie Chaplin, Mary Pickford, Douglas Fairbanks and director D.W. Griffith signed in 1919 when they decided to take control of their careers by joining to create their own motion picture company, the United Artists Corp. Until Thursday, that old contract appeared more a historical artifact than a template for the future. But in

announcing that it has struck a deal with Tom Cruise and his producing partner Paula Wagner to revive UA, MGM said it was harkening back to UA's storied history as a filmmaker friendly place where producers, writers, directors and actors can thrive in a creative environment.[21]

Unfortunately, as usually happens with companies driven by on-screen talent, Cruise, a consistently bankable superstar if ever there was one, was unable to deliver a hit film as his own producer. *Lions for Lambs* (2007) and *Valkyrie* (2008) both bellyflopped, although between each of these passion projects he reliably managed to consistently deliver hits for other studios. In August 2008, Wagner and Cruise stepped down, although they retained a percentage of ownership in United Artists. Sloan, who had admitted to Peter Bart that he too, like Kerkorian before him, was "enamored" with Leo the Lion, followed them out the door in 2009.

Inside that lion's lair, the CEO position was then split into smaller fiefdoms, and Stephen Cooper, a specialist in saving flailing companies (Krispy Kreme doughnuts being a recent success) was brought in to replace him. He lasted for about a year.

During this period, things were so bad that even Kerkorian, who again had continued to spin off the MGM name and MGM lion for his other holdings, was now suffering. His fortune, at one time estimated at $18 billion, was by the end of 2009 reduced to a "mere" $3 billion.

Kerkorian died at the age of ninety-eight on June 15, 2015. Peter Bart, who had worked at MGM during Kerkorian's first eventful regime there, struggled in print to explain a man he had worked under for years but never really understood. "While he bought and sold the once proud studio three times it was never clear whether he had any interest in movies or the movie business," he marveled. Bart then said about the man whom he remembered everyone on the lot always referring to as "the ghost" that "he was consistent in selecting a parade of misfits or miscreants to run his studio, and in finding unworthy buyers upon which to bestow his assets." Bart went on to assert that "it became a Hollywood joke that the only way to become Kerkorian's studio chief was to be fired for egregiously bad behavior by another company—Frank Yablans from Paramount, Jim Aubrey from CBS and David Begelman from Columbia (he narrowly escaped jail)."[22]

But Peter Bart, along with just about everyone he ever encountered, did praise his old boss's remarkably constant grace under pressure and his often remarked on inscrutability, both of which were qualities that had served Kerkorian well for a long time.

Kerkorian was probably happy during his last years that he was no longer saddled with the studio. In November 2010, MGM finally filed for Chapter 11 bankruptcy protection, although to the company's credit they quickly reorganized and emerged from that long, looming shadow less than a month later, with the aid of a private equity firm, Anchorage, run by investor Kevin Ulrich, who stayed on as chair of the board. During this period, Gary Barber and Roger Birnbaum were then the primary executives in the studio hot seat. Birnbaum stepped down after a couple years but remained at the studio as a development executive, but Barber would keep his chair until 2018, after which the CEO position was again split and divided up among division heads.

With the advent of the hard economic times for the studio and for the global economy, it seemed to Barber and Birnbaum somewhat insensitive to continue to maintain such expensive digs, however. In 2010, after emerging from their messy and public bankruptcy procedure, the company moved, yet again, to smaller and cheaper offices in Beverly Hills. Studio officials admitted they had been paying about five dollars a foot per month for their 200,000-square-foot principality in Century City but declined to say how much their new 144,000-square-foot address, at 245 N. Beverly Drive, was going to cost them, except to assert that it was "substantially less."[23]

In the twenty-first century, MGM's output has been similar to that of other so-called mini-majors, which are not, or in this particular case, are no longer, full-service studios but are larger than the production companies that develop projects for those studios or for stars. MGM officially ceased to be a major studio, officially at least, not when they shut down their distribution arm, when they sold off their lot, or when they sold off their library but in 2005 when they were partially purchased by Sony. The Motion Picture Association (MPA) has always worked with whatever the current definition of the major studios consists of to determine industry practices and to administer ratings. Because Sony already possessed a membership in this most exclusive of clubs, via their ownership of Columbia Studio, MGM was withdrawn under the assumption that Columbia and MGM would negotiate together. But when Sony and MGM parted ways, the latter was not invited back in. Today, MGM's old seat at the MPA table is, rather tellingly, occupied by Netflix.

The biggest financial news story in the world on May 26, 2021, was retail giant Amazon's announcement that, after weeks of negotiations, they were acquiring MGM, its logo, legacy, lion, and library for $8.45 billion. The agreed-on price was much higher than the roughly $5 billion that the legendary company was then estimated to be worth, making one wonder, perhaps with a bit of wistful romance, if the alure of that lion might have transfixed Amazon CEO Jeff Bezos just as it had Mayer, Kerkorian, Guber, Sloan, and perhaps even Parretti.

Not surprisingly, Leo the Lion was evoked in the first public statement after the deal was announced, when Ulrich remarked that "I am very proud that MGM's Lion, which has long evoked the Golden Age of Hollywood, will continue its storied history."[24]

In some ways, the sale was, for MGM at least, ideal. If the company had been purchased by another media company, Warner Bros., for example, it would have immediately and permanently been marginalized, which is exactly what had happened when Disney had swallowed MGM's longtime rival, 20th Century Fox, in 2017. But Amazon, seeking an entrée into Hollywood, in one expensive game of chess, immediately earned itself a place on the board. It will be interesting to see what they do with that place.

In 2018, in an earlier attempt to secure a slot in Hollywood society, Amazon had taken out a long-term lease on the former Thomas Ince Studio in Culver City, which Ince had constructed in 1918 after vacating what would soon be the longtime and long ago MGM lot. It is not at all unreasonable to believe then, that sometime in the near future, MGM's new parent company will relocate its media operations to this same campus, which is within sight of where, in 1924, Louis B. Mayer had first been given both his own place in Hollywood society and a prop key.

"MGM is a leading entertainment company focused on the production and global distribution of film and television content across all platforms" is MGM's own rather perfunctory and rather uninspiring self-definition on the company's website. So, it could be said that these words are the sum total, the result in a sense, of a dream that took root almost one hundred years ago in the minds of Marcus Loew, Nicholas Schenck, Louis B. Mayer, and Irving Thalberg, blunted into a single sentence by an anonymous copywriter and available for consumption on a media delivery system none of them ever conceived of.

That said, the concepts of "global distribution" and "all platforms" as quoted, would have intrigued Loew and Schenck—as much as the thorny road to those words, and much beyond those words, would probably have saddened Mayer and Thalberg. The recent sale of the company to Amazon, likewise, would have confused all four of them. "Amazon? You mean in the jungle? In South America?" L. B. Mayer might well have sputtered.

MGM itself, as we know it, may well yet turn out to be a finite entity, although the name, and that lion, will probably continue to roar forever on in some form. But that road, by turns glamorous and grisly, romantic and random, and paved with good intentions, rain puddles, and yes, sometimes even with yellow brick, will go on.

PART II

5

The "Other" MGMs

The MGM brand is historically most associated with motion pictures. In fact, it is without a doubt the single brand *most* associated with motion pictures. But unlike any of the other six big Hollywood studios, Leo the Lion has also been used to represent products as widely expansive as hotel casinos and resorts and as ephemeral as cocktail shakers and long obsolete VHS videocassettes.

Far from diluting that brand name, however, these alternate MGM products and services and companies, have in fact, oddly, paradoxically, tended to reinforce rather than to diminish, to emphasize rather than to distract from, MGM's potency as a specifically Hollywood-based icon. Whether the name was glued onto a replica of the HMS *Bounty* or a proposed Korean theme park, those three letters and that roaring lion still manage to evoke Hollywood, and all that Hollywood represents, better than any movie and better than any movie star, who has ever existed.

Yet many other companies and businesses and products have often used or suggested the MGM name or ethos. Some of these rather imitative entities are, or have been, licensed, sanctioned, or created by the studio (the now-generic word "studio" being here used with sad and intended irony), but others, such as a late but loved video shop in Chicago, tellingly named Metro Golden Memories, were unintentionally or purposely derivative. To catalog them all here then would amount to little more than a scattershot laundry list of products and services, licensed or not, which evoked, intentionally or not, a Hollywood Goliath that effectively no longer exists.

Even in the twenty-first century, examples of MGM's one-time dominance of popular culture, such as this fading sign in Buffalo, New York, can still be found, if one cares to look for them. *Rob Gold*

So, the MGM Auto Body Shop (in Culver City!) and something called MGM Products, which provides engineering and construction materials, MGM Apparel International, MGM Electric Motors, the MGM Tree Service in New Jersey, or MGM University in India (the letters here stand for "Mahatma Gandhi Mission") will not be dealt with here because we'll give them the benefit of the doubt as to coming by their names honestly—except for that Culver City auto body place because that's just too much of a coincidence.

But legitimately licensed offshoots should be acknowledged, even if only briefly, because these odd "shadow MGMs" have undoubtably contributed to the company's

Lots One and Two as they looked in the mid-1950s. The watchtower visible to the right of the studio was built in 1951 as a way for Culver City residents and tourists to view the Hollywood magic being made on the other side of the walls encircling the property. *Bison Archives*

overall cultural history and, for many of us, to our personal lives and personal histories as well.

REAL ESTATE

The MGM name is most associated with its longtime home in Culver City, which started out as a sixteen-acre former army barracks in 1915. The original name of the property was Triangle Studios, the triangle symbolizing the three original landlords, producers Thomas Ince, D. W. Griffith, and Mack Sennett, as well as the physical shape of the property, which aptly enough, pointed east toward Hollywood and

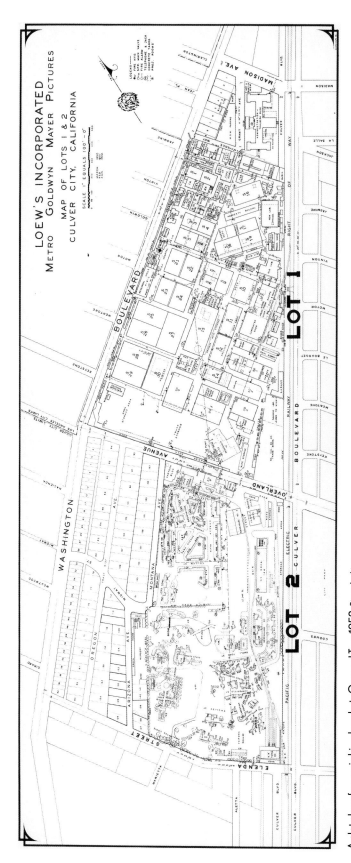

A plot plan of a magic kingdom, Lots One and Two, 1952. *Bison Archives*

eventually expanded into the junctures of Washington and Culver Boulevards, which it was wedged between.

In 1918 this lot was purchased by Samuel Goldwyn Pictures Corporation, which continued the expansion, adding an additional twenty-three acres to the property, although in 1922 Goldwyn himself was forced out, which led to the fateful 1924 merger with Metro Pictures and Louis B. Mayer Films.

The physical studio, by necessity, grew along with its influence. When Mayer and his partners acquired the property, it had expanded to approximately thirty-four acres. Another ten acres would be acquired on lands adjacent to this parcel by 1946. The backlot at this time was literally on the back end of this still-triangular property, along the edge of the land along Overland Avenue. But management's insistence on shooting everything, whenever possible, within the walls of the factory dictated that the factory expand to accommodate the variety of exotic outdoor settings that would then be required.

Conveniently, the land across from the studio on Overland Avenue was owned by none other than Joseph Schenck. Since officially leaving Loews for the West Coast, Schenck had had an eventful career, having released pictures through, or worked personally for, both First National and United Artists and later for what would later become 20th Century Fox. He was then (in the mid-1920s) also a co-owner and tenant at a studio in Hollywood that was about to become Paramount's new home. And, for

Lot Two's sprawling New York Street district backlot encompassed eight distinct New York "districts" and covered almost eight acres of real estate. *Bison Archives*

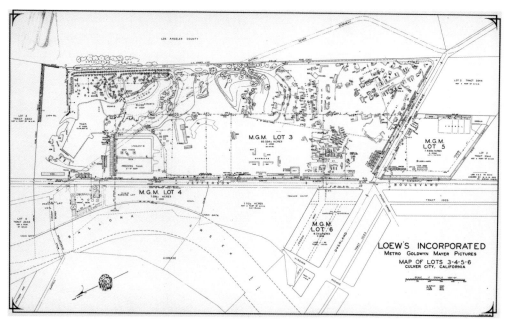

Lot Three, seen here in 1951, and in a 1952 map, was the largest backlot of all and contained some of the largest standing sets in the world. *Bison Archives*

what it's worth, through his marriage to Natalie Talmadge he was Buster Keaton's stepbrother. How he also acquired land in Culver City, conveniently across the street from his brother's studio yet, has never been explained.

We do know that this twenty-five-acre property was purchased by MGM in 1925 for a reported $375 an acre, which would have been a bargain price for undeveloped land in that era in that neighborhood. Inexplicably, however, internal and confidential studio records from 1969, when that studio was considering selling the property, indicated that this same plot had instead been purchased from Schenck at a total cost to Loews of some $202,312. This would have meant that MGM had in fact paid Schenck a considerably higher and, perhaps, unreported $8,092.48 per acre for the property. Eventually another twelve acres were purchased in parcels around this land until 1956, at which point the property, known as Lot Two, totaled thirty-seven acres.

Lot Two, like what was now by necessity being called Lot One before it, rapidly filled up with tangles and mazes of standing sets. The New York Street alone, built in 1936 and replacing a previous, older set constructed on Lot One, covered almost eight acres. So, by the mid-1930s, the studio was again looking for nearby land to expand.

The San Fernando Valley was first considered, but finally, in 1936, Joseph Schenck, as he tended to do, again remembered that he owned just the property that the studio needed. And that it was much closer, just slightly west of Lots One and Two and bordering Ballona Creek. Studio manager J. J. Cohn remembered the price this time as $275 an acre, although, again, records indicate the price actually paid was closer to $25,000 for the entire sixty acres, or some $420 an acre. Cohn also dismissively remembered that Schenck insisted on charging the studio additional money for the foliage already standing on the property. Specifically, he recalled that the cost per tree was twenty-five cents. Whatever its final price, this property, known as Lot Three, would also be extended, this time by some five acres, in 1939.

Separate parcels surrounding Lot Three, sensibly named Lots Four and Five (both purchased in 1940) and Six (purchased in parcels between 1940 and 1949) would be annexed onto the MGM plant through 1949, altogether bringing the studios combined production-based land holdings to approximately 175 acres.

In addition to owning much of Culver City, it should be noted that during this era, MGM, through its parent company, also owned or leased extensive properties and theaters in New York and in cities across the country, as well as offices in key cities around the world. Most of the appeal of the studio for its fans is centered on Hollywood, although the corporate intrigue in the New York properties in particular has been occasionally colorful too. For example, at various times, members of the board of directors there included actor Cary Grant and General Omar Bradley. Surely meetings there must have often been interesting.

In 1936, Loews also leased and, in 1944, purchased outright, an entire second studio in rainy Borehamwood, England. The property was originally used in the production of both films and aircraft, but MGM eventually consolidated and streamlined the operation to support, supplement, and conform with their Culver City operations. Eventually the lot covered 114 aces and included seven soundstages: a sixty-thousand-square-foot scene dock, dozens of support and clerical offices, and even its own generous backlot.

Much of the production in Borehamwood initially consisted of US films that it was determined would benefit from an authentic British locale; the classic *Goodbye, Mr. Chips* (1939) was a fine early example. Later on, when it became financially advantageous to film overseas, however, many studio epics (*Ivanhoe* in 1952) and period films (1954's *Beau Brummel*) found a home there too, with some productions being shot partially in Borehamwood and partially in Hollywood.

Other US studios sometimes rented the facilities in Borehamwood; homegrown British cinema, when it could afford to do so, also shot on the property. As at the parent studio, odd associations and coincidences, as well as productions, often haunted the soundstages. For example, MGM's much acclaimed *Julius Caesar* (1953) was shot in Los Angeles, but decades later, another, this time independent version of the same property shot in the UK studio. This time the star was Charlton Heston, an actor much associated with period-set MGM films. Heston's *Julius Caesar* (1970) would be one of the last titles to lens in Borehamwood in July 1969.

MGM British Studios was much beloved by those who worked there. Sir Sydney Samuelson, the first British film commissioner, praised the lot highly by stating that "whereas other studios were mostly what had become a hodgepodge of buildings over a period of years, MGM was designed and built as a production center with the quality and style expected of anything to do with Metro-Goldwyn-Mayer. Even Pinewood, that great place, had some shabby buildings dotted around the back lot."[1]

Assistant cameraman Keith Blake put it more bluntly. "MGM British was the best studio in the UK."[2]

Unfortunately, in 1970 the same financial belt-tightening measures that decimated MGM in the US eventually poisoned the company's British operations as well, leading to the studio being sold and then leveled with astonishing rapidity. This all happened exactly a year after, of course, studio management had announced publicly that they would do no such thing.

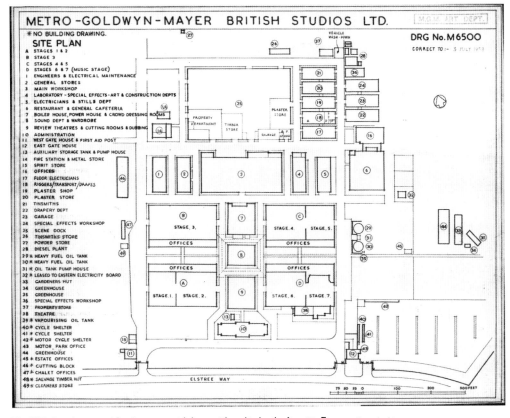

The UK's Borehamwood Studios were widely considered to be the finest in Europe. *Bison Archives*

Producer/director Brian Forbes remembers that "I fought vehemently against the closure, but was out-voted. James Aubrey ('the smiling cobra') one of the heads of MGM Hollywood came over to England with Doug Netter his sidekick, intent in selling off MGM's family silver. . . . It was a sad chapter in the history of the British film industry of the 1970's when that studio was demolished, and both the management and the craft unions allowed it to happen."[3]

Paul Mills, who had ironically just been promoted to the position of Director of Operations on the lot in January was the last employee of Borehamwood, lingering to tidy things up for the demolition until late in October 1970—after which *Daily Variety* dourly reported about Mills that "he has not mentioned any plans."[4]

Stateside, in 1967 the same cash-strapped company that was about to shut down their UK studio rather inexplicably still spent some $8.75 million to purchase fifteen hundred acres of land in the Conejo Valley, some forty minutes north of downtown Culver City, for the stated purpose of relocating and building an entire new facility there.

Company head Robert H. O'Brien hired Albert C. Martin and Associates architectural firm to design this new studio. A press release trumpeted that this new lot "would give MGM the distinction of being the first major motion picture company in the United States to build a completely new facility totally designed in terms of function, efficiency and operation for the making of feature pictures and television."

It should be noted that at the time, MGM was involved in a contentions battle with Culver City, which, although benefiting from the three thousand jobs and the $750,000 annual taxes that the company was then paying, was most unhappy about the block after block of sagging fences and unwashed studio walls that cut through most of their business district.

But this proposed studio move was more than just a leveraging ploy with the city. Ventura County, where the new property was located, accordingly rezoned the land for production use, and O'Brien went so far as to tell his department heads to prepare for a quick-coming moving day. Roger Mayer, who was an executive there at the time, remembered that "many employees even sold their homes and bought property in Thousand Oaks in anticipation of the move, which of course, never happened."[5]

The reason this massive studio transplant failed to materialize, which should have been obvious to all from the start, was financial. The cost of building an entire second studio, with its projected 1.5 million feet of interior space, fourteen soundstages, a film lab, screening rooms, and a new backlot, would have been prohibitive even for a healthy company. And MGM was not a then healthy company. The year before,

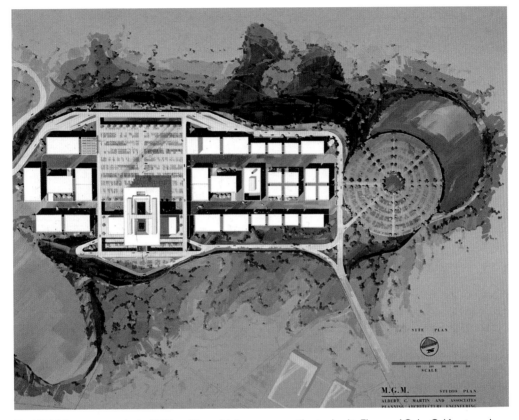

The MGM that never was. In the 1960s, millions of dollars were spent buying land in Thousand Oaks, California, and then designing this studio, which ultimately was never built. *Bison Archives*

O'Brien had successfully fought off a hostile and expensive takeover attempt by real estate magnate Philip J. Levin. And O'Brien himself would be ousted in 1969, effectively killing any still-lingering ideas of moving the studio.

The land the proposed "new MGM" was to be constructed on was ultimately purchased by Sharpell Housing and subdivided.

THEATERS

At its height, MGM, or rather Loews, only owned some 150 theaters, which was less than any of the other major studios. Warner Bros., for example, in the same period had its name on five hundred marquees. But the Loews chain of individual showplaces tended to be larger, more grandiose, and better saturated in major urban areas than any of its competitors.

For example, the Loews State Theater, part of the Loews State Building, where the company was headquartered, stood at the corner of 45th and Broadway in New York City and boasted a seating capacity of thirty-two hundred. The Loews Jersey Theater in New Jersey sported a rooftop that included a copper statue of St. George astride his horse. This shiny knight would be attacked by and vanquish a mechanical dragon every fifteen minutes. The Akron (Ohio) Civic Theater sported a Moorish-Mediterranean theme overall and romantically projected clouds and stars onto its vast auditorium ceiling. The Palace Theater in Louisville, Kentucky, was widely considered to be the finest in the southern US, as well as one of the largest, with a capacity of 3,273. But the biggest venue in this vast circuit was probably the Loews Metropolitan in Brooklyn, which could accommodate forty-one hundred patrons per show.

Many of these theaters were also equipped with Wurlitzer organs (from the silent era), orchestra pits, private boxes, multiple balconies, dressing rooms, smoking lounges, nurseries, and classical artwork and statuary, all there expressly for the amusement and pleasure of the circuit's guests.

And there were a lot of those guests to amuse. In 1922, movie theater attendance was already forty million people per week. And those numbers then just kept going up. Paid admissions peaked in 1930, even as the Depression was devastating the world's economy, with 110 million weekly paid admissions. But even in 1945, the last year of the war, the US Bureau of Internal Revenue reported that some 81.5 million patrons were going to the movies every week. And this was during an era when there were less than 140 million people in the country. Today, despite a much larger population base, weekly cinema admittance hovers at around ten million.

All these theaters unfortunately had to be sold off after the 1948 US Supreme Court consent decrees declared that studio ownership of theaters constituted a monopolistic practice.

As a newly separate entity, Loews Theaters soldiered on until 2005 when they merged with exhibition giant AMC, although some AMC theaters continued to use the name "Loews Cineplex Entertainment," or something similar, until as late as 2017.

Shorn of its exhibition arm in the US, MGM continued to own, or co-own, or lease theaters overseas for many years. Two notable and successful theater chains in India, for example, lasted until 1971.

Most oddly though, the last flowering of cinemas bearing the MGM name came about because of the 1990 buyout of the company by Giancarlo Parretti, which was

MGM (Loews) theater holdings once crisscrossed the world but were particularly dominant in US urban areas. *Author's collection*

otherwise disastrous for MGM. Parretti already owned the Cannon Group, which controlled several European theater chains. After the purchase, these theaters would therefore remain part of MGM even after Parretti no longer was, and after Crédit Lyonnais had taken over the studio.

Renamed MGM Cinemas, by 1994 this division's theater operations accounted for some 25 percent of all British movie houses. Ironically this era also represented the first time ever that the MGM name and logo had ever been featured prominently on theater marquees because in the US, it had always been the parent company, Loews, whose moniker had been featured on those theaters.

That name and that logo would continue to appear on marquees in the UK and in Denmark until 1995 when billionaire Richard Branson's Virgin Group purchased the chain and renamed it Virgin Cinemas.

For generations, MGM maintained distribution offices in every major city in the US. Even as late as 1968, for example, they also boasted overseas addresses in (alphabetically) Argentina, Australia, Austria, Belgium, Brazil, Chile, China, Columbia, Denmark, Egypt, France, Germany, Great Britain, Hong Kong, India, Iran, Iraq, Italy, Japan, Lebanon, Malaysia, Mexico, New Zealand, Pakistan, Panama, Peru, the Philippines, Puerto Rico, South Africa, Spain, Sweden, Switzerland, Thailand, Uganda, and even Viet Nam.

As the preceding paragraphs illustrate, with production facilities, booking offices, and theaters scattered quite literally worldwide, MGM's real estate presence, during and even after its long-ago peak was so vast that when Grace Kelly and her husband Prince Rainier of Monaco toured the studio in the 1950s, Rainier mentioned to Dore Schary that his entire country was five square miles.

"Jesus, that's not even as big as our backlot,"[6] Schary reportedly said. It was an exaggeration, but only to a point.

FILM PROCESSING

There was once, at the Culver City studio, hundreds of services available for the production of motion pictures. All these services were also available to other studios and to outside productions. Some of these divisions happily still exist, either through MGM itself or through other companies like Sony. For example, JC Backings is an independent company that still maintains and rents the inventory of the old MGM scenic arts shop. Perhaps unfairly, only one of these departments, however, ever achieved its own outside international fame throughout the world for providing the best of what they offered in the entire business.

For decades and for generations the pride of the industry, the MGM film lab enjoyed a long reputation as the busiest and most prestigious film-processing plant in all the world. Its services were much in demand and not just for the studio's own enormous output but also by other studios and across the industry as well. For example, in the 1940s, the MGM film lab was printing an average of 150 million feet of film annually for release prints, in addition to another twenty-five million feet of negative and twenty-nine million feet of prints for rushes. And the factory's enormous processing tanks were then consuming some 300,000 gallons of water *per day* doing so.

IMDB, sometimes less than a fountain of accuracy, currently offers only 150 films that were credited with "color by Metrocolor" (MGM's tradename for Eastmancolor), but surely, the number of films for which MGM contributed processing, postproduction, or lab work of one sort or another is many times multiplied by that number. During the studio's many lean years, that laboratory would usually continue to show a profit even when the rest of the operation itself failed to do so.

The original MGM laboratory building was an L-shaped structure built on the lot along Culver Boulevard. It was replaced by a much larger factory in the 1930s. In

The MGM film lab, seen here in 1936, enjoyed a long reputation as the busiest and most prestigious film-processing plant in all the world. *Author's collection*

1979, that building itself was completely and expensively rebuilt and expanded at the reported cost of $1.5 million. The old mailroom building and Stages 16 and 17 were removed at this time to accommodate these renovations. But in 1986, which was only seven years after all of this work to keep the department state-of-the-art, the entire studio property was sold to Lorimar, a television company with no interest in or aptitude for running a film lab.

Even allowing for this unfortunate event, however, there was an unusual stipulation buried deep in the minutia of that sale that stated that Lorimar would then immediately have to sell the entire film-processing division to something called CSD Acquisition Corp. The deal immediately returned to Lorimar a substantial $72 million of their $190 million purchase price for the property.

Unfortunately, it also turned out that one of the partners of the mysterious CSD Acquisition Corp. was a company named MacAndrews & Forbes. MacAndrews & Forbes also just happened to own a rival film lab, Technicolor. Both Disney, which interestingly enough would continue to use Technicolor for their lab services, and Warner Bros., which interestingly enough bought Lorimar in 1989, were also involved in this rather shady deal. So, the Metro lab, it appears, had been purchased only for the express purpose of closing it down and eliminating a rival, which is exactly what happened in 1989. Three hundred employees, many of whom had been working in the department for decades, subsequently lost their jobs.

Today, the former Metrocolor building has been gutted and turned into offices for Sony's technical operations and video game development staff. The building is now named after director Frank Capra, who only made one film at MGM (1948's *State of the Union*), who never worked in the building, and who probably never went inside; but like most Hollywood directors, he probably had some of his films processed there.

HOTELS AND CASINOS

Kirk Kerkorian set his sights on Las Vegas in 1962 when he started purchasing land on the Strip, which he subsequently leased to developers who eventually built, among other things, Caesar's Palace. His first personally built hotel was the International, which, when it opened in 1969, could boast of being the tallest building in Nevada and largest hotel in the world, at thirty floors high and with more than fifteen hundred rooms sprawling across sixty-four acres.

In 1973, Kerkorian opened the first MGM Grand hotel and casino, which once again was then the largest hotel in the world. The architect, Martin Stern Jr., had been encouraged to take his cue from the movies, so in addition to the MGM/lion emblems to be found throughout the property, specific films, like *Grand Hotel*, were evoked. But the Hollywood connection was also evident in the photographs of MGM stars that decorated the walls and the screening rooms, which constantly ran MGM movies starring those stars.

The hotel also included live venues for guests such as the Celebrity Showroom or the nine-hundred-seat Ziegfeld Showroom, which presented a live, movie-based extravaganza called *Hallelujah Hollywood* for a remarkable seven years. Even the restaurants, of which there were seven, were named after celebrities ("The Barrymore") or movies ("Café Gigi"). The entrées to be found inside these venues were also named, unsurprisingly, after MGM luminaries. Anyone for a "Cary Grant Sandwich"?

Perhaps most appealing, or disconcerting for film buffs, if not for the gamblers stampeding to the casino's 923 slot machines, was the hotel gift store, "The Nostalgia Shop," which peddled original movie props, costumes, scripts, and still photographs, all trucked up from Culver City and then cluelessly sold, sometimes at fire-sale prices, to whoever cared to root about in the bins and stalls and shelves where these once and future treasures were being palmed off. For example, although someone once ponied

MGM hotels, especially in the early years, were populated with mementos, souvenirs, and artwork designed to remind their patrons of the company's still tangible Hollywood ties, 2004. *Rob Gold*

up $975 for a pair of sandals allegedly worn by Charlton Heston in *Ben-Hur*, shrewd film fans could also have bought decades-old, original stills of MGM stars, manufactured in the MGM lab, for fifty cents each. William Wyler's personally annotated script for *Mrs. Miniver* reportedly sold there for twelve dollars. "Trinkets for the tourists"[7] was what one of Kerkorian's aides cluelessly called this.

In 1978 Kerkorian opened his second MGM Grand, this time, in Reno. As in Las Vegas, this second casino would be one of the tallest (twenty-six floors) and largest (1015 rooms) in the world. Although the theme in this hotel, as in Reno itself, was less overtly over the top than its flashier Las Vegas sister, the movie connection, and the prevalence of Leo the Lion as a mascot continued. Kerkorian would sell the hotel to Bally's in 1986 for $550 million as part of a restructuring move that would split the studio and the casinos into two sister companies. Although Reno's own showroom production, *Hello, Hollywood, Hello*, would continue to run even under the new ownership until 1989.

On November 21, 1980, the original Las Vegas hotel was destroyed in a tragic fire, which even today remains the deadliest disaster in Nevada history. The fire began in one of the hotel's restaurants early in the morning and spread through the walls into the property's vast, 140-yard-long casino, gutting it and trapping hundreds of guests upstairs. Seventy-five people trapped in their rooms, in stairwells, or waiting for stalled elevators were determined to have died from smoke inhalation alone. Eventually, the body count was determined to be eighty-seven people. Hundreds more, including fourteen firefighters, were injured or treated for burns or smoke inhalation.

Kerkorian, to his immense credit, was horrified over the disaster that had happened on his property and under his watch. Against the advice of his insurance company and that of his own lawyers, he took the unprecedented step of paying the families of the victims not only more than what they had requested but immediately and out of his own deep pockets. Eventually, the billionaire paid out a reported $69 million to settle fire-related claims that the insurance company had asserted were only worth $11 million. He didn't care.

The hotel itself was rapidly rebuilt and reopened in 1981, but in 1986 it was sold, along with the Reno hotel, as part of another corporate house-cleaning. In 1989 Kerkorian announced he was building a second, even larger, hotel in Las Vegas, which would again be named the MGM Grand. Completed in 1993, the complex with 6,852 rooms is even today the largest single hotel in the US.

Again, this newer, grander MGM Grand was branded as a Hollywood extravaganza even beyond its name. Life-size figures from *The Wizard of Oz*, a seemingly full-

On February 21, 1980, the original MGM Grand burned, resulting in what even today remains the deadliest disaster in Nevada history. *Author's collection*

The current MGM Grand hotel, which opened in 1993, is only the flagship of a fraternity of hotels and resorts that now encircle the globe. *Author's collection (taken from MGM Grand press kits and websites)*

sized Emerald City, a yellow brick road, and an Oz-themed buffet greeted visitors. Unfortunately, two years later, when Ted Turner acquired the studio, he also became owner of the studio's library, so references to *Oz* and other Turner-controlled properties then had to be removed or relicensed.

Kerkorian still owned the lion logo, however, or at least a version of it. So, guests continued to enter the casino through Leo's opened jaws and could then pose for pictures with live versions of the mascot as part of what hotel officials called the "mane attraction."

Neither of these amenities are available to today's guests, however. In 1998, the certainly unique lion head entrance was removed when it was pointed out that Chinese gamblers considered walking through a lion's mouth to be bad luck in their country. Although, where exactly would it be considered anything but? In 2012, the $9 million live lion compound was removed as well after a temperamental cat one day grabbed one of his trainers. That trainer was not badly hurt, but general liability issues, and the public's changing attitudes about how wild animals should be displayed, eventually doomed the endeavor. Today the hotel's Hollywood theme is evoked only through its name, the "classic" semi–art deco architecture, and in the rather redundantly monikered "studio walk" restaurant district.

The second "official" MGM Casino in Vegas (actually, it's in the nearby and unincorporated community of Paradise) is named Park MGM and opened in 2016. This second Vegas hotel is notable as a larger part of Kerkorian's, and then his successors, ongoing attempt to rebrand the MGM name and iconography outside that of its original intent and aside from any overt Hollywood connotations. Therefore, even the coveted MGM name itself is not always evoked in these properties. Several of the MGM Grand's Vegas neighbors, such as the Excalibur, Mandalay Bay, The Mirage, The Luxor, and New York-New York, for example, are all now owned, partially owned, or have been owned by Kerkorian companies.

But the actual MGM name and MGM lion do continue to be used on hotels and resorts around the world. Specifically, the company now operates the MGM Grand Detroit, which opened in 1999, and was billed as the first casino resort outside of Nevada. The Motor City MGM was followed in 2016 by the MGM National Harbor, which primarily services Washington, DC, but is actually located in nearby Maryland. Hotel-wise, if not movie-wise, the year 2018 has thus far been the biggest yet for the company(ies), having seen the openings of both the MGM Northfield Park in Ohio and the MGM Springfield in Massachusetts, neither location nor hotel being particularly movie themed beyond their names.

Your Photograph

IN COLOR
WITH THE LIVE MGM LION,
*DAILY, FROM 1 P.M. TO 5 P.M., IN THE
ARCADE LEVEL OF THE*

MGM GRAND HOTEL
LAS VEGAS

The Mane Attraction! From 1993 to 2012 guests at the MGM Grand in Las Vegas could pose for a photograph with Leo the Lion for "$10.00, including taxes." *Author's collection*

**8"x10" COLOR PHOTOGRAPH OF
YOURSELF WITH THE LIVE MGM LION:**

$10⁰⁰

INCLUDING TAXES

Additional 8"x10" color prints of same photograph, ordered at the same time, $7⁵⁰ each.

Your photographs will be ready for pick-up the following day at 1 p.m. If you cannot pick up your photographs at that time, we can mail the photo to your address.

**PRINTS ARE ALL PRESENTED IN ATTRACTIVE
SOUVENIR FOLDER!**

GRAND HOTEL
PHOTO STUDIOS

POST OFFICE BOX 14847, LAS VEGAS, NEVADA 89114

NOTE: We reserve the right to refuse service to anyone for any reason!

The MGM Grand in Detroit, Michigan, opened in 1999. *Author's collection (taken from MGM Grand press kits and websites)*

The MGM Northfield Park in Northfield, Ohio, opened in 2013. *Author's collection (taken from MGM Grand press kits and websites)*

The MGM National Harbor in Oxen Hill, Maryland, opened in 2016. *Author's collection (taken from MGM Grand press kits and websites)*

The MGM Springfield in Springfield, Massachusetts, opened in 2018. *Author's collection (taken from MGM Grand press kits and websites)*

All told, Kirk's three corporations, Tracinda (founded in 1978), MGM Resorts International (1986), and MGM Growth Properties (2015), continue today to be among the major investors and operators of hotels and resort properties in the world.

The reach of Kerkorian's brand is now international. The MGM Macau, originally the MGM Grand Macau, opened in 2007. Its success led to hotels in Australia and South Africa and eventually even to a corporate move into China that started with an MGM-branded hotel in Sanya and with a (planned) Cotai resort now on the books as well. There is now an MGM Resorts, Japanese division, too, although, again, none of their endeavors there specifically sports, or perhaps needs to, much in the way of either the MGM name or iconography.

Credit must be given to where it is due. Kerkorian's companies have done a good job of keeping the MGM name and, occasionally, the Hollywood connection that name infers alive throughout the world. They have done such a good job that some blurry-eyed casino patrons there might now be surprised to learn that MGM makes movies as well.

CONDOMINIUMS

In addition to its hotels, MGM Resorts has also dabbled in long-term housing. The Signature at MGM Grand consists of three 38-story towers containing a total of 1,728 units, although the land, adjacent to the Las Vegas MGM Grand property, has the capability for up to three more towers to be constructed there should the need arise.

However, it probably won't. The luxury condominium idea was not the success that the company hoped it would be. In 2004, when the project was announced, MGM offered potential buyers an opportunity to either live in their units or lease them out through a rental pool and then split the resultant revenue with the company. Unfortunately, the MGM Grand, which was, after all, next door, and the thousands of other hotel rooms on the Strip made this quasi-timeshare arrangement ultimately less than attractive for either party. In 2007 many of the buyers filed suit against MGM Resorts, claiming that they were failing to recoup the return on their investment that they had been promised.

Today the buildings still contain privately owned units, although much of the occupancy is now made up of high-roller gamblers in search of apartment-style luxury condos that are obligingly rented to them by the company, hotel-style, and by the night.

Opening in 2004, the Signature at MGM Condominium complex ultimately altered the Nevada skyline much more than it did the corporation's bottom line. *Author's collection (taken from MGM Grand press kits and websites)*

BASEBALL STADIUM

In 2014, MGM Resorts purchased the naming rights to a baseball stadium in Biloxi, Mississippi. The name they chose was MGM Park, and the entrance is adorned with— what else?—a golden lion statue.

Since 2014, Leo the Lion has proudly been the official greeter at Biloxi, Mississippi's, MGM Park. *Dave Cottenie (www.stadiumjourney.com)*

As the home of the minor league Biloxi Shuckers baseball team, named after that city's (apparently) famous way of opening their (apparently) famous oysters. The six-thousand-seat stadium also hosts concerts and college baseball games. "MGM Resorts International is proud to be an integral part of Biloxi baseball's launch,"[8] said George P. Corchis Jr., President and COO of MGM Resorts International's Southern Operations, at the time the deal was announced.

Corchis, however, did not explain why the company decided to become involved in such an unusual and far-flung venture.

AIRLINE

"Everything else should be called second class" was the motto for Kerkorian's short-lived but well-remembered attempt to take Leo the Lion airborne.

Like fellow billionaire and occasional studio owner Howard Hughes, Kerkorian was also an aviation pioneer and pilot, who after distinguishing himself as an airman in the Second World War, had founded what would become Trans International Airlines in 1947.

TransAmerica Airlines, as it was originally called, was a tiny charter service that specialized in ferrying gamblers to and from Las Vegas but, as reflected by its eventual name, ended up with European routes as well. Kerkorian was involved with the airline, on and off, as was his habit with all his endeavors, until 1968.

In 1987, the billionaire, again seeing a need among the wealthy to lose their money not just in Las Vegas but on the trip there as well, founded MGM Grand Air, the most luxurious airline of its era and a symbol of the entire excessive 1980s *Dynasty*-reflected period it sprang from.

There was even, aptly enough, a *Lifestyles of the Rich and Famous* TV show segment devoted just to the carrier, whose "all-star passengers include Tom Cruise, Kathleen Turner, Jaqueline Smith, Al Pacino and Elliot Gould," as that show's host Robin Leach fawningly gushed on-air. Sports teams, rock-and-roll bands, and corporate boardroom members on the go also made up much of the carrier's elite clientele.

MGM Grand Air's many gold-trimmed amenities included limousine and concierge services on both sides, in-flight gourmet meals served on expensive china, first run movies (presented on VHS!), a conference room, a rolling caviar cart, gold-plated faucets in the bathrooms, and, of course, a bar where, as a company promotional video informed us, "you can make new friends or business contacts."

From 1987 to 1994, MGM Grand Air established a standard for luxury air travel, which is remembered even today. *Author's collection*

Each flight was specifically limited to only thirty-three guests per Boeing 727 or Douglas DC-8. Those aircraft, by the way, had been originally manufactured to accommodate 189 and 150 passengers, respectively. "First class passengers have always had their own section, we thought it was time they had their own plane," the ads for the carrier rationalized it.

Flight attendants working for MGM Grand Air say that the job gave them a priceless education. "I learned how Hollywood works," says Gayle Giannotti, who was an MGM attendant from 1989 to 1993. "I learned that the stars were at the bottom of the pecking order. They'd spend the whole flight sucking up to the studio executives." Even so, the stars had their appeal, and romances between actors and crew were not unheard of. "Stars would invite the crew out all the time," says Giannotti. "After we landed, we'd end up going to some restaurant in Hollywood filled with celebrities. And when we'd come through the doors in our uniforms, they'd all cheer, 'It's the MGM flight attendants!' They made *us* feel like the stars."[9]

Unfortunately, for most people such opulence was easier to admire with Leach on television than to actually partake of. Most MGM Grand Air flights were unable to even fill those specially contoured thirty-three swivel seats they had been equipped with. The problem turned out to be that many of the jet-setters the airline had been created to accommodate could afford to charter their own planes and saw no particular need for the services of a public carrier, no matter how outrageously lavish that carrier might have been.

MGM Grand Air was shuttered in 1994, and its distinctive blue and white jets, with their gold Leo the Lion insignia disappeared, undoubtably leaving behind a lot of red ink. The airline is also survived by a great many fond memories by those who flew on it and by those many more who only dreamed of someday doing so.

THEME PARKS AND ATTRACTIONS

The impetus for an MGM-based theme park goes back to 1964 when studio management was trying to monetize their backlot, and so someone came up with an idea to offer a public tour. A not-so accurate script was written up, and guides, like future Culver City Historian Julie Lugo Cerra were hired. But like many of the studio's projects during this period, second-guessing, corporate interference, and financial concerns got in the way. Ultimately the effort was so haphazard that guests were simply

MGM's substantial backlots briefly became a tourist destination in the 1960s. *Bison Archives*

driven out to Lots Two and Three, unloaded from a bus, and told to "look around" amid the dilapidated sets for a little while. For this singular experience those guests were charged $7.95 for adults and $5.95 for children younger than twelve, although the company MGM shortsightedly hired to manage the operation, something called American Sightseeing Tours, ultimately took home most of the profit. The venture ran haphazardly for several years and then was quietly phased out, although author Stephen X. Sylvester who was lucky enough to take the tour, recalled that "the next day my parents took me to Disneyland, and I was so disappointed! MGM was so much bigger and so much better detailed."[10]

A few years later, Debbie Reynolds tried again to turn the backlot into a tourist destination. She was quoted in 1992 as saying that "I went up to the head of the studio, and I said, you can't let Lot Three go, because it's already a Disneyland. It's already there. You just add a turnstile and let people drive in and you charge 'em money. I'll be at the gate every day. I'll get other stars to come, we'll sign autographs. It's already made for you. Well, later on Universal did it. I mean if a little dumb girl from Burbank could see that, why couldn't they see it? And the shame of it is, why didn't they see it? It's too late now."[11]

MGM and Kerkorian eventually did get into the amusement park business. However, it was three thousand miles away in Orlando, Florida, in 1989, when the Disney-MGM Studios Theme Park, which was inspired by, if not based on, Universal Studios popular Hollywood studio tour, opened.

Disney-MGM Studios Theme Park was not, as the name suggested, a collaboration between the two entertainment giants but, rather, a deal by which Disney licensed the MGM name and logo because as Peter Bart put it, "the combination of the Disney and MGM names carried much more marketing clout than Disney alone."[12] The combined logo, which the Disney graphic artists came up with, depicted Mickey Mouse giggling nervously next to a roaring Leo the Lion, which marked the two Hollywood icons' first joint appearance, sort of, since MGM's movie *Hollywood Party* in 1934.

Mickey Mouse may have been laughing over this unlikely teaming up, but Kerkorian most certainly was not. The MGM logo, after all, was his most cherished possession, and the owner of that logo was, by all accounts, enraged that his executives had gone off without consulting him and given away that logo, and to another studio! According to Ron Grover, as quoted in his book *The Disney Touch*:

In the end, Disney all but walked away with Leo the Lion's mane. Disney received almost free rein in use of the famous roaring lion and the treasure trove of old MGM

Disney MGM Studios Theme Park opened in 1989. The contentious partnership between the lion and Mickey Mouse was inadvertently reflected even in the signage, which featured Leo rather menacingly bearing his fangs to the mouse's backside. *Werner Weiss (www.yesterland.com)*

movies. Most important, it got those rights for virtually nothing. Under the 20-year agreement, Disney was to pay only $100,000 a year for the first three years and $250,000 for the fourth year. The annual fee would increase by $50,000 in every year thereafter, with an eventual cap of $1 million for the yearly fee.[13]

Kerkorian demanded that this one-sided deal be torn up, but Disney chair Frank Wells refused to budge, explaining to Kerkorian's horror that in addition to the Orlando Park, his studio soon intended to build like-named attractions in Europe and much closer to home in Burbank.

Less troubling, but still frustrating, was that secondary revelation that Disney would indeed be allowed to plunder MGM's library as fodder for the park's attractions. This was most evident in one of its centerpieces, "The Great Movie Ride," in which guests entered through a copy of Grauman's Chinese Theater and were then entertained by animatronic re-creations of scenes from *Tarzan the Ape Man*, *The Wizard of Oz*, and *Singin' in the Rain*, as well as in sequences from Warner Bros. titles plucked from out of the MGM library like *The Public Enemy*, *Footlight Parade*, and *Casablanca*.

The twenty-year licensing agreement between the two studios expired in 2008, at which time the park had to be embarrassingly renamed and rebranded as Disney's

Hollywood Studios. All MGM-related attractions and signage inside then had to be removed as well. The only exception was "The Great Movie Ride," which would have had to be completely gutted to remove all of the MGM and MGM-controlled references. So, ultimately, these elements had to be expensively relicensed from then owner Warner Bros.

Fortunately, at least for Disney, as the park evolved from its original concept of being a Universal Studios–inspired "backlot" experience—with actual film content being created there alongside the rides, it became more of a traditional, if movie-inspired theme park experience. "The Great Movie Ride," therefore, eventually started to look rather passé. Its nostalgic glance backward at old films many a young guest had never seen became increasing out of line with the surrounding attractions, which were based on *Star Wars*, *Toy Story*, and *High School Musical*. So, the ride, which was the park's last original attraction, closed on August 13, 2017.

The California and European versions of Disney-MGM Studios Theme Park never materialized either. Although elements of the original park did later show up at Disneyland's California Adventure and Euro Disney Resort, Kerkorian and MGM in either case was not involved.

This mutually unhappy experience did not sour Kerkorian from an MGM-themed amusement park, however. One of the reasons he was so unhappy with the Disney partnership was possibly because he already had plans simmering on a back burner somewhere for his own "MGMland" or something similar. These vague schemes would not come to fruition, however, until 1993 with the opening of MGM Grand Adventures.

Built, aptly enough, adjacent to the Las Vegas MGM Grand, the thirty-three-acre amusement park, like Universal Studios and Disney-MGM, was largely Hollywood-themed. At the time, Las Vegas was in the middle of an effort to refocus its reputation as an adult's Disneyland into a place where parents could bring the kids and together enjoy family-friendly adventures, as well as then taking in a burlesque show and losing a mortgage payment at the roulette wheel.

Unfortunately, Kerkorian, or his designers, ultimately tried to create an amusement park based on Hollywood movies without referencing any actual Hollywood movies. The only MGM movie specifically referenced, maybe, was in the *Cotton Blossom* riverboat, which was borrowed, if not overtly, from *Show Boat* (1951), and which wasn't a ride anyway but a restaurant. Possibly the bad experience in licensing their characters to Disney made Kerkorian or his lawyers leery, or possibly it was felt that there was little left in the MGM library in 1993 that could be successfully adapted into a theme

The ambitious MGM Grand Adventures theme park under construction in 1992. *Josh Young (www.themeparkuniversity.com)*

King Looey makes a personal appearance for mildly excited MGM Grand Adventures guests in this Kodak advertisement from the early 1990s. *Author's collection*

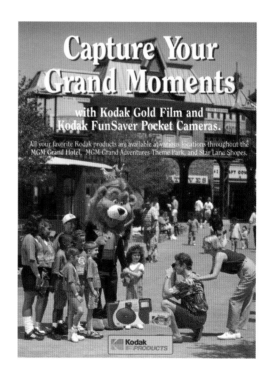

park ride—although, a James Bond ride, or attractions based on still-existing studio properties like *The Secret of Nimh* (1982) or *WarGames* (1983) certainly would have seemed ready-made to that task.

This lack of specific branding opportunities therefore gave the final version of the park a generally generic feel to it. When the park opened, the only recognizable characters exploited on the grounds were the Pink Panther, Popeye, and Betty Boop. To this rather meager menagerie a new character named King Looey, a crowned and tuxedo-clad cartoon lion specifically designed inhouse to attract the attention and the adoration of the children of the world, was added.

But these children seemed to recognize a market-survey-created character when they met one or at least when they met a badly costumed version of that character wandering about the often nearly empty streets of the park. Mickey Mouse, despite his latter-day reputation as a corporate shill first and an organic character second, at least had an established and earned lifelong personal connection with his audiences, which a newly minted cartoon character could not hope to compete with. The fact that assorted online sites and Las Vegas thrift shops are still stocked with dusty plush toys and milk glasses bearing the king's maned visage bears this out.

There was, incidentally, an obscure and apparently unrelated late 1940s comic book character with the same name as King Looey who was also a lion and also wore a crown, if not the MGM version's signature tux, but who was also similarly unsuccessful. And there is even a third and also unrelated King Louie (*sic*) costumed lion character who once worked as a spokes-lion for the Kentucky Kingdom Amusement Park in Louisville. The point here is that even had King Looey instead been MGM's well-established and well-loved Leo, rather than this new character (and why wasn't he?), a five-hundred-pound adult male lion is just not particularly cuddly, even when turned into an adorable plush toy or a costumed character. Which is another reason why this lion failed to endear himself to his targeted demographic, just as had apparently happened with his comic book and later theme park cousins.

The rides to be found in King Looey's Vegas domain were largely, with exceptions, equally unmemorable. Part of the problem, again, was the lack of recognizable franchises to attract audiences. But another underlying problem was the often uninspired nature of the attractions themselves, most of which were generic, out-of-the box carnival rides, largely designed by the Duell Corporation, which had worked on assorted Six Flags attractions, and second-stringer ride engineers who weren't good enough to "imagineer" for Mickey Mouse.

For example, on the "Backlot River Tour," guests boarded cruise boats that looked like they had been pilfered from Disney's beloved "Jungle Cruise" rides. (They had actually been purchased from an aborted version of the Universal Studios Florida "Jaws" attraction.) Yet instead of encountering robotic hippos and elephants, guests aboard them sailed through assorted and wholly fictitious movie sets.

For example, these boats were menaced by an amphibious "Swamp Creature" who resembled, but as per company lawyers, not too much, the creature from the Black Lagoon. Likewise, an *Indiana Jones and the Temple of Doom* adventure tableau was here named instead, and nonlitigiously, "The Temple of Gloom." Even those films which the studio *did* own some rights to were treated in the same generic fashion here, perhaps betraying an overall lack of corporate comprehension as to the contents of the studio's own library. Specifically, around the very next corner could be found an *Apocalypse Now*–inspired Viet Nam set, which, like the film, incorporated Wagner's (public domain) piece "Ride of the Valkyries."

It's tempting to hope that the park's nearby "Salem Waterfront" area, a nineteenth-century colonial district, was inspired by the same-named set on the actual MGM backlot that had been built for an ultimately unmade Clark Gable movie, *The Running of the Tide*, in 1950. But the identical name is surely, sadly, just a coincidence, especially because the architecture on display along this waterfront was largely Dutch-inspired and even included a windmill. The area also contained a "Haunted Mine" ride, in which guests explored an Indian-cursed cavern, although why there was an American Indian curse in play in Denmark was left wholly unexplained. Similarly, there was a New Orleans district to be found nearby, which included an effective, if again geographically challenged flume ride called "The Grand Canyon Rapids," but this one is at least remembered by guests as one of the genuine highlights of a day at the park.

Despite the MGM Grand Adventure's lack of marketable franchises, and a sometimes second-rate ride-development team, there were several other highlights to be enjoyed. "Deep Earth Exploration" was a *Journey to the Center of the Earth*–inspired underground trek which included 3D effects, physical sets, and aptly stomach-churning motion simulations, all of which are common amusement park tricks today but which had never been combined before in 1993. "Over the Edge" was another log flume ride, which included two harrowing twenty-five-foot drops, and "The Pirate's Cove" was a 950-seat auditorium that presented well-regarded live stunt shows throughout the day. There was also "Sky Screamer," which was then one of the world's tallest (250 foot) sky coasters.

Despite these pluses, and regardless of the park's minuses, the MGM Grand Adventure, and the larger experiment in making Vegas a family-friendly destination was not a success. Part of the problem, again, was Kerkorian, who, as he had proved with MGM Studios, did not mind spending money or pushing envelopes but had little patience to sit back and let his people's ideas, good or bad, play out. So, rather than let his park find itself, or find its audience, when initial attendance numbers were below projections, Kerkorian instead kept tinkering, second-guessing, and rethinking what he had already signed off on.

He also kept tinkering with the admission prices, raising or lowering them and sometimes charging additional ticket fees for certain attractions. In 1996, just three years after his park opened, he scrapped the expensive "Backlot River Tour" and "Deep Earth Exploration" rides to build a new MGM Grand hotel pool area and a convention center, cleaving the already compact park of nearly half of its original size. Although the following year, new, and much less innovative rides, like a Ferris wheel, (surely, surely not inspired by the Schenck bothers' long-ago Paradise Park attraction?) were added, even as it was announced that the operating hours would be reduced and the park closed entirely during certain seasons.

In 2000 the company started selling off, or trying to sell off, the remaining rides even as guests continued to pay admittance to ride on them. This practice, sadly, echoed that which had happened on the studio backlot, which had been demolished even while movies were still being profitably made there.

The following year, the park was inexplicably renamed The Park at MGM, which it was now announced would only be open for corporate events. The site's final closure, to the surprise of no one, came in 2002, at which point the few remaining rides and themed areas there were sold or demolished. The three Signature at MGM Condominium towers occupy the site of the former MGM Grand Adventure Park today.

Despite the partially self-inflicted bloody nose that the closure inflicted on its parent company, MGM was not quite done with theme parks. Not yet. In 2008, they announced that they were partnering with something called the Incheon International Airport Corporation to build a 16-million-square-foot theme park on Yeongiongdo Island in South Korea. The press release announcing the collaboration failed to mention if King Looey was to be involved as spokesperson. Unfortunately, like many MGM and MGM-partnered deals from this era, this one never happened either.

The same year the studio also partnered with Paramount, Universal, DreamWorks Animation, and Marvel in a licensing agreement to open a park in Dubai. Unfortunately, when "Motiongate Dubai," as it came to be called, finally opened in 2016, MGM had been replaced, rather ironically, by another studio named Lionsgate.

MGM has also licensed, more successfully, its name and its properties out to other theme parks and theme park developers, including a *Stargate*-based ride that has run successfully at both Space Park Bremen in Germany and at several Six Flags theme parks stateside. Another notable example was the MGM Studios Plaza in Niagara Falls, Canada, which featured a dramatic 3D Leo the Lion on its facade. Inside various interactive games and vaguely movie-based attractions were found, although the lion has now been removed and the site generically rebranded as Adventure City.

Over the decades, MGM has also been involved, if sometimes inadvertently, in other theme parks as well. In 1970, at the infamous MGM auction, two of the largest props on the backlot, the original *Cotton Blossom* riverboat from *Show Boat* (1951) and a three-masted sailing ship, probably built for *All the Brothers Were Valiant* (1953) were purchased by a Kansas City amusement park, Worlds of Fun, and trucked across the country as attractions. The schooner, sometimes called the *Victrix*, lasted there until 1993, but the *Cotton Blossom*, even though she was by this point listing badly and rotting badly, soldiered on, acquiring the nickname the "Rotten Blossom" by employees. Although, in 1995 she too was disassembled, except for part of the frame, which sank, or was abandoned there by the demolition crew. So, her rotting ribs remained visible just under the waterline for the next several years. Even today, guests of that park of a certain age still remember both ships fondly.

Also remembered, although now tainted by tragedy, was another full-rigged ship that the studio commissioned in 1960 for their remake of *Mutiny on the Bounty*. The Worlds of Fun ship has also been referred to by that name and that ship had played the *Bounty* in that film—if briefly, in some of the port-set backlot scenes. But unlike the older vessel, which remember was only a prop, this second *Bounty* was a purpose-built replica of the famous original.

This replica, considered to be the first tall ship built from the keel up for a motion picture (the studio's original 1935 *Mutiny on the Bounty* film had relied on existing vessels and models), was often referred to as a "full-sized copy" of the original schooner, which is incorrect, because the copy was actually considerably larger than the actual *Bounty* had been. She was, however, fully seaworthy, as evidenced by the ship's initial voyage, under her own power, from Nova Scotia, where she was constructed, through the Panama Canal and then, like the original, on to Tahiti, where much of the film was produced.

The *Cotton Blossom* and the *Victrix* on the MGM backlot later were both featured at the Worlds of Fun amusement park in Kansas City, Missouri. *(top and middle) Stephen X. Sylvester (via Brainard Miller); (bottom) Author's collection*

Unlike the actual *Bounty*, which had been burned by its mutineers in 1790, this second version, after filming, would go on to a long and adventure-filled second life as the star of other movies, of more around the world voyages, and as a tourist attraction.

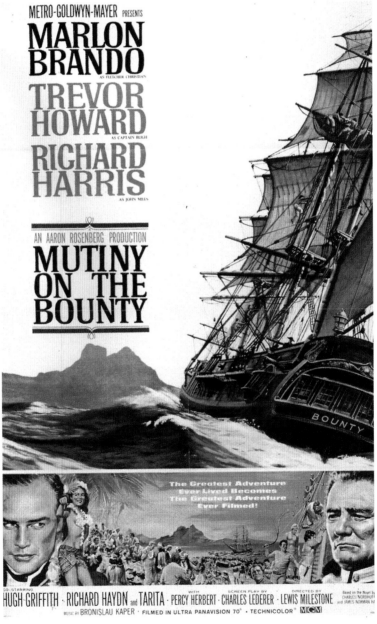

Mutiny on the Bounty (1962). *Author's collection*

MGM retained their ownership of the vessel and used it for publicity to promote the film, which turned out to be much less seaworthy than the ship was. After a world tour and a successful stopover at the 1964 World's Fair in New York, she was docked in St. Petersburg, Florida, and in July 1965 opened up to the public, who for a small admittance fee (initially ninety cents for adults and fifty cents for children) could cross through a giftshop and over a gangplank and explore.

Belowdecks, those tourists would be confronted with a kiosk that, when activated, would play prerecorded dialogue from the film. Although, most curiously, these soundbites did not come from the 1962 version, which the ship had originally been commissioned for, but rather from MGM's other, more successful 1935 version. So, it was the voice of Clark Gable as mutineer Fletcher Christian which would dramatically echo throughout the cabin—even though this was entirely the wrong actor in entirely the wrong cabin, no one seemed to mind.

During this era, the *Bounty* remained seaworthy, however, and was often rented out for other film productions and special events. In 1986, when Ted Turner acquired the MGM library he also somehow acquired the *Bounty* as well. Turner claimed that he had no idea he was the new owner of the ship at all until he started receiving bills for its repair. Although, as a lifelong yachtsman he probably was tickled that the ship had somehow been a part of the deal. In addition to taking a personal interest in the ship's welfare, he also starred her, along with Charlton Heston, in his 1989 cable TV remake of *Treasure Island*.

In 1993, Turner gifted the ship to a foundation in Fall River, Massachusetts, established for her care and preservation, although the filming and tourism aboard her decks continued. During this period Marlon Brando, who had played Fletcher Christian in the 1962 movie, expressed interest in acquiring the ship for use on his own Tahitian island, but not surprisingly, nothing ever came of this. Brando's interest in the ship, and in Tahiti, both went back to the film's troubled production. The *Bounty* replica originally had been scheduled to be destroyed for the production's climax, but the ship had been preserved when the star reportedly threatened to walk off the set if such a beautiful example of the shipbuilder's art were needlessly destroyed; Brando won.

In 2001, due to financial problems, the ship was sold to another foundation, but again, a lack of funds, a 2009 vandalism, and cross-purposed efforts to both modernize and restore the ship to its original eighteenth-century look took their toll. She continued to travel around the world while the latest owners tried to find a suitable buyer.

In October 2012, the *Bounty* was proceeding south from Connecticut to its old birth in St. Petersburg, when, ninety miles off the North Carolina coastline, she was

MGM's romantic and ultimately tragic replica of the HMS *Bounty* awaits its next adventure from its berth in St. Petersburg, Florida. *Author's collection*

trapped by Hurricane Sandy, started taking on water, and subsequently suffered an electrical failure. The Coast Guard was notified, but the raging storm made it hard for the responders to execute a rescue. The crew were eventually evacuated into life rafts just before the ship was pulled underwater by the storm.

Ultimately, two lost their lives in the disaster. One victim was Robin Walbridge, who had gone down with the ship he had captained for seventeen eventful and storm-swept years. The other casualty was named Claudine Christian, who claimed to be a descendant of the same Fletcher Christian who had seized the original *Bounty* in 1789 and thus first set this centuries-long romantic, tragic tale in motion.

RECORDS, RADIO, AND MUSIC PUBLISHING

MGM was the parent company of one of the world's major record labels and was the controller of a vast catalog of popular artists and songs spanning many genres and decades.

The roots of what became MGM Records goes back to at least 1928, when that name, or more properly the name Metro Goldwyn Mayer Records, was first affixed to promotional recordings called "air trailers," which were used only for publicity and radio and not distributed to the public at-large. During this period the company also, then using an outside manufacturer, occasionally sold records with MGM songs on it in their own theaters where their movies containing those songs were playing.

In 1934, MGM became involved in a lucrative facet of the music industry by buying two of the major music publishing companies of the time, Miller Music Publishing and Robbins Music. A third music publishing company, Leo Feist Inc., was added the following year, creating the so-called Big Three, and making MGM a powerhouse in the industry even before they had their own record label. Interestingly, in the 1950s the studio's longtime rivel, 20th Century Fox, would join with MGM as a Big Three minority partner as well.

The MGM Records division proper was not created until 1946 as a then innovative way of allowing the public to purchase and then take home soundtrack material from MGM movies. Considering that one of the unique facets of the movie industry, perhaps the single facet that had first attracted future moguls like Mayer and Goldwyn to it, was the concept of selling the public something that public would not actually own and could not take home with them; thus, the formation of a record division to sell

"Air Trailers," such as this 1940 Christmas edition, were designed for radio play and not distributed to the public at-large. *Scott Brogan (www.thejudyroom.com)*

outright the audible part of some of those films was an interesting, unheralded predecessor to what would become home video later in the twentieth century and streaming services in the twenty-first century.

The first MGM Records release was the soundtrack to the studio's picture *Till the Clouds Roll By*, which came out on March 1, 1947. *Till the Clouds Roll By* and MGM have often taken the credit for being the first movie-derived commercial record ever created, which isn't true; Disney had successfully released "Who's Afraid of the Big Bad Wolf" from *The Three Little Pigs* in 1933 and "The Whale Who Wanted to Sing at the Met" (with MGM's own Nelson Eddy) from *Make Mine Music* in 1946. Additionally, in 1941, RKO had scored a most unexpected hit with "Warsaw Concerto" from their film *Suicide Squadron*, and there were probably others. But Metro does deserve the credit for creating the first ever soundtrack *album* and for coining the word "soundtrack" itself to describe the idea of a record that was literally a recording, a *record* of what was heard in the film—although those songs from those films often had to be edited for time and occasionally new bridges or transitional material had to be layered into them to make them suitable for home use.

In the case of this initial album, performances by Frank Sinatra and Dinah Shore, both contracted to rival Capitol Records had to be excised as well. Also missing here were the vocals by an (unbilled) Trudy Erwin, who had dubbed Lucile Bremer's performances of "Who?" and "One More Dance" in the film. The problem of what to do about performers signed to a different label, or dubbed by unknowns, would continue to plague MGM soundtrack records for some time.

Till the Clouds Roll By, released in 1947, marked the debut of MGM's record label. *Scott Brogan (www.thejudyroom.com)*

At the time of course, the phrase "records" then referred to 78 RPM vinyl recordings. Unlike film elements, which were processed on-site in Culver City, these albums were pressed in a separate factory located at 120 Arlington Avenue in Bloomfield, New Jersey. This high-velocity pressing center, the parent company's name and clout, and their preexisting music publishing conglomerate immediately put MGM Records in the position of being one of the major labels in the industry. That label was yellow and often had Leo the Lion himself pictured in its center holding another record and with the slogan "the greatest name in entertainment," which itself would become an iconic music industry symbol.

In addition to their songs from their movies, the label also quickly started releasing scores from nonmusical films like *Quo Vadis*. Some of these titles included dialogue from those films too. Miklos Rózsa, *Quo Vadis*'s composer had been lured into a financially beneficial contract with the studio primarily because he knew that he could make additional income from soundtrack albums. His previous score for *Madame Bovary* (1949) represented the first dramatic, nonmusical film score to ever appear in its (generally) original form on vinyl.

The Wizard of Oz, of course, was a musical, but the successful 1956 album version also, again, included some of the film's dialogue, which was doubtless appreciated by fans of the film, which had just started its successful second life on television.

A large part of the success of MGM Records, however, was not associated with movie soundtracks but rather with its releases of music by performers not associated with the film division at all. In the 1950s, the label, often through subsidiaries, began distributing popular music by outside artists with great success. For example, in 1957, the company reported a loss of $7.8 million for their motion picture division, even as MGM Records dramatically posted a profit of $5.5 million.

MGM Records purchased a successful jazz subsidiary, Verve, and a classical division, but most notably in the 1950s, the company, on vinyl as well as on film, became one of the first to fully embrace rock and roll as the defining sound of that era. Musician Tom Petty who first came to Los Angeles during the 1960s remembered, rather inarticulately, that "going down Sunset Boulevard looking at the corridor with all the record companies, you know? In those days it was MGM . . . and all these labels that aren't there anymore."[14]

Despite the label being an undeniable mecca for the era's counterculture, the conservative nature of MGM overall sometimes made for a bad fit with rock-and-roll artists, especially in the late 1960s, when many of these artists complained publicly about censorship and about their contracts being bought up or sold to other labels without

Tommy Hines

their consent or knowledge. Most notoriously, in 1970 the label evoked a moral clause in eighteen artists' contracts and then fired them for allegedly promoting the use of drugs in their music, which drew condemnation from artists across the industry but praise and approval from President Richard M. Nixon.

By most accounts, MGM Records seems to have suffered, or benefited, depending on one's point of view, from surprisingly little interaction with its own film division, which one would think could have been mutually beneficial to both. For example, most of the successful songs in those successful MGM-produced Elvis Presley vehicles were released not by MGM, as one would expect, but by another label, RCA. In 1964, MGM Records released a Beatles single, "Please, Please Me," but that same year, the band's film debut, in *A Hard Day's Night*, came to fans courtesy of United Artists—although years after the fact, the company would distribute *The Complete Beatles* (1984), a retrospective documentary. Another example is the successful *That's Entertainment!* soundtrack album, which was released by MCA. Just as confoundingly, MGM also distributed the soundtrack recordings to American International Pictures's entire library and to films like *The Joe Louis Story* (1953) and *Born Free* (1966), none of which they (yet) owned or could otherwise benefit from.

To the company's credit, however, MGM Records did release several hits by Hank Williams—whose biography MGM filmed in 1964 as *Your Cheatin' Heart*. His son, Hank Williams Jr., found early success with the label as well, and so was also given a film vehicle at the studio in *A Time to Sing* (1968). Another example of the two divisions working in tandem involved the band Herman's Hermits, who made three somewhat successful films for the studio, each accompanied by MGM Record albums.

By the early 1970s, however, Kerkorian and Aubrey's hatchet men, who were decimating the rest of the company, also turned those hatchets to the underperforming MGM Records. In May 1972, the division was sold to the Dutch label PolyGram, which was then aggressively expanding into US markets. Although the record company had been losing money during this era (almost $22 million in 1972), Aubrey surprised everyone by announcing at the same time that he would also be selling the company's more profitable music publishing division, still called the Big Three. The reason given was to help pay for the $90 million MGM Grand hotel being built in Las Vegas. Ultimately the publishing rights for their library would go to United Artists, which MGM later and inadvertently reacquired by purchasing that company.

This PolyGram deal also included the rights to use the MGM Records name and logo for ten years and the rights to release the soundtracks for future MGM movies. Kerkorian, who was always intensely protective of MGM's trademark, could not have been pleased with this arrangement, which probably was one more factor contributing to James Aubrey's "resignation" the following year.

The company would not reclaim the rights to the MGM Records name until 1997, although the library itself is now split between the Universal Music Group, which had bought PolyGram in 1998, and Warner Bros., which controls the soundtrack rights to much of the old MGM library. MGM's current music division is now called MGM Music and controls the soundtrack and music publishing rights for their current catalog and some outside material.

Nearly concurrent with the launch of MGM Records, the studio rather timidly dipped its feet into radio stations and content as well. Warner Bros. had been the studio to move onto the airwaves most aggressively, just as they had pushed the motion picture industry into sound films, having founded radio station KFWB in 1925, which initially broadcast from their studio on Sunset Boulevard. Warner Bros. would remain the only movie studio to own its own radio network until 1948.

It should again be noted though that long before this, in the 1930s all of the studios issued those so-called air trailers promoting their films and, in a loose sense, getting those studios into radio broadcasting. The MGM air trailers were created by the

Publicity Department and shipped out to radio stations on sixteen-inch pressed discs under the banner, "Leo is on the air."

Also worth mentioning is that in 1938 MGM engaged in what was probably the first major effort by any of the studios to get into the thick of network broadcasting as a means of plugging movies on a broad scale. Louis K. Sidney (MGM director George Sidney's father), who had formally been the manager of Loew's Capitol Theatre, was brought from New York to Culver City to formally establish Metro's radio division in 1936. Sidney's primary job was supervising the production of the *Good News* radio series, which debuted in 1937 and was carried by NBC under the sponsorship of Maxwell House coffee. The show featured celebrity interviews, set visits, coverage of Hollywood events, and, of course, also heavily promoted current MGM products. The series, as innovative (and self-serving) as it was though, would run only until 1940.

Mickey Rooney and his *Andy Hardy* castmates performing in character on the air in 1939. Ten years later they tried it again, but audiences were indifferent. *Author's collection*

All of this is related to illustrate that MGM was not nearly as late to the table in the realm of radio as has been reported, although they would not actually brand a station with their own name until 1948 when they renamed New York's WHN (which they had purchased before the war) as WMGM—making the company only the second

Hollywood studio with its own branded radio station. Later that same year Metro aggressively opened their second station, KMGM, in Los Angeles. Others would soon follow, although ultimately the ownership of these stations would prove to be neither influential nor long-lasting. The New York station would only broadcast under those call letters until 1953 and its West Coast counterpart until 1963.

At about the same time, the company aggressively reasserted itself as a producer of original on-air content. *The MGM Theater of the Air* premiered on the airwaves in 1949. The first episode, broadcast on October 14, was an adaptation of the studio's movie *Vacation from Marriage*, which was already four years old. Deborah Kerr, who had starred in the movie, returned, and longtime studio lyricist/publicist Howard Dietz hosted, as he would for the rest of the series, which would be carried on Metro's own stations and then syndicated.

Critics at the time were largely unimpressed. A writer named Leon Morse, for example, in the industry rag *Billboard*, rightfully enough thought Marlene Dietrich an "unusual choice" for a 1949 adaptation of *Anna Karenina* but conceded that Dietz "presided over the proceedings in a polished manor."[15] Audiences also found the show tentative and uninspired, and it went off the air the following year.

By this time, MGM was producing other radio shows, however. Many of these efforts were, again, adaptations of (and advertising for) MGM feature films. But audiences even then seemed to realize that other programs, and even other studios, were doing the same thing better. For example, a radio version of the Andy Hardy series, with the participation of Mickey Rooney and most of the original cast, would have been a slam dunk in 1939. But ten years later, the radio version, now named *The Hardy Family*, only seemed quaint and tired.

That show, like most MGM radio efforts, and MGM radio stations, quickly folded.

TELEVISION

The same pattern, in general, defined the studio's early attempts to get into television. Years of resistance and false starts were again followed by badly timed, tentative, and bland TV efforts that failed to convince audiences that MGM really cared about being there at all. So, ultimately those audiences decided they didn't really care to be there either.

MGM-TV was founded in 1956, although their first effort in that medium, *The MGM Parade*, had debuted on ABC a full year before. Perhaps indicative of the stu-

Scene at the M-G-M Studios, when a group of ABC Television executives visited Culver City for a preview of "The MGM Parade," Metro's weekly TV show which premiered over the ABC network this week, with George Murphy as emcee. Shown (l to r): FRONT ROW—George Murphy, Mrs. Leonard H. Goldenson, John Balaban, Leonard H. Goldenson, Ann Blyth, Mrs. M. C. Callahan, Mr. & Mrs. A. H. Blank, Anthony Augelli, Mrs. Charles T. Fisher, Jr., Les Petersen. SECOND ROW—Robert M. Weitman, E. Chester Gersten, Mrs. Robert Hinckley, Robert Wilby, Mrs. John Balaban, Mrs. David Wallerstein, Sidney Markley, Mrs. Robert O'Brien, M. C. Callahan, Robert Huffines, Mrs. Robert Hinckley, Robert E. Kintner, Edward J. Noble, Mrs. Robert Huffines, Robert O'Donnell, Earl J. Hudson. THIRD ROW—David Wallerstein, Jo-Ellen O'Brien, Mr. & Mrs. Jerry Zigmond, John Coleman, Mrs. Harry Haggerty, Robert Hinckley, Mrs. Hugh McConnell, Robert E. Kintner, Harry Haggerty, Hugh McConnell, Robert O'Brien and Charles T. Fisher, Jr.

It's 1955 and ABC television executives from all over the country have come to Hollywood to celebrate MGM's TV debt, *The MGM Parade*. Two of them, Robert M. Weitman (second row) and Robert H. O'Brien (third row), would later become head of production there. Most of the visitors though were probably happy just to get to pose for this photo with actress Ann Blyth. *Author's collection*

dio's indecision and hesitancy about what to do about a TV show, or indeed, about what constituted a TV show at all, the series was produced by Jack Atlas out of the studio's trailer division.

Hosted by actor George Murphy, the resultant half hour was again, really more of an attempt to create an appetite among the public for MGM movies than a freestanding entity of its own. Often the series included clips from those movies and interviews with their casts, as well as a sprinkling of new, cheaply shot content.

After a derivative credit sequence featuring dancing girls and the song "That's Entertainment!"—both of which anticipated the feature film of that name by almost twenty years—Murphy would usually be introduced in a book-lined library. Several Academy Awards were also displayed amid these books, as if to denote the "classiness" of the presentation. Murphy would then, episode after tedious episode, ruthlessly shill both the studio's product and Pall Mall cigarettes . . . in that order.

To be fair though, Disney, 20th Century Fox, and Warner Bros. were all doing pretty much the exact same thing in their own television debuts at about the same time. Few in Hollywood had any inkling yet as to what audiences really wanted to see on television. And these movie studios had yet to realize that even though these audiences were presumably the same ones who were going to their movies, they had different expectations and needs when they were at home than they did when they put their shoes on and went to the cinema.

Walt Disney's show, *Disneyland*, was the only one of these self-serving anthologies that became a success, just as Disney was the only movie boss possessing any sort of understanding of the potential of this new medium. And surely, for MGM, the sting of being a Goliath brought down for the first time by an insignificant mouse was even worse than for its rivals because Walt's triumphant TV debut was on the same network, ABC, that *The MGM Parade* was then limping around on, making the latter's week-after-week public drubbing in the ratings even more acute.

To that end, *MGM Parade* largely switched to a new format involving the airing of classic MGM movies in its second season. It also got a new host in the classy personage of Walter Pidgeon. But nothing worked, and the show's cancellation in 1956 marked the second television-related black eye for the company. Prior to that, MGM had lost out on a piece of the successful Ed Sullivan series, then still called *The Toast of the Town*, when Sullivan, instead had affiliated himself with ever-rival, 20th Century Fox.

Because of the public drubbing that MGM-TV took during this era, it isn't at all surprising that the parent company enacted revenge of a sort the only way they knew how, by eventually mocking the upstart medium in their feature films. *Calloway Went Thataway* (1951) came first, before the studio had even dipped its toe in those unfriendly waters. But the studio would later take satiric jabs at television, or the television industry, in *It's Always Fair Weather* (1955), *Network* (1976), *My Favorite Year* (1982), and *Poltergeist* (1982). Other studios did the same. Billy Wilder's *The Apartment* (UA, 1960), for example, featured Jack Lemmon at home trying to enjoy MGM's *Grand Hotel* on television—if he could just get past all those commercials.

The failure of their first original series must have stung, but MGM-TV's primary reason for existence during this era was primarily then to license parts of their movie library for broadcast. In that regard, the division was more successful. Although, in 1957 the US Department of Justice brought suit against the studio for block-booking practices, that is, for forcing TV stations to buy movies they did not want to get to play ones they did. This had long been an issue with theater owners as well, although less so for MGM, because those owners were usually assured of a quality product merely because the MGM name was attached to it. But those days were apparently over. In this case, studio lawyers denied the charges, although they did subsequently allow stations to substitute certain titles in their syndication packages.

The TV division also announced plans to purchase, or establish, their own local affiliates, beginning with a partial buyout of KTTV in Los Angeles. Although again, as with in radio, these efforts did not amount to any significant inroads into this intimate and most confounding new medium.

Meanwhile, in the realm of original programming, the word "original" continued to be a problem inside that department. Early attempts at episodic TV, as opposed

The Thin Man (1957–1959) was one of many retreads of previous successes that MGM-TV adapted for the small screen.

Bison Archives

to anthologies, were remakes of old MGM movies like *The Thin Man* (1957–1959), *Northwest Passage* (1959–1959), *National Velvet* (1960–1962), *The Asphalt Jungle* (1961), and *Father of the Bride* (1961–1962). The all but creatively bankrupt unit also produced badly received TV versions of *Meet Me in St. Louis* (1959) and *Andy Hardy* (1962) during this era. None of these projects found any successes until *Dr. Kildare* (1961–1965), which, despite operating under the shadow of a long-running film series, eventually developed an aesthetic and an audience of its own.

During this period the most iconic TV series to come out of MGM were *The Twilight Zone* (1959–1964) and *Combat* (1962–1967), both of which, sadly, were only tenants renting space on the lot. *Twilight Zone*'s producer Buck Houghton once stated that the choice of a home base for his show was an obvious one because "MGM traditionally kept everything they ever made. Just about everything you could wish for in an anthology was there, including the backlot, which had New York streets and forests and lakes and you name it."[16]

MGM-TV itself did eventually find some financial success with their own productions during this period, but it was not through producing television series at all but rather industrial films and television commercials for well-paying clients like Standard Oil, Carlton Cigarettes, 3M, and Shell. All of these commercials, in turn, created a most interesting juxtaposition, if anyone then cared to notice it, of being able to see Greta Garbo emoting on the late show, sandwiched between ads for Burger King, with both products shot worlds apart and yet in the exact same place.

In 1961 MGM acquired NTA Telestudios in New York for the purpose of creating videotaped commercials for outside clients on the East Coast as well. Renamed MGM Telestudios, in 1964, its engineers built a $250,000 mobile video van, named "Leo," which included an innovative twenty-two-foot camera crane. At a press demonstration of their new toy in Times Square, publicity hungry studio executives rented a live lion cub and according to an article in *Sponsor* magazine "posed it sitting on the seat of the giant camera boom." The article then went on to tell its readers that "the cub proceeded to prove two things in rapid succession: (1) you can draw a crowd quickly in New York when you have a lion cub lofted in a cameraman's chair, and (2) the cub was not housebroken."[17] MGM Telestudios, and presumably that versatile, if soiled, mobile video van too, would be sold off in 1969.

Bright spots for MGM-TV, either artistic or financial, did eventually emerge in house, however. *The Man from U.N.C.L.E.* (1964–1968), *Medical Center* (1969–1976), *The Courtship of Eddie's Father* (1969–1972), and *CHiPS* (1977–1983) all had relatively long runs, paid the bills (most of them), and proved to the rest of the industry

CREATING A NEW IMAGE IN TAPE

The standout image in great picture-making is Metro-Goldwyn-Mayer's Leo the Lion . . . first in motion pictures, television and now *video tape*. All the attractions represented by the vast physical and creative resources of MGM have now been added to the industry's leading video tape organization, Telestudios.

More than ever, you can count on the finest production on tape—with MGM-TELE-STUDIOS. Be sure your next commercial is a roaring success—call George Gould and his staff of tape experts.

MGM TELESTUDIOS INC.

1481 Broadway · New York 36 · LOngacre 3-1122

In the 1950s and 1960s, MGM profitably, if shamelessly, rented their facilities for the production of television commercials and industrial films. *Bison Archives* that the studio, and particularly its TV division, could be a viable supplier of new product in that medium. Although ghosts from the studio's past still often outdistanced that new product. In 1976, MGM-TV licensed a single bicentennial screening of *Gone with the Wind* to NBC for its network TV debut. The movie, then thirty-seven years old, became the most widely watched program ever aired on a single network up to that time.

In 1982, the TV division was renamed MGM/UA Television, although the original name would be reaffixed to the letterhead ten years later when the United Artists name was corporately de-emphasized. Under that new/old name and others, it must be said the company is involved in a wide-ranging series of production, syndication, and distribution deals, internally and in collaboration with other studios, networks, and cable/streaming companies. Recent, and generally acclaimed, series the studio has been associated with include *Shark Tank* (2009–), *Vikings* (2013–2020), *Fargo* (2014–), and *The Handmaid's Tale* (2017–). MGM also owns, or is part owner of, three networks' MGM+ (which is currently not available in the US), MGM HD, and Epix, which broadcasts or streams the contents of their current library titles as well as both leased and original programming.

In the twenty-first century, MGM-TV still is a viable supplier of product in the medium.

HOME ENTERTAINMENT

Like other studios, in the 1970s, MGM began to license their product for private home viewing.

This was initially both difficult and expensive because the only way to do so at the time was on film. All MGM releases had been reproduced on 16-mm prints for decades. These films were then distributed for nontheatrical screenings at military bases, to film societies, for charity events, or for any venue where the larger and industry standard 35-mm format would have been impractical. Many stars owned their own 16-mm projectors and were given prints of their own movies as part of their contacts with the studio as well. It has been reported that one of Clark Gable's long-simmering issues with the company, and which eventually led to his departure in 1954, was that they insisted on charging him for his personal Technicolor print of *Gone with the Wind*.

In the 1970s, however, MGM started cautiously releasing their films on the smallest film format of all, 8-mm. Early releases were short subjects and *Tom & Jerry* cartoons.

Leo the Lion roars for cut-down versions of his previous triumphs on super 8-mm film, 1978. *Author's collection*

The addition of sound as an option on super 8 equipment in 1973 greatly expanded the type of content that could be made available for home collectors. The problem was that film, even when only 8-mm wide, was expensive, so the cost of a feature film, especially if it were in color, could total up to a couple hundred dollars or more, far beyond what a casual collector would be willing to pay.

The solution to this issue was certainly innovative. Distributers of films in this format came up with the idea of a "digest" version of feature films, meaning that the content would be edited to a more reasonable and cost-effective length.

And edited they were. The standard capacity of a super 8 projector's take-up reel was four hundred feet, or about seventeen minutes of film projected at the (sound) speed of twenty-four frames per second. Therefore, Dorothy had to go to Oz and back, Ben-Hur had to win that chariot race, and Gene Kelly had to sing in the rain in abbreviated versions. Although, to the credit of the editors responsible, it was surprising how much of the plot and flavor of the longer versions could still be preserved.

On rare occasions, the editors entrusted with this thankless job even tapped into little ironies that the longer versions were incapable of. For example, when *How the West Was Won* in super 8, Gregory Peck mentions to Thelma Ritter how sad it would be to see her fine hair "hanging from the waist of an Indian." The digest version's talented, but surely unappreciated, editor immediately then rather brilliantly slam cuts into a whooping tribe of American Indians attacking a wagon train, with, sure enough, a human scalp hanging on the chief's belt, an irony missed, and misplaced, in the longer version, where the attack scene came much later.

Most studios licensed their product to the same outside company, Ken Films of Fort Lee, New Jersey. MGM, however, in a rare later-day example of class, chose to do the job themselves. Starting in 1978 they released many of their current and catalog titles in this format packaged in lush-looking clamshell boxes, which opened, book-like, to reveal both a striking embossed version of the lion and the reel of film itself. Each digest print retailed for about thirty dollars.

Of course, as was the studio's habit during this period, all this effort came too late to make a difference, as home-video recording/playback machines were already on the market and would quickly and unceremoniously murder, for all but the most fervent fans, the hobby of collecting films on film.

MGM Home Video, with its own specially designed Leo the Lion logo, was established in 1975. Although it wasn't until 1979, that as part of a collaboration with CBS, the studio started marketing their films on VHS and Betamax, both of which offered consumers the ease of watching these films uncut and on their television sets, although the prices were originally again somewhat prohibitive, sometimes up to $100 per tape, because the manufacturers assumed that few people would want to own movies and so would rent them instead. Although originally the relationship between the studios and "video stores," where these movies could be acquired, was itself contentious.

Those prices quickly went down, usually to less than twenty dollars, when it was discovered that people were indeed buying and collecting, as well as renting, their all-time favorite films. Although the price point for a few of MGM's most beloved catalog titles remained prohibitive. For its home-video debut in 1985, for example, *Gone with the Wind* retailed at an epic ninety dollars.

In 1982, MGM, without CBS, began distributing their library, as well as their UA and Warner Bros. catalog on VHS (Betamax having by then gone the way of super 8). Taking a cue, or a corporate memory from their super 8 days, this product was again marketed in a clamshell box, this time with the graphics printed in front of a yellow background.

The 1986 Ted Turner deal stripped MGM of much of that library, however, so subsequently the studio started outsourcing their home-video product, with both vintage and contemporary MGM movies first being released by Warner Bros. This deal ended in 2005 when a consortium of investors led by Sony bought MGM—although Sony's

The same movie, *Strike up the Band* (1940), in its 1985 and 1991 MGM home-video incarnations. *Scott Brogan (www.thejudy room.com)*

(temporary) rights to distribute MGM product on video would be one of the few tangible assets the Japanese company would acquire through this ill-fated deal. Both Fox and, again, Warner Bros. have also distributed MGM's product in recent years.

For a time during the VHS boom, the studio licensed its name and logo to a brand of blank videocassettes as well, on which collectors, presumably, could record MGM movies off the airwaves. Under the studio's name and under Leo's picture on the box, these collectors were reassured that the product inside was "studio grade"—whatever that meant.

Unfortunately for those collectors, these blank tapes and the VHS players they operated with were replaced entirely by higher-resolution digital DVDs in 1996, Blu-ray discs in 2006, and, most recently, by streaming services, through which virtually the company's entire library is now instantaneously available. Therefore, it is now possible, if anyone in the world is interested, to watch, say, *The Ice Follies of 1939*, at home and on demand, at any time.

LIVE THEATER

Considering that Loews roots were in exhibition rather than production, that many a Hollywood movie concerns itself with making it on Broadway, the many stage productions Hollywood later filmed, and the many stage performers who were plucked from the Great White Way and brought West, hopefully to be groomed for screen stardom, it is somewhat surprising that MGM, like its sister studios, long-evidenced so little interest in the legitimate stage.

Historically, Hollywood has sometimes coproduced or financed theater productions, if only for the purpose of later bringing them to the screen. For example, in the 1930s, Warner Bros. helped finance both the Biltmore theater on Broadway and an original production of *The Amazing Dr. Clitterhouse*, which they filmed in 1937. In the 1970s, Universal opened a division in New York with the (largely unsuccessful, it must be said) goal of producing plays that could later be adapted into films. And in 1978, Paramount invested in a play called *Platinum* and then rehearsed it in their stages in Hollywood before bringing it to Broadway, where it resoundingly flopped. That studio tried again in 1983 with a show called *My One and Only*, which was more successful, but about which then CEO Michael Eisner has said that "it took more time than anything I was doing at Paramount. I decided, never again. This is a hobby we can do without."[18]

For its part, MGM occasionally leveraged licensing agreements with theatrical producers interested in creating stage versions of their films. So over the years, the studio granted whatever rights they owned at the time for live productions of *Some Like It Hot* (renamed *Sugar* for the stage), *Singin' in the Rain*, and *The Wizard of Oz*. There have also been at least three different musical stage versions of *Gone with the Wind*. Despite this, whichever executives were then mismanaging the company expressed little interest in pursuing this potential income stream further.

That changed in the 1990s when Disney unexpectedly revitalized Broadway by producing a series of hyper-successful live-action versions of their animated classics on the stage, leading to a stampede of other studios hoping to monetize their old libraries as Broadway hits as well. Therefore, MGM On Stage, a specialty division within the company was created in 2002. And, yes, this new unit did design its own unique version of the lion logo.

Darcie Denkert, a two-decade veteran of the studio and one of Hollywood's first prominent female lawyers, was chosen to head up this new division. Unlike Disney, MGM On Stage, did not attempt to produce its own properties outright but, instead, developed and then licensed them out, while retaining a certain measure of control as to how they were then presented.

Denkert told the press that her studio viewed legit theater as a way to create what she dramatically called a "halo effect, while freshening up their library."[19] And Hollywood at-large apparently approved. For example, Peter Franklin at the William Morris Agency cautiously rhapsodized to *Variety* in 2004 that the creation of MGM On Stage was "[a] very exciting turn of events for a movie company."[20]

The energetic Denkert seemed to be just the person to make it work too. Within two years she had a remarkable twenty-five titles from the studio's four-thousand picture library in development as stage properties.

Unfortunately, most of these properties would never make it to New York, and when they did, the results were mixed. MGM On Stage's inaugural production, *Chitty Chitty Bang Bang*, did run for ten months in 2005. A musical version of *Dirty Rotten Scoundrels* with John Lithgow followed, opening in March 2005 and running into September 2006—accounting for 626 performances on the boards in all. A legit version of *Legally Blonde* then ran for eighteen months in 2008–2009, even with mostly negative reviews. *Promises, Promises* (based on the 1960 film *The Apartment*) opened in 2010 and itself ran for 291 performances. The last official MGM On Stage production, *Priscilla Queen of the Desert: The Musical* (produced by Bette Midler) itself vamped through 526 performances in 2011–2012.

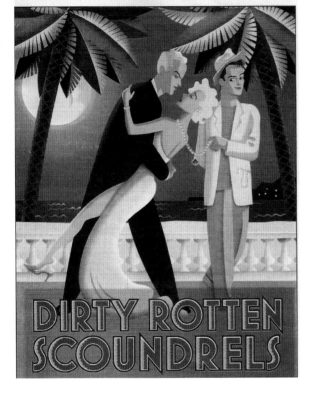

Dirty Rotten Scoundrels, a 2005–2006 theatrical version of their 1988 feature, has been one of several successful and semi-successful MGM On Stage adaptations since 2002. *Author's collection*

As these numbers prove, some of these projects *were* successful, but none ever managed to become the triumph that Disney's stage version of *The Lion King*, for example, had been.

In 2005, Denkert would write a book, *A Fine Romance*, about the intersection of Broadway and Hollywood, although it modestly included little about her part in finally bringing the two together. Rather ironically, her book was then itself adapted into a musical revue, which is still presented annually by the Motion Picture and Television Fund, to which she largely donated both the book's and the live-production's profits.

Denkert retired from MGM in 2012. She passed away in 2016. Dean Stolber, her longtime MGM On Stage collaborator, would go on to produce one more theatrical property based on an MGM movie, *Network*, in 2018.

MGM INTERACTIVE

MGM Interactive was founded in 1994 as an attempt to tap into the burgeoning video game industry. At the time it was thought to be an effective way to cross-promote with the studio's latest features—by creating games based on elements from those features—and then in creating features based upon those games.

The division's first release was called *Blown Away* and was (if loosely) based on the same year's, same-named, Jeff Bridges flop movie. Distributed as was the way at the time on a CD-ROM for use on a home computer, it pleased few gamers of the era, who saw little reason to replay it once its repetitive bomb-squad-related puzzles had initially been solved.

The gaming industry, such as it existed then, was not impressed either. The magazine *High Score*, for example, bluntly carped that "the game sucks. Film companies should not do computer games."[21]

Despite this, MGM Interactive soldiered on. As expected, they developed yet another variation on the studio's logo, this time with their division name unfurled above Leo's head. Although in this instance it is unclear if the lion's presence was an asset at all because at the time media companies, as with television previously, had yet to discover that gamers were largely a new and sometimes separate market. The most successful video games of the era had titles like *John Madden Football* and *Mortal*

Blown Away, the first MGM Interactive effort, was based on a recent movie about the delivery of a bomb. Unfortunately, the game version delivered one too, 1994. *Author's collection*

Kombat and were not (yet) based on movies at all. Yet MGM Interactive, not comprehending the difference, even created traditional "trailers" for their product, complete with movie-like on-screen critical raves—or at least they did when they could find those raves.

Another early effort, *Wirehead* (1995), was not based on a movie but felt like it was. Actual actors were hired for the linking material separating the gaming sequences. So, players had to watch long, scripted sequences to get to the so-called virtual movie material.

Of course, any new industry in its fledgling years can be forgiven for experimenting a bit to, hopefully, create its own rules and patterns. This was no more remarked on by players of the 1990s than silent sequences in sound films had been in movies of the 1920s. Yet as had happened with the company's early ventures into radio and TV, there was often a hesitant, tentative quality to MGM Interactive releases during this period that other video game companies, and even other movie studios, largely avoided. It was as if the writers and designers at MGM Interactive were themselves working somewhat outside their comfort zones and did not fully understand either the product or its audience. After a few more original games (anyone remember *Tiny Tank*?) they retreated back into the relative safety of only adapting their own films into the new format.

But even then, some of MGM's choices were questionable. For example, in 1998 MGM Interactive produced a video game based on their hit film *WarGames*, which would have been a good fit had that film not already been fifteen years old at the time!

Eventually, unsurprisingly, their gaming release schedule consisted pretty much entirely of many virtual experiences based on James Bond and *Rocky*, with a few other library titles like *Robocop* and *The Great Escape* occasionally trotted out in video game form as well. Only intermittently was the synergy between the two mediums the company had hoped for actually attained. One rare example was the James Bond film *Tomorrow Never Dies* (1997), which, for its VHS home-video release included original footage of the character "Q," enacted, as in the film, by Desmond Llewelyn, playing and promoting a new video game based on the movie. Unfortunately, that game, for unknown reasons would not actually come out for another two years!

The division's early ambitions went well beyond video games. In 1996 MGM announced that they would also be creating original programs to be released on the internet, describing themselves as "the first Hollywood based company to create online content not tied somehow to promoting a film or TV show."[22] Unfortunately, although MGM could produce the content, which was, after all, what they did, there was no infrastructure yet in place to broadcast, if that's the right word, this material online. Ultimately, they did produce one webisode of one prospective series, *Angel House* (1997). But the technology to broadcast sustained content over the internet was then still in its relative infancy, and they had no practical way to attract potential viewers into sampling it, so, those viewers didn't.

The experiment was yet one more example of the company managing to come up with often forward-looking ideas and doing so despite MGM's perceived "old-fashioned" reputation. But then that company confoundingly, ultimately, lacked the follow-through or the finances to pursue those new ideas to their conclusions. Of course, more than a decade later in 2007, Netflix, a tech company and Hollywood outsider, would use the same basic business model MGM had pioneered in launching their streaming service and change the world.

As with MGM itself, hesitancy, financial problems, and corporate infighting eventually rendered MGM Interactive, which had been started with so many promises of creativity and innovation, rather a rudderless appendage of the larger company, which itself was often then in free fall. In 2005, MGM quietly stopped using the MGM Interactive name and the logo they had designed to go with it and fired most of the staff who had worked there.

In the future, MGM would, and still does, continue to put their name on video games, almost all of which still star either James Bond or Rocky. Although today the actual development, production, and distribution of these projects is now licensed out to other, more *interactive* companies.

MERCHANDISE

A good measure of interest in any subject is the amount of merchandise, either factory or home manufactured, that the subject generates. On an average day, eBay, the popular online auction site, lists more than 115,000 items that happen to include the letters "MGM" in that order in an item's description. Many of these whatsits are not studio specific of course and instead focus on a single MGM film or MGM star. But there are a lot of surprises to be found out there too—which is indicative, presumably, of the passion that people feel for the subject.

A lot of this plentiful swag now comes out of various MGM resorts and casinos. A visit to the gift shop at any of these venues will reward any collector with merchandise branded with Leo the Lion, although this merchandise is all specifically, and legally,

Ars Gratia Artis? These MGM Grand lions are aptly majestic, at least until a closer inspection reveals that they were actually made in Taiwan. *Rob Gold*

Beautiful, six-foot-tall collector's edition poster created to commemorate the 1974 release of *That's Entertainment!*, but which surpasses even the scope of the film it celebrates by including dozens of nonmusical MGM moments as well. *Scott Brogan (www.thejudyroom.com)*

A collection of MGM-based wristwatches. *Author's collection*

A deluxe MGM cocktail kit, originally given to studio guests and exhibitors, already stocked with gin, vermouth, and even olives. *Author's collection*

Recently spotted at an eyeglass store in North Hollywood was this promotion for "Oliver Peoples's Cary Grant sunglasses," as worn in MGM's *North by Northwest*—and as retailed for $551. *Stephen X. Sylvester*

tied to those particular venues rather than to the Hollywood studio, which probably confuses fans of both.

Merchandise related specifically to the studio, or rather to the now-named "entertainment company," has always been out there as well. Exhibitor and sales conferences, to which theater owners and managers would be invited to the studio for a weekend of partying, also netted these besotted businessmen trinkets to take home from their visit to Hollywood; although T-shirts emblazoned with the brand would not become popular until the 1960s, there are still MGM watches, lighters, ashtrays, shot glasses, and martini shakers in attics and in private collections to commemorate these long ago, and surely remembered, events.

Like other studios, MGM was surprisingly slow to catch on to the idea of marketing items associated with specific MGM movies. Outside of publicity and promotional materials and, later, soundtrack albums, it was, shockingly, hard to find toys related to *The Wizard of Oz*, for example, for a long time. And if such items did exist, they

During MGM's Santa Monica period, visitors were induced to visit the "studio" and then buy a souvenir or two. *Author's collection*

were made only as special promotions or handmade by fans and thus unlicensed by the company. Cartoonist William Hanna believed that this seemingly missed opportunity was largely a result of studio bureaucracy. "When we were at MGM, we never did much about merchandise tie-ups There were too many executives and lawyers to go through," he once sadly recalled.[23]

One such off-lot example of merchandise associated with a specific movie was the so-called, *Gone with the Wind* lamp. In the 1940s, inexplicably there occurred a widespread trend among (mostly) female consumers to acquire just such a thing. The connection these lamps actually had to the movie was unofficial, although certainly hoped for by their (unlicensed) manufactures. These whatsits were either free-standing or tabletop units and were elaborately carpeted over with gaudy crushed velvet and beads and ornate embroideries. These items, let's be honest, looked like something that would have been found while touring a 1940s Georgia whorehouse. But because of those (perceived) *Gone with the Wind* connotations, these eye-rolling abominations would prove to be phenomenally desirable, particularly among suburban would-be Scarlett O'Hara's, for the next twenty-five years! Countless thousands of these grotesque eyesores would subsequently be sold solely on the strength of that tenuous connection. And even today, hundreds of bed-and-breakfasts across the US still contain survivors from the craze.

For a long time, it did not occur to anyone at the studio to actually sell generic MGM logo items to the public either; although there was a studio store near the barbershop on the lot that did so, it was inaccessible to the general public, which of course made these branded items all the more desired by members of that public.

But when the studio moved across the street in 1986, tourists continued to visit the neighborhood and were attracted by the big MGM sign, which was on the roof of their new building and was visible all over the city. These tourists must have been confused that this sign was now in slightly the wrong place, but they were delighted that they could wander into this office building's lobby without a gate pass—because now there was no gate.

There wasn't much to see in that lobby. Although, the studio store, what there was of it, was then in a corner and to the right of the front door. This store did contain more than three hundred branded items, which sold better during this period than most of the studio's films did. T-shirts, in particular, with the lion silk-screened on the front, or embroidered on the pockets, became beloved, bittersweet souvenirs for visitors. For the record, the lion now playing Leo on most of this merchandise was named Zamba.

When the studio's operations eventually moved again to an office complex in Santa Monica, the company not only again made the store accessible to the public, but even printed up and distributed flyers on Hollywood Boulevard specifically dedicated to attracting tourists, and their money, who were eager to see "MGM." "You haven't been to Hollywood until you visit the new MGM Studio Store," these adds confusingly promised and even included a helpful map out to Santa Monica.

Lamps were not among the items for sale.

6

MGM, as Depicted . . .

MGM was by no means above dropping its own name into a script or a song on occasion. In *Strike Up the Band* (1940), for example, Judy Garland brazenly rhapsodized about the studio by name ("Metro-Goldwyn has Mayer . . ."). Likewise, the "Triplets" number in *The Band Wagon* (1953) took care to remind audiences that "MGM has got a Leo," and the "Stereophonic Sound" number in *Silk Stockings* (1957) specifically plugged their Metrocolor process in its lyrics. Other examples abound. As late as *De-Lovely* in 2004 and beyond, for example, the studio was still referencing itself.

The only slightly less brazen alternative to all this blatant name-dropping was to instead shout out an on-screen reference to one of the studio's stars. *Broadway Melody of 1938* (1937), for example, featured young Garland singing specially written lyrics of "You Made Me Love You" to a portrait of Clark Gable. This altered version had originated for a Gable birthday party on the lot and Garland's rendition of it had been such a success that both she and it were then featured in the film. Decades later, when introducing the song for *That's Entertainment!* James Stewart had the nerve to assert to us that this version, retitled "Dear Mr. Gable," "was a milestone in its day. It was the first time a studio permitted a song to be dedicated to one of its stars."

Stewart's ghostwriters, however, could not have been more wrong. As far back as *The Hollywood Review of 1929*, audiences had been told, in song, that "Lon Chaney's Gonna Get You If You Don't Watch Out." That said, it is certainly because of the success of "Dear Mr. Gable," that this practice became afterward so self-servingly prominent and is perhaps why Gable in particular would be name-dropped in the

Broadway Melody of 1938 gave us Judy Garland singing "Dear Mr. Gable" to a photograph. Decades later, James Stewart, in *That's Entertainment!*, immortalized the moment. *(top) Pho-tofest; (bottom) Bison Archives*

studio's own films countless times, as well as in in-house caricatures and cartoons in the following years. The song also caused Gable himself to complain off-screen that for the rest of his life he kept expecting them to pull Garland and that song out from behind the cake every time he had a birthday.

MGM, like other classic-era film companies, also tended to cast itself, or versions of itself, in its own films. Surprisingly, however, the studio, all studios actually, were initially and uncharacteristically modest about using their own names when representing the motion picture industry on-screen. So, early MGM movies with Hollywood settings, perhaps to protect guilty parties lurking inside, would repaint the sign above their gates. Thus, the gates in front of MGM have been labeled "High Arts Studio" (1928's *Show People*), Independent Art Studio (1933's *Going Hollywood*), Monarch Studios (in both 1933's *Bombshell* and 1939's *The Ice Follies of 1939*), Mango Pictures (in 1939's *Honolulu*), Mammoth Studios (1945's *Bud Abbott and Lou Costello in Hollywood*), Paul Hunter Productions (in 1955's *Love Me or Leave Me*), Climax Pictures (in 1957's *Jailhouse Rock*), and, eventually and unforgettably, Monumental Pictures, for *Singin' in the Rain* (1952). Even in MGM's last days on the lot, that lot was still occasionally using an alias for itself. Perhaps the last time this happened was its appearance as "Worldwide Studios," for TV's *The Phantom of Hollywood* in 1974.

Two Buster Keaton features, *The Cameraman* (1928) and *Free and Easy* (1930), were early anomalies, however, in that both times, the studio is identified on-screen as being at MGM. In *The Cameraman*, the film's Tong War climax, although set in a tenement, was also of course, shot on the MGM backlot—a sort of mirror-image double dipping in its choice of locations.

After Buster, however, one has to go all the way to *Anchors Aweigh* (1945) to find the studio playing itself as itself and under its actual name. The success of *Anchors Aweigh*, both as a movie and as a promotional tool for the company, then made it possible for other movies, notably *Till the Clouds Roll By* (1946) and *Words and Music* (1948), to use the studio's name and physical presence as locations . . . and ultimately as adverting as well. This tactic continued even into the 1970s, with *Alex in Wonderland* (1970) and, of course, the *That's Entertainment!* series.

The idea of the studio as a physical place on a map and in Hollywood has been perpetuated by that studio hundreds of times, even after that studio no longer *had* a studio, and *none* of those things were true. For example, in the animated kid's TV series *The Lionhearts* (1988), in *That's Entertainment III* (1994), in *Get Shorty* (1995), and again, in the British-made *De-Lovely* (2004), MGM is still pictured, Oz-like, as still being a magical yet real place. Although by this time the company had to rent, rather

Art imitating life imitating art? The actual studio colonnade facing Washington Boulevard and an idealized "Monarch Studios" version as seen in *The Ice Follies of 1939. Bison Archives*

embarrassingly one would think, their old studio, or some other studio, and repaint the signage there, if however briefly.

MGM has also continued to appear in biographical pictures created by, and filmed at, other studios. Usually these films depicted a nonspecific studio street or some equally generic backlot set, which of course could have been anywhere, with another of those "Metro Goldwyn Mayer" signs prominently visible somewhere in the mise-en-scène. Certainly, most audiences wouldn't know the difference. Many of the films to be discussed here later were guilty of this subterfuge. *Gable and Lombard*, for example, was shot at Universal, *Rainbow* at Paramount, and *The Scarlett O'Hara War* at Warner Bros. We won't here dignify by name the projects that lensed in Canada or Australia but will mention that it works both ways. Scenes set at Paramount Studios for 1955's *I'll Cry Tomorrow*, for example, were shot at MGM.

A MAYER IN THE MOVIES (AND ONSTAGE!)

Worldwide, it is apparent that there are few more beloved corporate entities than MGM. Frank Capra once remarked that in the 1930s the mere appearance of the MGM lion on a theater screen "brought anticipatory applause."[1] David Picker who worked for Loews echoed this, "as Leo the Lion roared in all his glory the audience would burst into applause just because it was an MGM movie. Those were the days."[2] Actor George Murphy marveled that "when that shaggy lion flashed on the screen to signal the beginning of an MGM picture audiences knew they were in for a treat."[3]

The mystique of the MGM lion, however pictured or depicted, seemingly defies time and somehow retains its potency even today. *Bison Archives*

Even today, decades and worlds after that era they were speaking of had ended, Leo's odd charisma is still intact. In 2014, studio CEO Gary Barber remarked to the press at a Chinese Theater ceremony that "when that lion roars, it's just the magical feeling of something great gonna happen."[4]

Sometimes the mystique of the beast can also be potentially blinding. In 1988, producer Peter Guber, who was then toying with the idea of buying into the studio, remembers that "at a small coffee shop in the Hilton hotel, Kirk [Kerkorian] pulled out a buck slip with the famous MGM lion logo stamped at the top," he recalls. "Then Kirk began casually to narrate his MGM story and its glorious past, all the while scribbling the terms of the deal on the pad, below the lion. The emotional pull of this iconic company's logo and history virtually blinded Guber," he tells us, oddly, in the third person, in his 2011 book, *Tell to Win*.[5]

Today, as the studio's physical presence has been dissipated into a single upscale office complex in Beverly Hills, tourists reportedly still come to that address from all over the world, just for the privilege of photographing the signage above the front door. So, it is probably safe to say then, without fear of contradiction, that except for a few hundred disgruntled writers and actors, virtually everyone loves MGM—or at least the *idea* of MGM anyway.

It is indeed odd then, that the man who most represents such a beloved US company, Louis B. Mayer, should be so widely disliked.

Certainly, there was nothing particularly cuddly about Mister Mayer. He was often ruthless in his business practices, and his temper could be volcanic indeed. But it goes beyond that. Today, in the #MeToo era, he has been vilified as a sexual predator as well and as the "monster of MGM."

Perhaps this duality, this image of a demon presiding over a papier-mâché paradise, a kingdom of glamour and glitter and beguiling lies with a huckster sociopath at its vortex appeals to both cynics and romantics, who are, after all, often the same people. Perhaps this is even why so many of the studio's most famous films somehow reflect this same idea. *The Wizard of Oz* is, after all, about a charlatan who rules over a magical kingdom. *Gone with the Wind* is about a beautiful corrupt empire built on the concept of enforced servitude. *Brigadoon* (1954) is about an enchanted community, all-too susceptible to destruction by the outside world. And many musicals concern themselves with performers willfully and fictitiously creating onstage falsehoods. So, *of course*, fans of these films would appreciate this take on MGM's rise and its fall. So, Mayer becomes, time and again, in dramatized retellings of the story, its epicenter, and often as not its villain.

The quantity of Mayer's on-screen appearances is surprising, as the five-foot-six, fireplug-shaped executive was neither physically attractive nor charismatic, at least not by any standard definition of those terms. Yet Mayer has been repeatedly depicted on the big and small screens and been featured in comic books, cartoons, and on the stage as a sort of avatar to illustrate the glories and the evils of classic Hollywood.

Despite possessing the talent and good looks that should have made him irresistible to screenwriters, Irving Thalberg has seldom been impersonated on-screen, although future uber-producer Robert Evens was unwittingly cast well in the *Man of a Thousand Faces* (1957). Here Thalberg (right) counsels James Cagney, who portrays screen legend Lon Chaney. *Photofest*

Certainly, Irving Thalberg would have seemed to be more fitting as a symbol of the studio because of his creativity, his youth and charisma, and the quick, dramatic, and tragic trajectory of his life. Yet, Thalberg has only been portrayed on the big screen once, aptly, by future mega-producer Robert Evens, in the Lon Chaney biography *Man of a Thousand Faces* (1957), which being a Universal film, otherwise ignored

MGM completely. Thalberg has also popped up on the small screen occasionally, portrayed by John Rubinstein in *Moviola: The Silent Lovers* (1980), by Seth Fisher in *The Last Tycoon* (2016–2017), and by Ferdinand Kingsley in *Mank* (2020).

One of the few other backstage MGM people who have ever gotten any attention in narrative cinema, and that has been limited, is Joseph Schenck, of all people, who shows up briefly as a character played by David de Keyser, in *Valentino* (1977). Then there are Mayer's Cerberus-as-secretary, Ida Koverman, and his notorious fixers, Eddie Mannix and Howard Strickling, who are often seen skulking in the background of studio-set movies and whose surprisingly numerous and consistent appearances will be discussed later.

Unsurprisingly, trailing in last place as far as screen appearances is Mayer's one-time heir apparent, Dore Schary. Schary rates a mention here only because he did appear as a character in an *I Love Lucy* episode from 1955, "Don Juan Is Shelved." Schary had been referred to several times in the series previous to his appearance, and the real executive had initially wanted to play himself, although other commitments eventually got in the way of his acting debut. So, the role was ultimately enacted by actor Philip Ober, who was married to *Lucy* costar Vivian Vance.

Like Mayer, Schary also did host, as himself of course, several nonfiction MGM-themed promotional films during his reign at the studio, including a tribute to himself on television's *This Is Your Life*, an episode of Ed Sullivan's popular variety show, and a one-hour documentary, *The Metro-Goldwyn-Mayer Story* (1951), which he claimed in his autobiography he emceed with two broken ribs, which might partially excuse how immobile and wooden he is in it. But Schary's tenure in Mayer's job has subsequently held little appeal for novelists or filmmakers. Amusingly, Schary's apparent lack of charisma is reflected even in *I Love Lucy*, with the actress playing Lucy's mother (Kathryn Card) repeatedly asking her daughter, "Who is Dore Schary?"

In popular culture no one has ever had to ask who Louis B. Mayer is. L. B. Mayer is MGM. And MGM really is only Mayer. He represents and characterizes the company to an ever-greater extent than any of its stars, who, seemingly unlike Mayer, lived lives outside the studio gates. The preceding "M" and the preceding "G" in the studio's name, hyphenated or not, are apparently only but thunderclaps before the crescendo. So, it is proper and apt then, that it is primarily, if not exclusively, through Mayer's appearances on-screen and in print, that we will look at MGM's odd and vast ripple effect across popular culture.

Mayer, as a screen character, has never been given a starring role in any film in which he is represented. No biopic of the man's literal and dramatic rags-to-riches scramble to

The first actor to portray Louis B. Mayer, and the only one to date to do so twice on the big screen, was Jack Kruschen, seen here in a 1961 portrait. *Author's collection*

the heights of success has even been attempted. And in most of his frequent on-screen appearances, Mayer is little more than a stock puppet master, sometimes beneficent, sometimes satanic. Often, he is kept mostly off-screen or in shadow. Sometimes he is never seen at all. For example, in *Postcards from the Edge* (1990), Shirley MacLaine's domineering movie-star mom reminisces to her daughter that, "I remember when I was fifteen years old. Mister Mayer called me in for a meeting. He was sitting on the toilet. We had to conduct the whole meeting with him on the toilet. Now you can be sure that he wouldn't have done that to John Garfield."

As indicated, the Mayer depicted on-screen is usually something of a rascal, although not without a snake-oil salesman's slippery charm. Consequently, as Hollywood's biggest dog. Other characters tend to resent him. In the recent series *The Last Tycoon* (2016–2017), Kelsey Grammer remarks that "I heard a joke today. . . .You're on an elevator. The doors open suddenly, in walks Hitler, Mussolini, and Louie B. Mayer. You've got a gun with two bullets in it. What do you do? Easy, you shoot Mayer twice." And in *Mank* (2020), writer Herman J. Mankiewicz remarks about Mayer that "if I ever go to the electric chair, I'd like him to be sitting on my lap."

Mayer's first actual on-screen impersonation was in a movie about Jean Harlow. The film, aptly called *Harlow*, was one of two dueling Harlow biopics that both came out in 1965. This second, alternate *Harlow* was a low-budget affair, although unlike the more expensive competing version with Carroll Baker as the star, this Harlow, played instead by another Carol, Carol Lynley, clashes with an actual and named Mayer rather than the pseudonymous mogul in the Baker version. Ethnic (here meaning Jewish) character actor Jack Kruschen played the screen's first-ever Mayer, although the effectiveness of the character, the role, the actor, and the movie is blunted by the crude, overly dark "Electrovision" process the film was shot in.

The relative failure of the dueling *Harlow*'s of 1965 perhaps helped to ensure that the next big screen Mayer would not arrive for another eleven years. In the early 1970s, the US was in the midst of a so-called nostalgia boom, which included a hunger for, and a perceived interest in, the legendary figures of old Hollywood. What no one seemed to notice during this era was that "old Hollywood" had not really been that long ago yet. Judy Garland, for example, had only died in 1969, and many other classic stars and executives from the era were still alive. Unfortunately, during this period it became more of an asset to look like one of those stars than to actually be one. A beautiful young actress named Morgan Brittany, for example, played Vivien Leigh, who she somewhat resembled, three times during this era, even as many of the real Leigh's costars were then reduced to doing denture commercials on television.

One of Brittany's Leigh impressions came in *Gable and Lombard* (1976), which featured James Brolin and Jill Clayburgh trying hard in the title roles, although Clayburgh's firecracker-fast line delivery makes her verbal characterization more reminiscent of Barbra Streisand than the actual Carole Lombard. Like *Harlow*, either version, *Gable and Lombard* plays fast and loose with the facts. For example, Gable's mustache, which would not become a permanent part of his persona until the mid-1930s is here sported throughout the film by Brolin.

Allen Garfield, as Mayer, is at least presented as being properly clean-shaven. His characterization though, like the tone of the whole film, seems to be trying hard for a fast-paced, effortless screwball comedy vibe, which is all too evident even in Garfield's dialogue. "There's a scene in *Libeled Lady* where Harlow has a button on her blouse unbuttoned, and they can see she has breasts. What do they think she has Clark, bottlecaps?" he quips at Gable and then he pauses, as though waiting for the audience to laugh. That said, Garfield's humorous, even warm-hearted L.B. probably played well to 1970s audiences who were trying to convince themselves that the 1930s were the "good ol' days."

The TV film *Rainbow* (1978) starred Andrea McArdle, the star of Broadway's *Annie*, as a teenage Judy Garland. The film is notable for giving the Oscar-winning character actor Martin Balsam the chance to play Mayer. Sometimes the casting of a certain acter can signify a "fictious" character's implied identity, which was certainly the case here. Balsam had first played a Hollywood hotshot, here named "Danny Weiss," in a 1959 *Twilight Zone* episode, "The 16-mm Shrine," and then went on to memorably essay another movieland slickster, one "O. J. Berman" in *Breakfast at Tiffany's* (1961). But

The go-to guy to play movie executive types for two generations, Martin Balsam, is seen here (center) intimidating George Peppard and Francesca Bellini in *The Carpetbaggers* (1964). *Author's collection*

his first actual studio president had been the fictitious "Bernard B. Norman" in *The Carpetbaggers* (1964).

Part of the overheated plot of *The Carpetbaggers* involved this executive's interactions with an overtly Jean Harlowesque 1930s actress, as played with trampy style by Carroll Baker. When Baker then played the star herself in 1965, Balsam, significantly, was *again* cast as her boss. This time, in this *Harlow*, the Mayer character was named "Everett Redman." But because many in the audience presumably knew that Mayer fulfilled that function, specifically as the boss of Jean Harlow in real life, it was obvious to those audiences who the character/actor was intended to evoke. Balsam's future performances as Mayer-like characters, such as agent "Harry Granoff" in *After the Fox* (1966), would ultimately continue to reinforce this impression about this actor for decades.

In *Rainbow*, Balsam is introduced in his office, misrepresented here as being decorated in brown leather and wood, listening implacably to Garland's audition recording.

Ultimately, his interest in Garland is presented as being financial, and not sexual, in nature. Although he, or his studio, is explicitly represented here as getting her addicted to pills. As a film, *Rainbow* is smart enough to keep this Mayer and his machinations largely off-screen, realizing, as noted previously, that the character works most effectively as an all-powerful and omnipotent godhead. Because of this well-executed conceit, and due to his connivingly cold portrayal, Balsam's Mayer(s) remains, even today, among the most impressive interpretation(s) of the character on-screen.

The perceived interest in all things nostalgia in the 1970s had just about flickered out when Garson Kanin's book *Moviola* appeared in 1979. Kanin was a longtime Hollywood insider who had written or directed many well-respected hits for the screen and on Broadway, so his novelistic weaving of fact and fiction impressed critics and audiences with its insider's look at famous movieland events and personages. In 1980, three of the book's stories were adapted into a network miniseries. In two of these episodes, "The Silent Lovers" (about the doomed Greta Garbo–John Gilbert affair) and "The Scarlett O'Hara War" (regarding the search for Scarlett), Mayer would appear as a character. The third story, "This Year's Blonde," was about Marilyn Monroe and so Mayer-free.

As Mayer, the miniseries producers cast Harold Gould, who was then well-known for playing the father of the title character on television's *Rhoda*. Gould is, by far, the most trim and dapper Mayer ever seen. The actor had already appeared as a studio overlord in Mel Brooks's *Silent Movie* (1976) and had long specialized in playing sly, well-dressed old foxes, so his altogether new and rather charmingly bemused take on the character ultimately served both he and that character well, subsequently earning him an Emmy nomination. It also eventually earned him several more Mayer-derived roles, such as in *Tales from the Hollywood Hills: Closed Set* (1988).

Unfortunately, *Moviola*, overall and once again, played fast and loose with the facts. Kanin's pulpy approach does not

Busy character actor Harold Gould presented television audiences with an unusually dapper and affable Mayer in *Moviola* (1979). *Author's collection*

always suit the material well either. In "The Scarlett O'Hara War" for example, Tony Curtis's vivid, wheeler-dealer David O. Selznick is depicted as having an illicit affair with Joan Crawford, which in 1939 would certainly have surprised both of them.

Incidentally, the usually reliable Kanin's questionable judgment is also evident in the source novel, which betrays its publication date by climaxing with an episode in which a failing old film studio is single-handedly rescued by producing a film about disco. That scene, at least, was not dramatized in the miniseries.

Before moving on with Mayer's on-screen life, it should be noted here that it was "The Silent Lovers" section of *Moviola* that offered viewers the first-ever on-screen depiction of MGM publicist Howard Strickling and General Manager Eddie Mannix, here played respectively, if briefly, by Frederick Combs and Barney Martin. In 2004, Strickling and Mannix would be the subjects of a controversial book, *The Fixers: Eddie Mannix, Howard Strickling and the MGM Publicity Machine*, by J. Fleming, which would document their alleged, illicit, and sometimes illegal cover-ups of scandals for Mayer. Because of the book's notoriety, both Strickling and Mannix would be depicted on-screen again, by Bob Hoskins and Joe Spano, in *Hollywoodland* (2006) and elsewhere. Mannix, this time without Strickling or Mayer in tow, would also be turned into a fictional character for *Hail Caesar!* (2014). This Coen brothers' film version of Mannix (Josh Brolin) works not at MGM but for something called "Capitol Studios." Yet he still confusingly scolds a misbehaving actor by telling him that "Nick Schenck and this studio have been good to you," making well-read viewers wonder what sort of parallel-world Hollywood the film is set in.

Following in the wake of the *Moviola* trilogy, the next on-screen Mayer was to be found up to his neck in Munchkins in *Under the Rainbow* (1981). The film was a would-be comedic riff on the making of *The Wizard of Oz*, with Jack Kruschen, from the second of 1965's dueling *Harlow* pictures, back for a curtain call as a more genial Mayer, although Kruschen's understandably exasperated studio boss is perhaps, wisely, only identified on-screen as "Louie." For the record, this on-screen Louie is the first and, to date, only Mayer to sport a mustache.

Titans (1981–1982) was a short-lived Canadian TV series whose admittedly novel gimmick involved journalist Patrick Watson's time traveling throughout history to interview various "titans." In one episode, he gets a chance to sit down and chew the fat with Louis B. Mayer, who is played by Canadian actor Al Waxman. Waxman would reprise the role twenty years later in *Life with Judy Garland: Me and My Shadows*.

Mommie Dearest (1981) offered audiences Faye Dunaway as Joan Crawford and Howard Da Silva as her boss. Note the carefully re-created white office and group shot of Louis B. Mayer and his stars adorning the wall. This attention to detail unfortunately did not extend to the movie's script. *Author's collection*

The same year as *Under the Rainbow* and *Titans*, a theatrical feature about Joan Crawford, *Mommie Dearest* (1981), debuted. The film's screenplay was based on Christina Crawford's gossipy, best-selling biography of her mother. Between documenting her mom's crimes against Christina and against wire hangers, the film also found time to give us a couple vignettes involving Crawford's old boss. Howard Da Silva plays the mogul, and the character is presented somewhat sympathetically—although when this particular Mayer fires Joan, he has already had her dressing room emptied and refuses to be seen walking with his former star out the studio gates. As cold as that sounds, compared to Faye Dunaway's shrieking harpy-from-hell version of Crawford, putting Vlad the Impaler behind Mayer's desk probably would have evoked sympathy. Da Silva, incidentally, had once been a victim of the Hollywood blacklist, which the real Mayer could probably have squelched, had he been inclined to do so.

Three years later, *Malice in Wonderland* (1985), an amusing TV film about the catty rivalry between Hollywood gossip queens Hedda Hopper and Louella Parsons,

Malice in Wonderland (1985) largely concerned itself with the battles between gossip queens Louella Parsons (Elizabeth Taylor) and Hedda Hopper (Jane Alexander), although Richard Dysart's Louis B. Mayer was seen lurking about as well. *Author's collection*

played here respectively by Jane Alexander and, aptly enough, Elizabeth Taylor, came out. Among the many Hollywood luminaries name-dropped or depicted on-screen was Mayer. Here, L.B., as played by Richard Dysart, is depicted as being the first to set the two as rival columnists, a juicy, perhaps even authentic, detail that was taken from George Eells book on which the screenplay was based. Therefore, both Mayer and MGM are featured quite prominently in the subsequent mayhem. In addition to the many celebrities impersonated in the film, Mayer's formidable secretary Ida Koverman is depicted by name for the third time on-screen (following Rue McClanahan's sympathetic Ida in *Rainbow*, and preceding Rosemary Dunsmore's icier one in *Life with Judy Garland: Me and My Shadows* [2001]). Also, briefly on view in *Malice in Wonderland*, unsurprisingly, are again, Mayer's favored toadies, Mannix and Strickling.

RKO 281 (1999) was another television feature, made in foggy London of all places and dramatizing Orson Welles's battle to film *Citizen Kane*. David Suchet, playing Mayer with owlish glasses and quiet authority is depicted briefly, along with fel-

David Suchet's Mayer in *RKO 281* (1999) was particularly Machiavellian. *Author's collection*

low empire builders Samuel Goldwyn, Darryl F. Zanuck, Jack L. Warner, David O. Selznick, Walt Disney, and Harry Cohn, all trying to decide how to deal with upstart Welles and his masterpiece. The scene as presented is certainly fascinating and would in fact be approximated later for the book *The Ben-Hur Murders* and for television's *The Last Tycoon* (2016–2017). In the latter, the subject of the summit was Adolf Hitler rather than Orson Welles.

Apparently, the genesis for all of these admittedly intriguing, meeting-of-the-mogul-minds scenes is to be found in Neal Gabler's definitive book *An Empire of Their Own*, which hinted at occasional and high-stakes poker games between some of the studio bosses. True or not, the premise of *all* of these alpha dogs ever being in the same room at the same time is highly fanciful, if for no other reason than that some of the participants, Goldwyn and Mayer, for example, in reality could barely abide one another, and Walt Disney, during the era depicted in *RKO 281* at least, would not yet have been important enough to earn a place at the table for such a movieland Malta conference.

There is a similar scene in yet another biographical TV film, *The Three Stooges* (2000), which was coproduced by actor (and admitted Stooge fanatic) Mel Gibson and shot in Australia. Mayer, played by David Baldwin, shows up in a fictional sequence set in a 1933 nightclub in which the boys, new to Hollywood, manage to amuse Mayer—as well as Jack Warner and Harry Cohn, leading to all three of them offering the Stooges jobs at the same time. "The business boys at my studio can have a contract ready for you by morning," Mayer tells them, to which Cohn snaps, "Don't listen to that junk dealer!" Improbably, the Stooges then proceed to choose little Columbia Studios over both Warner Bros. and MGM. This scene does jibe remarkably well with the boys' legendary bad business sense, if not so much with the actual facts.

Amusingly, *The Three Stooges*, just like the Three Stooges, would be televised to impressive ratings, at least among men, although there would be little significant viewership inside any female demographics.

An episode of the long-running *Wonderful World of Disney* TV series, "Child Star: The Shirley Temple Story" (2001), dramatized the star's best-selling memoir. The film included a brief sequence involving Temple and Mayer, played by John O'May.

The following year, Mayer tangled with yet another child star in *Life with Judy Garland: Me and My Shadows* (2001). Filmed in Canada, the movie continued the long run of TV movies about celebrities that had essentially begun in 1978 with *Rainbow*. As with *Rainbow*, the subject here was of course Garland, played as a child by Tammy Blanchard and as an adult by Judy Davis, both of whom would win Emmys for their effort.

Mayer is, again capably impersonated by Al Waxman. "I have loved you as a father loves his child, and you have been a bad girl, but I forgive you," he scolds her at one point, before stroking Garland's quivering chin with his fat fingers. For good or ill, the possibly subtextual meaning of this gesture would be further explored on-screen in more disturbing and explicit ways and soon.

But not too soon. In 2001, the same year as *Life with Judy Garland*, another, and much more wholesome, Mayer would make a wholly unexpected appearance in *Golden Dreams*, a 70-mm, twenty-two-minute short commissioned by Disney to run as an attraction in their new California Adventure amusement park. And run it did, continuously, for the next seven-plus years, ensuring that the project would be experienced by a combined audience probably larger than any other Mayer depiction in any media.

The director of *Golden Dreams* was Polish ex-pat, and Oscar nominee (for *Europa, Europa* [1990]), Agnieszka Holland. Holland's selection was a surprising and audacious choice for what amounted to, essentially, playing ringleader for a theme park attraction, which of course is exactly why the imagineers at Disney hired her for the gig in the first place. Whoopi Goldberg starred as "Califia, the Queen of California," who was initially seen as an animated art deco statue next to the screen on which the film was to be projected. Mayer was played by actor Richard Balin, who escorts viewers on a tour of Lot One in 1939. Several actual Mayer quotes, and several MGM stars, as portrayed by impersonators, are briefly introduced along the way. For his part, Balin comes across as such an altogether jovial and grandfatherly host that one ends up wondering why the studio didn't use an actor to play their own Walt Disney, whose image was more appropriate for such an interpretation as its Hollywood spokesperson instead.

Mayer was also treated pretty well in a 2004 episode of the then popular *Biography* TV series in which he was briefly impersonated by actor Angelo Fierro. Fierro, who is of Sicilian decent, would also play Samuel Goldwyn that same year in another episode of the series. Apparently, the reasoning here being that one ethnic movieland mogul looks pretty much identical to another.

The rehabilitation of Mayer as a kindly uncle character continued in *De-Lovely* (2004), which holds a place unique among all the Mayer-movies before or since in that the film was actually made by his own old studio. Yes, *De-Lovely* was an MGM musical—and what's more, this L.B. even sings!

In 2004, MGM was once again in questionable financial straits and less than eager to return to the genre they were most associated with, musicals having become evermore monetarily dicey over past decades. Nonetheless, the studio finally ponied up the comparatively modest $15 million budget the project required, reportedly because of pressure by producer/director Irwin Winkler, who then wielded a great deal of clout with management there, owing to his hyper-successful *Rocky* franchise. Although in his autobiography, Winkler charitably only describes MGM as coming aboard "with some nostalgia."[5]

Winkler had wanted to film a musical biography of Cole Porter for a long time, using contemporary artists to interpret the composer's impressive catalog of standards. One of these standards, "Be a Clown," is performed by Kevin Kline as Porter and British actor Peter Polycarpou as Mayer, who here implores the composer to write a funny song as they dance across the MGM lot, which of course no longer existed as such. So, it's bitterly ironic that, after decades of Warner Bros. and Universal and Australia and Canada portraying MGM, here at last was an actual MGM movie, made by MGM, and yet the studio scenes this time were again shot in the UK. The number apparently

Peter Polycarpou's Louis B. Mayer performs "Be a Clown" with Kevin Kline's Cole Porter in *De-Lovely* (2004). It is possible that this scene, surely based on a true incident, may have been fictionalized here, if only slightly, for dramatic effect. *Photofest*

is meant to take place in 1947 when Porter was at MGM for *The Pirate*—although historical authenticity is hardly a concern in a film where Mayer wears a rubber clown nose, impersonates Groucho Marx, and dresses up as Napoleon.

The cinematic Mayer was back to his old tricks, however, in *The Aviator* (2004), which was a high-profile, Academy Award–winning biography of billionaire Howard Hughes. Mayer, played by Stanley DeSantis, is used to represent the Hollywood power structure that Hughes (Leonardo DiCaprio) tries to crash during the production of his aviation epic *Hell's Angels* (1930). Mayer is characterized as trying to preserve the status quo by refusing to rent outsider Hughes some production equipment. Director Martin Scorsese, who had directed *New York, New York* (1977) and parts of *The Last Waltz* (1978) on the MGM lot, had the clout, the will, and the money to shoot the film in Los Angeles, where most of it is set. He also returned, briefly, to the old MGM (Sony) Studio for some exteriors.

Curiously, the earthy MGM star Ava Gardner, played by Kate Beckinsale, is represented in *The Aviator* as being an ethereal and sometimes imagined muse for DiCaprio's addled Hughes. Previously in the TV movie *The Rat Pack* (1998), Deborah

Kara Unger, also playing Gardner, had appeared to Frank Sinatra in an identically ghostly manner—the power of stardom.

The microbudget *Fried: The Autobiography of Louie B. Mayer* (2014), despite its title, was actually a scattershot and largely improvised spoof of, among a great many other things, *King Kong*. The plot, if that's at all what it was, concerned itself with a wild gorilla (played with the aid of no expensive and cumbersome monkey makeup whatsoever by one Megan Stogner) that is brought to the jungles of Hollywood and transformed into "Louie B. Mayer, the most successful producer in the history of cinema." All of the familiar producer-themed tropes, save for that still-ever-omnipotent-still-ever-present cigar, are bravely cast aside, although possibly only to satisfy certain budgetary problems. Nonetheless, this film, if again that's at all what it is, is still notable for offering us the first-ever *female* Mayer. And as a special bonus, Samuel Goldwyn also makes an appearance. *Fried* probably possesses other virtues too, although I can't personally verify this, having been unable to ever make it to the end.

More traditional, and better financed, was *Trumbo* (2015), which starred Bryan Cranston as blacklisted screenwriter Dalton Trumbo, who takes on Hollywood studios, the US Congress, and even big John Wayne in defense of his beliefs and then pays dearly for doing so. Mayer, as the establishment's obvious biggest, baddest wolf, would, one would expect, therefore, be portrayed as a fire-breathing ogre to stack the dramatic deck to favor Trumbo's righteous, outgunned little guy. Interestingly though, this is not the path that John McNamara's deft screenplay chooses to follow. Instead Mayer, played by Richard Portnow, is depicted as being coerced by columnist Hedda Hopper (Helen Mirren, all smiles and acid) into allowing the blacklist to decimate an industry he had built. "Forty years ago, you were starving in some *shtetl*. The greatest country on earth takes you in, gives you wealth, power, but the second we need you; you do nothing. And that's exactly what my readers expect from a business run by kikes!" Hopper almost spits the words at Mayer, who is presented as being blackmailed, against his will, and with the rest of the studios, to then turn on Trumbo and his friends.

Television took a crack at F. Scott Fitzgerald's *The Last Tycoon* in 2016–2017. Here Mayer is played as a crass bore by Saul Rubinek, although again, all of the other characters are presented as being in awe of his immense power and influence. Rubinek is introduced in the second episode of the series, not in his office, but rather on a set and squatting in a director's chair, marking the cinematic Mayer's first-ever media appearance in such a workaday setting. Rubinek's story arc continues through the run of the show, which like Fitzgerald's book, was ultimately left unfinished due to the series's abrupt cancellation.

Mayer's contribution to the TV series *Feud* (2017) was limited, literally, to a single memorable line. The story is a dramatization of the battles between stars Joan Crawford (Jessica Lange) and Bette Davis (Susan Sarandon). In the second episode, Crawford's attempt to secure the lead in *Madame Curie* (1943) is thwarted by Mayer. "Either I play that egghead dame or I walk," Crawford shouts at Mayer (Kerry Stein), who is seated at the end of a long table. "Then I suggest you start walking then." He says bluntly, ending the MGM phase of Crawford's career, and Mayer's participation in the plot. Despite its brevity, the scene is more dramatic than its equivalent in *Mommie Dearest* or in the sanitized account of her own dismissal that Crawford gives us in in her autobiography. Again, with Mayer, less is usually more—or not.

Although in *Feud*, Mayer's role is almost comically brief, like the real person, Mayer still casts his long, plump shadow over the rest of the story. Decades and episodes later in the series, J. L. Warner (played by Stanley Tucci) is seen sputtering that "Goldwyn is finished. Mayer is dead. And Selznick is just one pastrami sandwich away from a coronary. . . . I'm the last goddamn dinosaur. And I'm up to my tits in tar." This near coda to the series implies that like Crawford and Davis, Warner and Mayer probably, actually, had more in common than they ever would have admitted.

Judy (2019) returned to the Garland biopic formula, which had been minted with *Rainbow* and perpetuated in *Life with Judy Garland*. This time, however, the producers chose to focus on Garland's final concert engagement in London, with only occasional flashbacks to Hollywood and, of course, to the production of *The Wizard of Oz*. A stylized re-creation of the yellow brick road set was therefore commissioned, which is represented as being almost comically cramped, probably more a result of the film's relatively small budget than any particular attempt at stylization. Young Garland (Darci Shaw) here has several disturbing scenes grappling with "Mister Mayer."

Mayer is Richard Cordery, who stands almost a foot taller than the real man did. The height discrepancy does make his scenes opposite this diminutive Garland all the more harrowing, however. And harrowing they are. If (some of) the previous portrayals of Mayer in media had been benign, even charming, here the Mayer as monster trope is back, and he is more savagely evil than ever before. "Your name is Frances Gumm. You're a fat-ankled, snag-toothed rube from Grand Rapids. Your father was a faggot, and your mother only cares about what I think of you. Now do you remember who you are, Judy?" Cordery's Mayer virtually hisses this sentence into her face. Unsubtly

Judy (2019) featured Darci Shaw as Judy Garland from the era of *The Wizard of Oz* here disturbingly offered up as a sacrificial goat to Richard Cordery's predatory, pedophilic "Mister Mayer." *Author's collection*

reminding her and, us, that a deal with the devil can indeed give one passage to Oz but can swallow an innocent soul up in the process.

It gets worse. The most controversial of these MGM-as-hell flashbacks depict Mayer's groping of Garland's breast while the two of them are alone. These rumors of possible improprieties with Garland, who was sixteen at the time, had been depicted on-screen, if ambiguously, before. But *Judy* represented the first time these allegations would be fully visualized for movie audiences.

This scene apparently was taken from Gerald Clarke's biography *Get Happy: The Life of Judy Garland*. The book quotes an unpublished Garland memoir, which Clarke discovered. To quote Clarke then, and Garland:

Whenever he complimented her on her voice—she sang from the heart, he said—Mayer would invariably place his hand on her left breast to show just where her heart was. "I often thought I was lucky," observed Judy, "that I didn't sing with another part of my anatomy."

That scenario, a compliment followed by a grope, was repeated many times until, grown up at last, Judy put a stop to it. "Mr. Mayer, don't you ever, ever do that again," she finally had the courage to say. "I just will not stand for it. If you want to show me where I sing from, just point!" To her surprise, Mayer reacted not with anger, but with tears, sitting down, putting his head in her hands and crying. "How can you say that to me, to me who loves you?" he asked, looking so miserable that Judy found herself consoling him. "It's amazing how these big men, who had been around so many sophisticated women all their lives, could act like idiots," she was later to write.[7]

The scene in *Judy* is a pretty harrowing representation of these passages. And that scene's inclusion in the film is dramatically understandable, even necessary to explain how the adult Garland (an Oscar-winning Renée Zellweger) grew up to be so damaged. In the world outside the film, the sequence, sadly, now resonates as well. Although one can only hope that the #MeToo movement has now given female victims of similar abuse by powerful men more of a voice in the twenty-first century.

But is it true?

Historian and author, Alicia Mayer, to whom Mayer was a great uncle, does not think so. When film producer Harvey Weinstein was publicly accused of sexual molestation of more than sixty women in 2017, the press, including Hollywood trade publications, which should have known better, immediately started drawing parallels between Weinstein and Mayer. Even though the truth, she claims, does not support these comparisons.

There were at least three studio moguls who were "known" in this regard, but Louis B. Mayer was not one of them. The closest he came to this was pursuing bumbling relationships after the end of his 25-year marriage, and ultimately marrying Lorena Danker in 1948. They were together until his death in 1957 . . . to call him a sexual predator, to put him in the same tweets, posts, headlines and articles as Harvey Weinstein is wrong, libelous. It's lazy journalism too.

What is also tragic about these slanderous headlines, equating Louis B. Mayer to Weinstein, is that L.B.'s love for his mother Sarah, deeply influenced how he treated women. One of his closest friends and advisers was a woman lawyer, *his own doctor* was a woman, and there were women in leadership roles at M-G-M from very early on, including Ruth Harriet Louise, the first woman to ever run the still photography department at any studio. Probably his closest friend was my great-grandmother, Ida Mayer Cummings, and he was happy to conspire behind the scenes with the Queen of Hollywood, Mary Pickford, to fundraise for good causes. The fact is, Louis B.

Contrasting imagery: "Bad" Louis B. Mayer in 1943, obese, powerful, and chewing an omnipotent, ever present, cigar. *Bison Archives*

And "good" Louis B. Mayer, with wife Margaret rather touchingly picking (hand-colorized) fruit while visiting Garnett Grove in St. Augustine, Florida, circa late 1910s or early 1920s, photographer unknown but likely Philip A. Wolfe. *Courtesy Alicia Mayer and Family Collection*

Louis B. Mayer, with one of his closest associates and advisors, Ida Mayer, holding a plaque recognizing his contribution to the Los Angeles Jewish Home for the Aged (as it was called then) in 1952. *Courtesy Alicia Mayer and Family Collection*

Mayer held women in high esteem and expected others to do so too. I think it's very clear that he valued the counsel of women. Sex-fiend monsters don't tend to care what women think.[8]

Alicia Mayer has several sources with which to back up her defense, including actresses Joan Crawford, who she quotes as saying unequivocally that "at Metro we were lucky because Mr. Mayer didn't believe in the casting couch routine."[9] And Ann Rutherford, who she paraphrases as saying that Mayer, in fact, "ran a family-oriented studio, and that he took care of his people."[10]

Alicia has also talked to Daniel Mayer Selznick, Mayer's grandson, who told her unequivocally that "Louis B. Mayer may have been the ONLY major studio executive who DID NOT engage in intimate relations."[11] Alicia Mayer is also understandably skeptical of the accusations against her great uncle by actress Joan Collins, who has claimed that Mayer tried to take advantage of her circa 1963—six years after he had retired to the great white office in the sky!

But what about Garland's specific and horrifying allegations? Again, to quote Alicia Mayer: "Regarding Judy Garland, it was my understanding that she had later rescinded her accusations about Louis B. Mayer, saying that she regretted them deeply and that there was never anything insidious about her treatment by Louis B. Mayer personally, or the studio."[12]

Selznick agrees with this, saying that "when my mother took me to see Judy [Garland] at the Palace, we went backstage, and Judy was very upset about the negative things she had read about Louis B."[13]

It should also be noted that at Garland's wedding to Vincente Minnelli, Mayer not only attended but also gave the bride away. In his autobiography, Minnelli says that he and Garland and the Mayers used to occasionally go out together socially, including an apparently pleasant night the four spent at the Hollywood Bowl. Although this could have been only a political move on their parts, Minnelli makes no allusion to this being the case.

A careful reading of Garland's statement about the incident could also indicate that she might indeed have been trying to pass off the incident as a bad joke ("I often thought I was lucky that I didn't sing with another part of my anatomy"). Garland was a great raconteur, and she was never one to let the truth get in the way of a good story, as her repeated tales about amorous munchkins and scene-stealing cowardly lions prove.

There is also ample, if anecdotal, evidence that for emphasis Mayer was known to poke *other* actresses, and perhaps actors too, in the head or the heart to dramatically make whatever point he was emphasizing. Betty Garrett mentioned this, comically, in her memoirs and in her one woman show. Garrett seems, from the tone in which she describes the anecdote, to have found her boss's finger-poking habit, awkward, but not offensive, and most certainly not sexual.

Yet it is Judy's story, and *Judy*'s story, true or not, that people will choose to remember. And nothing about that story, as recent events have proven, is particularly funny.

After the problematic and tonally creepy Mayer on display in *Judy*, it is perhaps a relief that the most recent Mayer on-screen is again presented as being ruthless and manipulative and slippery—but at least he keeps his hands to himself.

Mank (2020) was a classy, lovingly crafted biography of screenwriter and uber-wit Herman J. Mankiewicz. The film contains beautiful performances throughout, all captured in beautiful Oscar-winning black-and-white, and filmed in, as the credits beautifully inform us, Hollywood, California. In particular, star Gary Oldman, although vocally sporting a Burgess Meredith growl, is subline as the title character. That said, the film is on historically slippery ground in its widely disproven assertation that it was Mankiewicz, with little input from Orson Welles, who wrote *Citizen Kane*. Perhaps because director David Fincher (using a screenplay by his father, the late Jack Fincher) is aware that he is working from a dubious historical position, most of the film is made up of flashbacks to Mank's previous Hollywood adventures, prominently including Mankiewicz's always amusing interactions with occasional boss-taskmaster, Mayer.

Gary Oldman and Tom Pelphrey can only trot along in the wake of Arliss Howard's volcanic Louis B. Mayer in *Mank* (2020). *Author's collection*

Oddly, perhaps to play up the *Mank* screenplay's *Citizen Kane* parallels, Mayer is described (in dialogue) as somehow being the inspiration for *Kane*'s "Bernstein" character, which is odd indeed because Mayer, even as presented here, is nothing at all like the sycophantic lapdog played by Everett Sloane in the older film.

If anything, *Mank*'s Mayer is instead perhaps the most physically aggressive Mayer ever presented. One of the first times we see him he is beating up an unfortunate actor, presumably John Gilbert, for insulting the sanctity of motherhood. Immediately he then stomps out of his office and across his studio (mercifully, the former MGM lot again largely plays itself)—spitting orders to Mank and to Mank's brother Joe (Tom Pelphrey) and to every other unfortunate minion he passes on the way. He then rushes into a meeting with his employees—famously talking them into accepting that notorious 50 percent pay cut, after which they collectively cheer him for asking it of them. Remember that all of this happens in one scene.

This dynamo Mayer is played by Arliss Howard with, as can be expected, a great deal of verve and energy. So, it is perhaps the fault of the older Fincher's screenplay, rather than of Howard's exuberant performance, that despite the generous screen time the character is afforded, he ultimately comes across as a conscienceless cipher with, yet again, no evidence ever presented of his having any internal life at all. This Mayer, from first scene to last, is simply no more and no less than a great white shark in a great white office operating at the top of the food chain on impulse and instinct rather than out of any strategy or intellectual chess.

Apparently, that characterization is exactly how the two Mankiewicz's, as well as the two Finchers, and apparently most audiences, ultimately want us to see him.

In addition to being a supporting character in films, Mayer as a character has also appeared or been evoked occasionally on the stage, including, most intriguingly, the unsuccessful Broadway musical *In Hell with Harlow* from the 1990s, by Paul L. Williams, which, true to its title literally dramatized a divine reckoning between the blonde bombshell and those in her orbit, including her old boss.

Although the mogul is also an onstage character in Buddy Kaye and Mort Garson's musical *When Garbo Talks* (2001), more often he remains a characteristically omnipotent off-stage presence. In Ron Hutchinson's *Moonlight and Magnolias* (2004), Selznick, writer Ben Hecht, and director Victor Fleming, are besieged by phone calls from, among others, Mayer, while they are writing the screenplay for *Gone with the Wind*. And in her popular one-woman musical revue, *Betty Garrett and Other Songs*

(1974), the star impersonates Mayer poking her, renewing her contact—and stepping on her toe.

The producer also received catty on-stage shoutouts from Judy Garland characters in both *The End of the Rainbow* (2005) by Peter Quilter, and *The Judy Monologues* (2010) by Darren Stewart-Jones, the first of which eventually would morph into the Oscar-winning movie *Judy*.

Likewise, both *A Day in Hollywood/A Night in the Ukraine* (1979), a musical comedy written by Dick Vosburgh and Frank Lazarus, and the revue *Hello Hollywood, Hello* (1978–1989) in Reno, Nevada, by Donn Arden, have referenced and name-dropped either Mayer or his studio, as have, for that matter, the many Hollywood-themed floorshows at the MGM Grand hotel(s) in Las Vegas and elsewhere.

But Mayer's biggest contribution to legitimate theater would come, again off-screen, in the person of his daughter, Irene Mayer Selznick, who produced *A Streetcar Named Desire* (1947), one of the seminal successes in Broadway history.

A MOGUL IN THE MOVIES

Ultimately, the collective result of all of these sometimes contradictory and conflicting cinematic Louis B. Mayers, from 1965 until today, is one of filmmakers using the character different ways to make points about a man and his times. It is all together rather remarkable then that none of this varied tinkering has yet rendered him unrecognizable, no matter what sort of vivisection is performed on his persona performance to performance and film to film.

Because of all these mixed messages, one is left wondering how exactly the now pervasive almost all-encompassing Mayer-as-monster stereotype first took root because only a few of the impersonations detailed have overtly presented the mogul as any sort of sexual predator at all. In fact, several of these Mayers in these films were charming, even endearing, if in a rascally uncle sort of way.

The answer, perhaps, is not to be found in movies featuring Mayer, so much as in movies which don't. A good example is the Carroll Baker *Harlow*; where as noted, it is obvious to everyone that it is Mayer being portrayed on-screen, but pseudonymously. Martin Balsam, of course, was the past master of this, to the point where eventually, anytime he appeared in a Hollywood setting, he would play a mogul, often *the* mogul, named on-screen or not. It is these near-Mayers, or almost Mayers who perhaps have done so much damage to the real man's reputation.

That said, the truth is that any portrayal of a classic-era studio head, positive or negative, no matter who plays him, could be interpreted as or twisted into being Mayer. For example, John Marley played two different but similar movie bosses in the 1970s, tangling with the legendary comedian in *W. C. Fields and Me* and, notoriously, with Vito Corleone's "family" in *The Godfather*. But neither time is his character explicitly, or symbolically, intended to evoke Mayer. In fact, *The Godfather*'s "Jack Woltz" was allegedly modeled instead after rival Columbia Studio's big cheese, Harry Cohn. Not that that matters because audiences would have thought of the better-known Mayer first anyway and so then assumed the worst.

The archetype of the powerful, predatory, often overtly Jewish, and often vulgar, cigar-chomping film tycoon is truly omnipotent. It may have partially sprouted from Fitzgerald's *The Last Tycoon*, which featured a character, "Pat Brady," who was specifically, if not ethnically, styled after Mayer. The book has been dramatized for television several times, most recently in 2016 with Kelsey Grammer as Brady, and was given a big-screen treatment in 1976 with Robert Mitchum in the role. Mitchum was a close enough approximation to the stereotype, but Grammer's sometimes crass, but still urbane interpretation seemed instead to be based on Christopher Plummer's dapper but sinister studio head from *Inside Daisy Clover* (1965). As noted, the 2016 *Last Tycoon* covered its tracks by also featuring Mayer himself as a supporting character.

The reliable "it must be Mayer?" equation continues even today. The Coen brothers' film *Barton Fink* (1991), like the Carroll Baker *Harlow*, similarly referenced another MGM-specific star, Wallace Beery. But Beery's boss was instead called "Jack Lipnick." Michael Lerner's convincingly Mayer-like performance earned the actor an Oscar nomination. Lerner had previously played Hollywood reptiles in both MGM's *Alex in Wonderland* (1970) and television's *F. Scott Fitzgerald in Hollywood* (1975), so his promotion here to full mogul status would have, again, resonated with any audiences who subconsciously remembered the actor operating in this milieu before.

Perhaps it's due to this blurring of the lines between actor and character and actor and role and to the great number of Hollywood-related movies out there, that eventually, these films, surely almost a genre onto itself by now, eventually seem to exist all together and in the same vast collective universe? This is a universe where Balsam seems to (almost) always play the big cheese, and Red Buttons keeps showing up (well, at least twice) as a confidant to whatever star's life is being then dramatized.

Another example is gossip queen Hedda Hopper; she had been an actress before turning to her poison pen, and she even occasionally played herself in movies like *Sunset Boulevard* and, weirdly, in the TV series *The Beverly Hillbillies*. And again

Robert Mitchum, center, is not specifically playing anyone named Louis B. Mayer in *The Last Tycoon*, yet the big desk, the white suit, and the ever-orbiting clique of yes-men surrounding him capably suggest otherwise, 1976. *Author's collection*

weirdly, her actual appearances as herself are slightly less Hopper-like than the subsequent films in which her antics and her big hats are dramatized by performers like Tilda Swinton, Fiona Shaw, Alice Backes, Rue McClanahan, Melinda McGraw, and Helen Mirren.

No matter who plays Hopper, however, it feels like a continuation of the same caricature by one talented actress after another, and this helps to lend a weird sense of continuity, of verisimilitude, to all these ripped-from-the-headlines dramatizations and airings of dirty laundry, battles with rival Louella Parsons, and whitewashings of sordid Hollywood dirt she always performs. Judy Davis, one of the best of these hat-wearing Hoppers in *Feud*, also played Judy Garland in *Life with Judy Garland*. Although unfortunately, she was not also brought on as Hopper in that project, thus denying the talented actress the opportunity to torture herself. By far the most brazen of all the Hedda/Louella caricatures though, was in *Won Ton Ton: The Dog Who Saved Hollywood* (1976), which featured Ethel Merman as a columnist in, yes, a big hat, who is identified as "Hedda Parsons."

And in this Hollywood-set universe, studio chiefs are even more omnipotent than gossip columnists. Jacqueline Susann's trashy novel *Valley of the Dolls* (1966), of course, included a transparently veiled character obviously based on Mayer, nicknamed "The Head," who clashes with a character obviously based on Garland. But sadly, when the book was filmed in 1967, the "head" character was omitted from the screenplay. Surely depriving Balsam of a juicy supporting role.

Other movies with would-be or might-be Mayers could surely include *A Star Is Born*, featuring the character of "Oliver Niles," played by Adolphe Menjou in 1937 and by Charles Bickford in 1954. The surprisingly honorable, even romanticized studio chief on view in these two films may well be due to the influence of the 1937 picture's producer, David O. Selznick. Selznick was Mayer's son-in-law. He also possessed a great deal of genuine respect for both Mayer and for Mayer's breed. In life, Selznick continued to feel that respect for that breed even after he divorced Mayer's daughter in 1949.

MGM's own *Singin' in the Rain* (1952) delightfully offered Millard Mitchell as studio head "R. F. Simpson," who is presented as being indecisive and befuddled but also basically decent. This "head," however, was surely more a wink at the film's producer, Arthur Freed (it even included Freed's characteristic "I cannot quite visualize it" catchphrase), than as a caricature of the actual and then-departing and then-diminished Mayer.

Other legendary Hollywood-set films, maybe *all* legendary Hollywood-set films, also contain veiled or coded references to Mayer. For example, Billy Wilder's *Sunset Boulevard* (1950) has a character named "Sheldrake" (Fred Clark), who, as Mayer and Thalberg did, admits to turning down *Gone with the Wind*, because, as he mournfully puts it, "who wants to see a Civil War picture?"

Sometimes though, the Mayer figure is hidden or split among multiple characters. MGM's own post-Mayer classic, *The Bad and the Beautiful* (1952), featured Kirk Douglas as one "Jonathan Shields," a decidedly not-so-nice producer. But the Shields character doesn't resemble Mayer so much as Selznick, who had by then already run, and run into the ground, his own studio. Yet intriguingly, *The Bad and the Beautiful* also contains references to Shields's unseen father, "Hugo Shields," another mogul, about whom his own son says, "he wasn't a heel, he was THE heel." It is this disreputable ghost figure, crossed with Selznick's own father, pioneer mogul Lewis J. Selznick, who seems to echo Mayer quite nicely. Incidentally, the same film also offers us a *third* Mayer in the person of Walter Pidgeon's put-upon "Harry Pebbel" character, a B-film producer made up of disparate elements of both Mayer and of an actual B-film producer, Val Lewton—echoes upon echoes.

And there are many more echoes. In United Artists's *The Big Knife* (1955), Rod Steiger played the crass "Stanley Shriner Hoff," who like Mayer could "cry at the drop of an option,"[14] to quote filmmaker Alain Silver. Although director Robert Aldrich admitted that the character in Clifford Odets's source play on which the film was based, again probably owed more of his personality to Harry Cohn, whom Odets had suffered under. But, of course, audiences wouldn't have known this and would probably have seen Mayer instead. Like many other actors who played moguls, Steiger would go on to play other surely Mayer-inspired studio bosses on television, namely, one "Michael Kirsch" in *The Movie Makers* (1967) and "Oliver Easterne" in the miniseries *Hollywood Wives* (1985).

Rod Steiger's mercurial movie boss in *The Big Knife* (1955) manages to intimidate even physically larger foes like Jack Palance, much as Louis B. Mayer was famous for doing. *Photofest*

But by the mid-1950s, the traditional mogul archetype was finally wearing thin. Films about filmmaking in the 1960s and beyond tended to be set in Europe rather than Hollywood, which is where many films were then being made. So, United Artists's *The Barefoot Contessa* (1954), MGM's *Two Weeks in Another Town* (1962), and even foreign art-house hits like Francois Truffaut's *Day for Night* (1973) needed to present no overt Mayer-types because in these films the studio head would presumably have been torturing his minions back in Hollywood during this period. Jean-Luc Godard's *Contempt* (1963) is the only film from this continental offshoot genre that offered audiences a recognizable Mayer stand-in, in the person of Jack Palance's "Jeremy Prokosch." Prokosch is presented as being a philistine US producer who finances and then disrupts a film shoot in Italy. Palance, true to form, had earlier costarred in *The Big Knife*.

But by this time, even home set movies, except for parodies, now had no use for the traditional cigar-chomping mogul stereotype because with the end of the studio era came the rise of a theory, first popularized in the US by critics like Andrew Sarris, that it was the director, not the producer at all, who was the film's true auteur, or creator of that film.

This theory flew directly in the face of everything that the old film studios like MGM and old film czars like Mayer had believed in. For example, director Fred Zinnemann, who had suffered under Mayer personally, recalled that his old boss "considered producers the single most important element in picture making. Next came the star, then the story. In fourth place was the director."[15] But during this era, due to the immediate popularity of this alternate director-centric concept, at least among well-read *cineastes*, moguls, producers, and even the studios themselves now suddenly seemed increasingly quaint, even irrelevant.

The most prevalent on-screen example of this "director is God" school of cinema was *The Stunt Man* (1980), which unintentionally and unironically was partially shot at MGM, and featured Peter O'Toole as director "Eli Cross," who as his name suggests, evokes both Jesus and Satan to his awestruck cast and crew, both of these characteristics, in a prior era, would surely have been used only to describe Mayer and his ilk.

Weirdly, when an impresario or studio chief was depicted during this period, he was now represented as a sunglass-wearing hipster type, more Phil Silvers or Zero Mostel than Balsam. Even more weirdly, many real producers then started trying to live up to this stereotype in a desperate attempt to appear young and to remain relevant.

For example, MGM's own *The Phantom of Hollywood* (1974) based its studio boss, this time named "Roger (rather than Eli) Cross," not on their own Mayer-created

The Stunt Man (1980) chose to anoint the director, not the producer, as god-like. Here Peter O'Toole descends out of the sky on a camera crane and into the life of an untrusting Steve Railsback. *Photofest*

archetype, but on the floundering company's actual manager, James Aubrey. Aubrey's real-life daughter, Skye Aubrey, in a delightfully perverse casting choice, also appeared as the sleazy executive's daughter. Peter Lawford, who would have known more than a few secrets about the real MGM by that time, played the part of Cross, without a big cigar but, instead, sporting a trendy, 1970s ascot.

As the original, Mayer-influenced stereotype evolved into yet another, even more outlandish stereotype, this second mogul archetype immediately itself became cartoonish, and much quicker than the first, even to the point of being mocked in actual cartoons. The 1960s animated TV series *The Flintstones* and *Rocky and Bullwinkle*, for example, savagely milled this crumbling archetype into the ground for preteen audiences long before those audiences' parents realized how silly it all really was.

Also ironic was the fact that with the coming of the 1970s nostalgia wave, it was the original Mayer caricature that returned to prominence. And this unexpected cultural shift was again reflected not only in live action but in animation. *Who Framed Roger Rabbit*'s (1988) studio boss R. K Maroon, played (in live action) by Alan Tilvern, for example, represents a producer archetype that would not have been out of place decades earlier as befitting the film's period setting.

In the 1980s it became harder to take seriously the traditional mogul stereotype. In *Who Framed Roger Rabbit* (1988), for example, Alan Tilvern's studio boss (left, with Bob Hoskins), is ultimately outsmarted by a not-so-bright cartoon bunny. *Author's collection*

Later and likewise, the children's film *Movie Critter's Big Picture* (2003) featured a puppet-populated movie studio headed by one "Louie B. Mole," who was, yes, an actual mole. Then there is the theatrical cartoon feature *Cats Don't Dance* (1997), which similarly and tellingly christened its studio boss character "L. B. Mammoth." *Cats Don't Dance*, significantly, was dedicated to Gene Kelly, who, like Lawford, had known the real McCoy.

In the 1970s, there was also an ongoing and parallel trend in depicting comedic studio chiefs, as if to underscore the idea that Mayer and his breed could no longer be taken too seriously. MGM's *Hearts of the West* (1975) offered Donald Pleasance as "R.

J. Neitz," who was actually a publishing rather than movie czar, but the Hollywood setting made the effect of the characterization the same. *Won Ton Ton: The Dog Who Saved Hollywood* (1976) featured both Art Carney and Ronny Graham as rival moguls. Carney's "J. J. Fromberg" certainly resembled a more-than-usually-addled Mayer, but Graham's "Mark Bennett" was presumably intended as a messy pie-in-the-face to the memory of actual producer Mack Sennett.

The 1970s also gave us Mel Brooks's *Silent Movie* (1976), which featured Sid Caesar and Harold Gould as studio chiefs, and *Nickelodeon* (1976), which costarred Brian Keith as an early movie mogul named "H. H. Cobb." The following year *The World's Greatest Lover* (1977) offered audiences one "Adolph Zitz," played by Dom DeLuise. But Zitz was a caricature of Paramount's Adolph Zukor, right?

After *The World's Greatest Lover*, the comic Hollywood cycle mostly flickered out. *¡Three Amigos!* didn't come along until 1986, but it did feature Joe Mantegna as the unforgettably named movie boss "Harry Flugelman." Although the Oscar-winning *The Artist* (2011) has kept the tradition alive somewhat, including among its characters John Goodman as studio honcho "Al Zimmer."

Nickelodeon (1976) offered Brian Keith (flanked by minions Ryan O'Neal and Burt Reynolds) as a producer at the dawn of the studio age, although the bluster and the cigar are already in place.
Author's collection

Concurrent with this comic trend, more serious Mayer-inspired studio chiefs have continued, and continue, to throw their girth and cigar ash about in serious features as well. An early return to the archetype was MGM's *The Legend of Lylah Clare* (1968), in which one "Barney Shehann" (Ernest Borgnine) very Mayer-like, asserts that "I make movies, not films" from within the sanctuary of his Oscar-studded *green* office (it was the 1960s). *Ed Wood* (1994) gave us a mogul named only "Mr. Feldman," played by Stanley DeSantis, who screens a (very) bad movie and then complains that "this has gotta be a put-on. This is probably another one of Billy Wellman's practical jokes?"

Then consider Orson Welles as the godlike, self-serious "Lew Lord" in *The Muppet Movie* (1979) and contrast his characterization with Darren McGavin's mogul-on-the-skids role of "A. D. Nathan" in *Tales from the Hollywood Hills: A Table at Ciro's* (1987). Both of these projects, represent both Mayers, Mayer unbound first and then Mayer in slow eclipse.

Between those extremes the repetition of the archetype is amusingly endless. Remember Leslie Neilsen's little-seen "John Bracken," head of Century Studios in *Brackin's World* (TV 1969–1970)? Remember Allen Garfield's "Harry Sylver," the mercurial big boss of Silver Screen Pictures in *The Lot* (TV 1999–2001)? And did you catch Rob Reiner's "Ace Amberg," the piggish monarch of Ace Studios in *Hollywood* (TV 2020)? They all, all of them, and many, many more, are made up with a touch of Mayer. Many are made up, or perceived to be made up, of more than just a touch.

Not all of these would-be Mayers are presented as being the ogre that the real man has been occasionally and recently portrayed as in the press, but some of them certainly are—whatever their on-screen names might be. So, it is these rather extreme

Rob Reiner in the miniseries *Hollywood* (2020) again reinforced negative and hedonistic mogul stereotypes. It should go without saying that the light here encircling Reiner's head most certainly does not represent a halo. *Author's collection*

and apparently unfair characterizations, along with often lock-step portrayals in print, which seem to cling to the character, and to the person behind the character, to this day.

MAYER AND HIS STUDIO ON THE PAGE: NONFICTION

MGM has had an enduringly long and colorful life on the printed page. Perhaps this literary tenacity is because, as in the movies, every book ever written dealing with classic Hollywood ultimately has to grapple somehow with the lion in the room. Often the studio is used as a metaphor for the business in total. For example, Arthur H. Lewis's collection of essays about Los Angeles, *It Was Fun While It Lasted*, published in 1973, climaxes with the author wandering about amid the debacles of the studio's notorious auctions, which he then uses as an unsubtle metaphor for the death of Hollywood.

There has been so much nonfiction written about the US entertainment industry that people tend to forget that virtually all of it has appeared in the last fifty years before which there had been surprisingly few books, serious or sensational, about the subject, especially when one sets aside books and fan magazines telling of the lives and scandals of specific movie stars. In 1960, critic Bosley Crowther was able to tell us that "there is a surprisingly meager body of solid literature on Hollywood producers, the motley executives who played roles clairvoyants and attempted to ride some sort of herd on much more conspicuous and publicized writers, directors, and stars."[16] Consequently, almost all that has been written about the studio itself has appeared after that studio's ultimate erosion was already well underway.

Dealing with all of this Metro-centric nonfiction, some of which is excellent and much of which is biased, however, is both unnecessary and redundant because again, by using Mayer as our primary guide, it is possible, with a few diversions, to chart a through line to the other side of all of this verbiage and to make a few MGM-specific observations on the way.

The Lion's Share: The Story of an Entertainment Empire (1957), written by the same esteemed reviewer, Crowther, who is quoted, was the first serious book ever published about Hollywood as seen through the prism of a single studio. Lillian Ross's *Picture*, about the making of *The Red Badge of Courage* and published in 1952, had grappled with some of the same personalities, but it was *Lion's Share*, along with Crowther's *Hollywood Rajah: The Life and Times of Louis B. Mayer* (1960), that together represented the first sustained, collected impressions of the studio created by someone outside that studio's gates.

Bosley Crowther, the dean of New York film critics for decades, was generally dismissive of Hollywood and of Louis. B. Mayer in particular. Although his bad temper may well have been born of envy, as he eventually became an executive at Columbia Pictures, 1960. *Photofest*

In *Lion's Share*, accordingly, Crowther is indeed critical of the product, if occasionally admiring of the factory that created that product. But little of this begrudging admiration comes through in *Hollywood Rajah*, where his take on Mayer is highly critical, condescending, and inflammatory. He, even, at one point accuses his subject of possessing a "psychopathic need for power." When referring to Mayer's sexual appetites, however, Crowther did, and perhaps reluctantly, here concede to his readers that "Mayer could not be counted among the more wanton types."

Crowther, as a self-professed liberal, New York–based journalist, and early, vocal proponent of European cinema, had a complicated relationship with Hollywood. He enjoyed the craft and talent that went into studio product but derided how the industry then wasted that talent. For example, in a 1948 lecture he attacked "meaningless musical comedies, pseudo-historical, tough guy and other such pictures," archly concluding that "nine out of ten of these are a mockery to the adult mind."[17] But maybe his pique against Mayer was actually born of envy? In 1968, after being fired from the

New York Times, Crowther would cross over to the dark side and take a job in upper management at Columbia Pictures.

In both books, Irving Thalberg, as would ever-happen in the future, comes across much better than Mayer does. It should be mentioned though that Norma Shearer, Thalberg's widow, had cooperated with Crowther. Perhaps her input explains his resultant, fawning portrait of the Thalbergs, which caused at least one wag to suggest that the first book should have been retitled *The Lion's Shearer*.

Until the advent of Crowther's one-two punch against Mayer. The mogul had been treated pretty well in the press. There had been no published whiff of scandal or improprieties associated with his name or reputation, although Ross's *Picture* had done the executive no particular favors. So, sadly, it is Crowther's vindictive portrait of Mayer, supplemented with the gossipy innuendos and accusations in Kenneth Anger's *Hollywood Babylon*, which had been first published (in Europe) at about the same time, that seems to have cemented the overall characterization of Mayer as an omnipotent ogre in print.

Crowther's books, if not all of his assumptions, are respected, if little read today. But Anger's work has since been so widely reprinted that although Mayer scarcely appears in it, his character, largely off-stage or not, is by association implied to have been complacent in every scandal, miscarriage, abortion, and unsolved murder ever committed in classic Hollywood. And it matters not that most of the book's salacious accusations have since been so widely discredited that author Karina Longworth literally labored for an entire season on her podcast, *You Must Remember This*, at debunking the book's many libelous and inaccurate accusations; the damage had been done.

After Ross, Crowther, and Anger were done raking him over the coals, there was little biographical interest in Mayer until Samuel Marx's *Mayer and Thalberg: The Make-Believe Saints* (1975). Marx's book has a uniquely intimate and personal perspective because the author knew both of his subjects personally. Yes, Myrna Loy once dismissed Marx as "a flunky,"[18] but the fact that Marx was there at all gives his words a great deal of weight. His generally tough-love look at his old bosses did little to correct old misconceptions about them, although regarding Mayer's perceived sexual proclivities, Marx tells his readers that "there were rumors that he slept with stars, but they were spread by people who didn't know him, because it was precisely what he would not do."[19] Tellingly, Marx concludes his account with Thalberg's death.

After Marx's shared study, there would be no full-length biography of Mayer at all until Gary Carey's *All the Stars in Heaven: Louis B. Mayer's MGM* (1981). It was Carey who began Mayer's partial literary rehabilitation. He pertinently notes

Samuel Marx's shared biography of his two former bosses, published in 1975, certainly benefits from having its author in the room when the stories he tells were happening, but he too, ultimately, seems to want to buy into the legend. *Author's collection*

in his text that in the 1960s as Hollywood was written about and reevaluated by its survivors, ridiculous and scandalous stories about Mayer "were taken as truth, partly because they were so amusing that people wanted to believe them, partly because the American public had been primed to believe that anything and everything was possible in Hollywood."[20]

Unfortunately, as Carey notes, people wanted to believe what they wanted to believe, and the truth is, even after *All the Stars in Heaven* debunked some of these myths, it failed to destroy them. Carey ends his portrait with an anecdote about being approached by someone writing a thesis about MGM who asked him, "Why was Louis B. Mayer such a villain?" His response is worth reprinting.

First of all, this man wasn't a villain. If you want a villain, go look at the head of ITT or General Motors or the head of whatever . . . just because Mayer stepped on some toes or because he browbeat some actresses into playing parts they didn't want to do, or because there was a certain amount of conniving around—this made him a villain? Then God help us all. Mr. Mayer was a great showman, and he loved and believed in what he was doing. He created something that was unique and which is wonderful and of lasting value."[21]

Furthermore, when Irene Mayer Selznick, Mayer's daughter, wrote a clear-headed autobiography, *A Private View* (1983), she described her father as "probably the most unsophisticated, straightlaced man in town,"[22] and although her often conflicted impressions of the man would have admittedly been different from those of his underlings, these words hardly seem to describe the character usually depicted in popular culture. Yet again, though, it just didn't matter.

More biographies, all of them worthwhile, followed. Diana Altman's *Hollywood East: Louis B. Mayer and the Origins of the Studio System* was published in 1992. Memorably and not at all sarcastically she anoints her subject as the "Zeus of film pioneers."[23] Altman also took care to point out that "if the old man had really been such a monster, how is it that so many people had worked for him for thirty, for forty, years?"[24] Seemingly, by this point, however, had a biographer discovered evidence that Mayer had devised a cure for polio and rescued orphans from burning buildings it would not have changed public perceptions about him.

Sadly, recent media comparing Mayer to Harvey Weinstein make this point all too well. Had any of these so-called journalists consulted any of these books, even those highly critical of their subject, these comparisons would certainly never have happened.

The following year (1993), Charles Higham's *Merchant of Dreams: Louis B. Mayer, M.G.M and the Secret Hollywood* took a slightly different tack, however. Similar to E. J. Fleming's later *The Fixers: Eddie Mannix, Howard Strickling and the MGM Publicity Machine*, Higham does little to paint Mayer in a human, let alone humane light, although ultimately, he does make a real effort to show his subject a perhaps begrudging amount of respect.

The most recent biography of Mayer has been Scott Eyman's balanced and fair *Lion of Hollywood: The Life and Legend of Louis B. Mayer* (2005). Well-rounded, even-handed, and sympathetic, the book does not shy away from either its subject's virtues or his flaws, which is, after all, everything one can ask for in a biography.

After Crowther's fawning portrait of him, Thalberg has continued to be treated much better on the written page than Mayer ever has. Thalberg's deification began practically before he died, and the semi-regular presentation of the Irving Thalberg

Memorial (Academy) Award has done much to keep his name in front of the general public. The first book-length look at the legendary producer's life and legend was, aptly enough, called *Thalberg: Life and Legend* (1969) published by Bob Thomas, which romantically emphasized his last tycoon persona. Marx's *Mayer and Thalberg: The Make-Believe Saints* followed in 1975.

Later biographies by Roland Flamini (1994) and Mark A. Vieira (2009) have gone a long way to humanize Thalberg's saintly boy-genus image, although, unlike Mayer, whose public persona has flowed and (mostly) ebbed over the years, Thalberg's image has remained remarkably consistent, that is, as stalwart, passionate, and driven, throughout his bibliographical life.

There are by now a great many general works about the studio as well. Although, again, other than those already mentioned, and some movie star autobiographies, which will be dealt with later, these books did not start to appear until the 1970s. *The MGM Years* (1971) by Lawrence B. Thomas was apparently the first "modern" MGM book. From the title one would think this would be a narrative account of the whole studio, but Thomas instead concentrates primarily on its musicals, as did, more transparently, Hugh Fordin's *The World of Entertainment! Hollywood's Greatest Musicals* (1975).

Like Frodin's book, *The MGM Story* (1975) by John Douglas Eames was first published as part of the company's golden anniversary. Its popular and critical success led to reprints and updates in 1981, 1987, and in 1990 for the studio's sixty-fifth anniversary. *The MGM Story*, in any edition, is a massively suitable spectacle, with every MGM release to that time chronologically listed, described, evaluated, and represented by a photograph. Eames seminal and successful approach led to books on other studios, all of which would follow the same durable format.

MGM eventually became the topic of another high-quality, coffee-table book. *MGM: When the Lion Roars* (1992), by Peter Hay, which would also inspire an epic, same-named three-part documentary on the studio. As in *The MGM Story*, Hay dealt mostly with the company's library. But there was also much more production and corporate detail included, although oddly, unlike the TV series, which carried us into the (1990s) present, Hay chooses not to, or was instructed not to, deal with the studio's post-1959 output at all, except in a brief epilogue, omitting the dramatic possibilities of the studio auctions, for example, and ignoring the many evictions and eviscerations that came after.

Because collectively, Eames and Hay did such a good job of illustrating the big-picture aspects of MGM, it would fall to concurrent and later historians and authors to

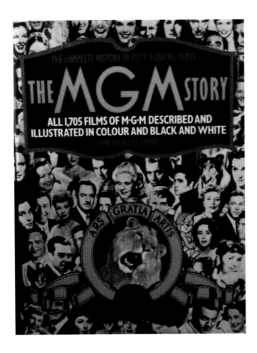 

The MGM Story (1975) by John Douglas Eames and *MGM: When The Lion Roars* (1992) by Peter Hay each grappled with the studio's history and legacy in different ways and remain fundamental works on the subject today. *Author's collection*

fill in the remaining gray spaces and minutia about the people and the personalities and the films that the company produced. Surely most people who read these books, and indeed most people who wrote these books, started out by reading Eames or Hay first. Collectively, these less general MGM-specific books have succeeded in doing a good job of flushing out the ghosts and glories, as well as the grit and dirt, which made up the studio era.

There are now MGM-centric books about virtually every aspect of the factory, its operations, and its colorful personnel. Ida Koverman, Mayer's secretary, now has her own biography. The Dore Schary regime has its own worthy book-length study. The studio's Art Department and Cedric Gibbons are the subject of their own book. The Costume Department, and even specific costume designers like Irene and Adrian, now have multiple biographies devoted to their works. The Publicity Department, and notoriously, Eddie Mannix and Howard Strickling, have likewise been profiled. Dorothy Penedel of the Makeup Department has her own biography. Lassie's trainer Rudd Weatherwax is the subject of a biography. The Special Effects Department and Arnold "Buddy" Gillespie have been given their own book. Tex Avery, William Hanna, and Joe Barbera of the Cartoon Unit also are the subjects of biographies or autobiographies. The famous "little red schoolhouse" on the lot is the star of a book, as is the studio's backlot. There is even a book-length work about MGM's Cinemascope releases, of which, as the author admits, there were only seven.

Perhaps the most uniquely focused MGM-centric book so far has been *The Best Is Yet to Come: A Life That Went from the Lion of Metro Goldwyn Mayer to the Lion of Judah* (2017), which details former distribution executive Bill Barber's conversion to Christianity.

A subcategory of all of this has been those books that deal specifically or critically with the studio's films, as Eames did in his early and groundbreaking work. To date there have been three (!) separate books with the title *The Best of MGM*, each dealing with the movies that came from the movie studio. Specific genres and production units' and stars' films within the studio have been given their own book-length treatments too.

There have also been entire books about individual MGM films, beginning with Ross's seminal writings about *The Red Badge of Courage* and followed by, among others, commemorative, popular, academic, or analytical books about the production and impact of *Greed* (1924), *The Student Prince in Old Heidelberg* (1927), *The Crowd*, (1928), *Marie Antoinette* (1938), *Boy's Town* (1938), *The Next Voice You Hear* (1950), *An American in Paris* (1951), *Singin' in the Rain* (1952), *2001: A Space Odyssey* (1968), and the James Bond series. And, of course, written studies of *The Wizard of Oz* and *Gone with the Wind* are now so numerous that each could fill up a long shelf in the library.

Several studio-centric works have had the audacity to title themselves *The Best of MGM*. This one, from 1981, despite its dull cover art, is worthwhile. *Author's collection*

Also of note, in the 1970s, a whole series of individual volumes were published, collectively titled *The MGM Library*, which reprinted the screenplays of at least half a dozen MGM classics, which was probably welcome to fans and scholars in those long-ago days before home video.

It should be mentioned that MGM itself has sometimes published or licensed books or booklets about individual films for the purposes of publicity or to garnish Oscar consideration. For example, *Singin' in the Rain* of all things was the subject of a comic book adaptation in 1952.

This practice of the studio selling books to sell movies goes back to the 1920s when souvenir programs from roadshow-styled pictures like *Ben-Hur* were sold at the theaters where these films played for twenty-five cents, which was then more than the price of a ticket for most of those movies. This practice became something of a cottage industry late in the 1950s and early in the 1960s, when short, well-printed hardcover tribute programs associated with several of MGM's big-budget productions were sold in the theaters where these films played as, again, souvenir keepsakes for patrons. Many of these tribute books, associated with epics like *Quo Vadis, Ben-Hur, How the West Was Won, The Wonderful World of the Brothers Grimm, Mutiny on the Bounty*,

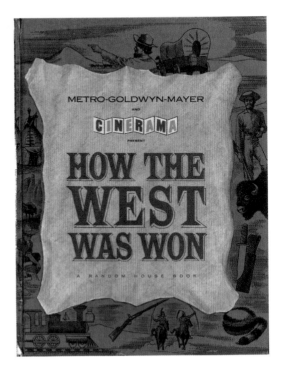

Starting in the 1950s MGM began publishing hardcover souvenir programs for their roadshow-style super productions. This one, for *How the West Was Won* (1962), apparently was almost as successful as the movie, judging from the number of copies still available at garage sales. *Author's collection*

and probably surprised to find itself in such epic company, *The Boy Friend*, still show up constantly in flea markets, garage sales, and on eBay, where they usually sell for only a few dollars because they once sold so well and are still so plentiful.

MGM, of course, and later Ted Turner, have also licensed artwork, from these films and others, for the original novels on which their subsequent movies had been based. Countless readers first encountered Rhett Butler and Scarlett O'Hara, for example, not on-screen but while reading paperback copies of *Gone with the Wind* that featured Clark Gable and Vivien Leigh making sparks on the cover. The first such edition of that particular book, fully authorized by the studio, came out in 1940 when the film was still in its first release.

Internally, MGM also published, under various names, an in-house newsletter/trade publication for employees and exhibitors. The most famous of these was *The Lion Roars*, which ran only during the years of World War II but is much cherished today by collectors due to its eye-catching graphics and striking covers, which usually featured a stylized Leo the Lion and whichever star then had a movie coming out. Hay's *MGM: When the Lion Roars* (1992), would decades later, revive this motif for its own cover.

Like most large companies MGM has often sponsored an internal newsletter for its employees and contractors. These arbitrary samples of those newsletters, with various names and agendas, span the decades from the 1940s into the twenty-first century. *(left) Tommy Hines; (right) David Bowen*

MAYER AND HIS STUDIO ON THE PAGE: BIOGRAPHICAL

It is the talent that worked at the studio that has accrued the largest, the lion's share, if you will, of the writings about that studio. Every major, and nearly every minor, luminary who ever worked on the lot by now has at least one biography to call his or her own. Cheeta the Chimp, from the *Tarzan* series, and Toto from The *Wizard of Oz*, for example, have now each authored their own, presumably ghostwritten, memoirs.

But for the purposes of illustrating one sample branch of this vast biographical tree, I am focusing on autobiographical works by the stars themselves. These stars, after all, were presumably well-positioned to comment, firsthand, about their experiences with MGM, and with Louis B. Mayer.

This autobiographical trend among MGM stars can be traced largely to early in the 1960s after Mayer's death and as it became ever obvious that an era in Hollywood had indeed died as well. This is apparently the time when many survivors of that era first tried to grapple with what it had all meant, personally certainly, but also professionally and psychologically. Some of these autobiographies were probably ghostwritten, many were overwritten, badly written, or self-serving. But they all reflected the opinions of those who were there, as opposed to the opinions of those of us who came later. So, for that reason they all deserve our attention, if not always our outright respect.

It should also be stressed that these books' portraits of these stars' old boss consistently and almost without exception have contradicted and refuted Ross's and Crowther's portraits of Mayer as an eccentric at best or as Anger's blood-sucking, baby-eating gargoyle at worst.

One of Mayer's biographers, Gary Carey, claimed that these autobiographies all "cast Mayer and other studio executives in a vicious or ridiculous light,"[25] which isn't really true, although it should be mentioned that few of these supposed tell-alls ever suggest that the mogul was any sort of sexual predator. On the contrary, collectively or individually, these books all express respect for, at the very least, Mayer's business acumen—which, again, makes one wonder exactly how those Mayer-Weinstein comparisons first took root.

This is probably a good time to mention that many stars would have had little interaction with a man who was, after all, their boss's boss's boss. Some of the autobiographies sited here describe little direct interaction with Mayer at all, leading a reader to assume that these interactions were apparently either unremarkable or unreportable. For example, Rita Moreno only tells us how soft and well-manicured L.B.'s hand was when she shook it. Groucho Marx, who wrote several dubious but amusing memoirs, sums up Mayer basically by only saying that "I didn't like him,"[26] while his brother Harpo only tells us that Mayer used to call Nelson Eddy "Eddie Nelson."[27] Buster Keaton, like Groucho, had every right to not like Mayer, but in his 1960 autobiography, he appeared to bear his old boss no ill will for the eventual wreckage of his career.

Then there are the autobiographies where no particular opinion about the old man is expressed at all. For example, singer Marni Nixon interacted with Mayer but gives us more insight into Ida Koverman. Marie Dressler, Billie Burke, Ingrid Bergman, Ginger Rogers, Howard Keel, Leslie Caron, Claude Jarman Jr., Carleton Carpenter, and Ricardo Montalban only mention Mayer in passing, either because they were children, were overly discreet, came at the end of his tenure, or had little cause to interact with the boss at all.

Perhaps the first full-length memoir to deal with Mayer as a character, although it came out decades before the era of the tell-all, was Lionel Barrymore's family biography *We Barrymores* (1951), published when the mogul was still (barely) on his throne. The book includes a chapter tellingly titled "A Bow to Louis B." Its author admits at the start of this chapter that "the mind's picture of a great studio chief [is] that of a cold and shrewd executive who dangles careers on strings, plays with actors like puppets, and discards them when they begin to unravel around the edges,"[28] which gets the reader's hopes up for something really dishy. Instead, he goes on to warmly assert that *his* mogul was nothing like that, that Mayer always found time to council Barrymore, frequently loaned him money, and even saved the actor's career from premature conclusion when Mayer insisted that Barrymore not be tossed onto the scrap heap when he lost the use of his legs. Mayer did this simply by insisting that the roles Barrymore usually played be rewritten to be enacted from behind a desk or in a wheelchair. In an era when even the president of the US largely concealed a similar handicap, this stand for the rights of a much-marginalized minority is both admirable and, for its time, remarkably forward-thinking. "Mr. Mayer," Mr. Barrymore emotionally tells us, "did what he did, and there is, of course, no way to express my gratitude."[29]

The next major MGM star to release an autobiography was Fred Astaire. Astaire's memoir, *Steps in Time* (1959), was an unsurprisingly classy affair, which significantly and disappointingly, for our purposes, only mentioned Mayer in the context of his stable of racehorses.

But the same year gave readers silent star Mae Murray's *The Self-Enchanted* (written by Jane Kesner Ardmore but authorized by the star), which offered up a mogul concerned with much more than just racehorses. Murray had been a hot commodity up until her fourth husband, a minor European aristocrat named David Mdivani, suggested to her that she break her contract with the studio. Disastrously as it turned out, she heeded his advice, leading effectively to her being blacklisted in Hollywood. Eventually seeing the error in taking her husband's counsel, Murray would then write Mayer a letter pleading to come back, which he refused to even consider, leading surely to Murray's statement in her book referring to Mayer as "an unforgiving, ruthless and vengeful man."[30]

A fuller, and largely more positive view of the mogul was Joan Crawford's *A Portrait of Joan: The Autobiography of Joan Crawford* (1962). While Mayer had been dead for half a decade by this point, the great star still tastefully, if not excitingly, toes the studio line, praising her old boss's wisdom and his fatherly advice.

Mickey Rooney's first autobiography *I.E.* followed in 1965. Rooney, like Crawford, is deferential, consistently referring to Mayer as "Mister Mayer" both here and in his otherwise more explicit 1991 follow-up, *Life Is Too Short.* "I'd liked Louie B. Mayer for a long time, and in his way, he'd liked me too,"[31] being a typical Rooney statement. In neither of these books is there anything of the Mayer-as-monster trope at all. Rooney is, in fact, much harder on Dore Schary, who is usually perceived as the kinder, gentler executive.

Rooney would be even more complementary in the documentary *MGM: When the Lion Roars* (1992), saying for the record that "he meant everything in the world to me, he gave me my place in the sun. I love Mr. Mayer very much."[32] Likewise, when he received an honorary Oscar in 1982, Rooney got a laugh from

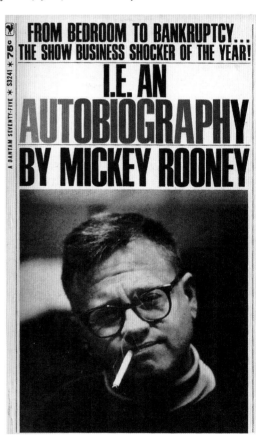

Mickey Rooney apparently thought so much of his life story that he told it twice. *I.E.* (1965), although not particularly concerned with MGM itself, also seemed less interested in tidying up inconvenient facts than the latter, *Life Is Too Short* (1991), was. *Author's collection*

the audience when he said that "I'd like to even kiss Louie B. Mayer." It should be mentioned that on both occasions, being able to see him saying these words on camera is rather moving—although Rooney was, after all, nothing if not a consummate actor.

Lena Horne had such a public and contentions relationship with the studio that one cannot help but wish that her 1965 autobiography (cowritten with critic Richard Schickel) was less inclined to toe the party line, Mayer-wise, than it is. "He was a short, chubby man, and by now everyone is familiar with the tales of his temperament," she begins, promisingly enough, but then she reassures and, let's admit it, somehow disappoints her readers by asserting that "on this occasion—as upon most of the very few others that I dealt personally with him—he seemed very genial and fatherly to me."[33] Anyone notice a pattern emerging here yet?

Hedy Lamarr's *Ecstasy and Me: My Life as a Woman* (1966) was allegedly ghost-written. Although these possible rumors may stem from the book's occasional literary conceit in slipping from the first to the third person and in questionably including a preface and introduction by the star's medical doctor and her psychologist, respectively! Despite its alluring title, Lamarr's narrative again offered nothing scandalous, at least not about Mayer, who she, perhaps disingenuously often describes as "a friend."[34] That said, she does mention this friend patting her on the bottom on their first meeting, although she makes little of it or of his comment to her that "you'd be surprised how tits figure in a girl's career."[35]

Lillian Gish's memoir, *Lillian Gish: The Movies, Mr. Griffith and Me* (1969), deals with the star's MGM period in some detail, recounting, for example, that when the studio brass first summoned her for a meeting, her mother mistook Irving Thalberg for an office boy! She also tells us that Mayer thanked her once for giving him his start as an exhibitor by appearing in cinema's first blockbuster, *The Birth of a Nation* (1915). Gish details how she was impressed by Mayer's acting as an honorary pallbearer at D. W. Griffith's funeral in 1948. Gish does, however, also tell her readers about Mayer's less generous side, including his threatening her with his famous line, "If you don't do as I say, I can ruin you."[36] Although she brushes his words off and leaves MGM with, apparently, no psychological wounds or hard feelings.

There were certainly no hard words to be found about Mayer in George Murphy's autobiography from 1970. On the contrary, he calls his old boss "one of the great men of his time," one of the "outstanding figures in his industry," "a great human being," and a "great man." He also praises his "dear friend"[37] Mayer for his patriotism and his largely unheralded work to promote racial and religious brotherhood in the entertainment industry. Although the fact that the studio boss and the future senator were much aligned politically possibly contributed to those opinions.

Ann Miller told her story in *Miller's High Life* (1972), which offered a far more personal look at the mogul, whom she claimed she had a brief romance with in 1944, right after Mayer had left his wife, Margaret (the Mayers would ultimately divorce in 1947). Miller's account, although certainly more intimate than any other star's, is still respectful, even loving. "He was my idol, both personally and professionally,"[38] she gushes. Miller also claims that when she announced her engagement, to someone else, Mayer was so bereaved that he attempted suicide—although others have since tried to refute her claims, which are apparently unsubstantiated except by her. Most of Mayer's biographers ignore them completely. Even if true, though, these actions, although gossipy, still hardly represent those of a consummate Hollywood playboy.

Marion Davies's charming, posthumously published memoir, *The Times We Had* (1975), dishes little dirt and spends little time in the company of her one-time boss. Although this is hardly surprising, considering the favorable, and free, mentions in her boyfriend William Randolph Hearst's newspapers that came with her services while she worked at MGM. Basically, she just tiresomely tells her readers that "I was very fond of Irving and of L.B."[39]

In her own memoir, Lena Horne earlier had mentioned that Davies sat in with Mayer on Horne's first audition for him. This would have been in 1942, long after Marion and Hearst had left the studio, which probably affirms that Mayer and Davies had indeed remained friendly over the years.

In her book, Davies also wryly tells us that when she left MGM for greener pastures at Warner Bros., that "I don't think Louis B. Mayer minded losing me so much. He did mind losing Mr. Hearst, if you know what I mean."[40] We do.

Gloria Swanson largely avoided both Mayer and his studio, due no doubt to Mayer's dislike of Joseph P. Kennedy, who was once both her personal and professional partner. In her memoir, *Swanson on Swanson* (1980), however, the star does mention seeing her masterpiece *Sunset Boulevard* at a screening in which Mayer was in attendance. And although Mayer reportedly hated the picture because of its acidic anti-Hollywood bias, he apparently never told her this on that surely memorable night. End of encounter.

Jackie Cooper's autobiography *Please Don't Shoot My Dog* (1981) contains little Mayer, understandably, because a child star would not have been expected to negotiate for himself in that white office. That unpleasant task instead fell to Jackie's mother, on whom he asserts Mayer had a crush. Cooper also asserts, using rather flimsy evidence, that the boss had the stages across the lot bugged to better spy on his employees.

The MGM section of this book ends when hat in hand, a newly mature Cooper himself asks that same boss to put him under contract again—and to pay him only if he felt that he was earning his keep for MGM. The fact that Cooper would have been willing to come back and under such humiliating terms indicates that life under Mayer could not have been *that* bad. In any case, it didn't happen. He writes that after making that offer, he never heard from Mayer again.

A self-named autobiography by June Allyson in 1982 portrays her old employer as stern and paternal. She also remembered frequent Mayer-basher Judy Garland telling her that Mayer had been consistently kind to her and had even once given a personal loan to her when Garland was destitute.

In 1982, Lana Turner's memoir, *Lana: The Lady, the Legend, the Truth*, was published. Turner's impressions of her boss were not exactly, if we can here use a newer term, "politicly correct." But those impressions could hardly be considered, in terms of their era, either scandalous or salacious. In one early scene Turner does remember being summoned into Mayer's office, with her mother in tow and being admonished for being seen dancing in nightclubs while still a teenager. Turner says that Mayer proceeded to then tell her that perhaps "the only thing you're interested in is . . ."[41]—and then crudely pointing to his own crotch, leading to a serious scolding from Turner's mom for talking like that in front of her daughter. Turner, apparently untraumatized by this display, seldom bothers to refer to Mayer again for the duration of her, let's admit it, eventful, three-hundred-plus page biography. Unaddressed by Turner here, perhaps not surprisingly, is Esther Williams's later assertion that Turner used to sit on Mayer's lap and call him "Daddy." Mayer also reportedly asked Luise Rainer (and perhaps others?) to assume the same position. Rainer at least, declined.

"Mayer was wily, but he wasn't crude like Schenck. I liked Mayer. I didn't trust him, but I liked him," Myrna Loy says in her memoir *Being and Becoming* (1987). Then the star proceeds to tell several bemusing, affectionate tales about her old employer, including an anecdote about Mayer's reported phony fainting during a negotiation, and rather oddly, his once confiding in her that "Myrna, you're like one of my family. If you were my mother, my wife, my mistress I couldn't be more sincere."[42]

Loy also, again, has Garland gushing to her about Mayer's compassion. "Schenck and the others wanted to throw me to the wolves . . . but Mayer sent me to Boston for therapy. He tried to help me, while the others cried: 'Off with her head!'"[43]

Jane Powell's and Debbie Reynolds's respective autobiographies, both published in 1988, almost identically painted Mayer as a friendly and protective mentor, perhaps because Mayer was older, maybe wiser, by the time they came along. "In a way, I loved him," Powell says, in her book *The Girl Next Door . . . and How She Grew*. "Oh, I'd heard all sorts of terrible stories about him, but I thought he was a wonderful man. People make him sound like an ogre—he has been called 'a monster'—but he wasn't like that at all to me. I was his little daughter."[44]

Reynolds, in her first memoir, *Debbie*, doesn't dispute this. "He seemed rather cuddly and sweet, although other people have expressed different opinions about Mr. Mayer. For many he was nothing less than a tyrant, who ruled the studio with an iron hand. But he was always nice to me and from what I could see he was extremely polite and solicitous in the company of women,"[45] Reynolds asserts.

Shirley Temple's short stay at Metro is documented in her autobiography *Child Star* (1988) in which she describes a single harrowing day in which she is most crudely propositioned by Alan Freed even while, in a different office, her mother receives some unwelcome attention from Mayer. Although in the case of the older Mrs. Temple, Mayer's "proposition" involved little more than his sitting on a couch with her and taking her hand.

Kirk Douglas, as only an occasional MGM actor, apparently never had personal access to Mayer, but he does share a secondhand, if telling, story about him in his first autobiography, *The Ragman's Son* (1988). Douglas asserts that during the making of *The Bad and the Beautiful* (1952) he was excited to meet former

Like Mickey Rooney, Debbie Reynolds wrote several memoirs over the course of her long career. Her Frist, *Debbie* (1988), most concerned itself with her years in Culver City, however. *Author's collection*

star Francis X. Bushman, who was playing a small role in the movie. Bushman then confided to Douglas that this was the first time he had worked at MGM in twenty-five years! Surprised, Douglas, who was playing a character partially based on the just-departed Mayer, asked why. Bushman responded that "I was doing a play once, and Louis B. Mayer came backstage to see me. I was taking off my makeup and he had to wait a couple of minutes. He ran off in a huff and said, 'that man will never work at my studio again.' And I never did."[46]

In her autobiography, *Ava: My Story* (1990), the salty Ava Gardner was unsurprisingly less sentimental than many of her fellow leading ladies had been. Gardner implies, well, she actually pretty much states outright, that she "didn't like" Mayer. Although Gardner does, in her fashion, concede that "MGM was a damn sight better when the old man was around."[47] That said, her problems with her longtime employer were seemingly of a financial rather than a personal nature.

In her typically no-nonsense way, Katharine Hepburn begins her discussion of Mayer in her 1991 memoir *Me* (as well as in a 1993 documentary version), by asserting that "L. B. Mayer and I were friends. He was the head of Metro-Goldwyn-Mayer. I liked him and he liked me. I sold him quite a number of properties. He gave me a lot of freedom and I gave him a lot of respect. L.B. had a sense of romance about the

Ava Gardner's autobiography from 1990, like its author, was frank, salty, and blunt, although Louis B. Mayer receives no particular amount of scorn. *Author's collection*

movie business and the studio system." She also tells us flat out that "L.B. Mayer was an amazing man."[48] That said, Hepburn does concede that at a certain level her boss lacked personal charm, which she speculates might have been one of the reasons he was so disliked by so many, if not by Hepburn.

Hollywood bad boy Orson Welles never wrote an autobiography, although Peter Bogdanovich did the next best thing, when he published *This Is Orson Welles* (1992), as recorded by Bogdanovich during his frequent conversations with the late star. In one chapter Welles asserts to Bogdanovich that writer Ben Hecht had told him that in the 1930s, before Welles ever came to Hollywood, Mayer had put a team of secretaries to work trying to track down Welles in New York because someone had told Mayer that Welles was somehow "exotic," perhaps along the lines of a (male) Hedy Lamarr, and so might have been a valuable addition to his stable of stars. Unfortunately, by the time that the mogul's flunkies actually located Welles, Mayer had forgotten what he had originally summoned him for. Too, bad. It's interesting to speculate how Orson Welles would have fared at MGM.

A dubious but interesting assertion comes later in the same book when Welles tells Bogdanovich that "the old studio bosses—Jack Warner, Sam Goldwyn, Darryl Zanuck, Harry Cohn—were all friends, or friendly enemies I knew how to deal with. They offered me work. Louis B. Mayer even wanted me to be production chief at his studio—the job Dore Schary took. I was in great shape with those boys. The minute the independents got in; I never directed another American picture except by accident."[49]

"Mayer was the absolute and merciless king of the jungle," Buddy Ebsen remarked in his modest memoir *The Other Side of Oz* (1993). He stresses that Mayer was never mean to him in their dealings, just frighteningly, omnipotently powerful. He also remembers Arthur Freed sycophantically hovering around Mayer as he paced his studio. "If you kicked L. B. Mayer in the ass, Arthur Freed would get a bloody nose,"[50] Ebsen wryly remembered.

Jeanette MacDonald wrote an unpublished memoir in 1960. Fortunately, we can thank author Sharon Rich for salvaging it, along with the star's personal correspondence and even her desk diary, and then bringing it all to light starting with *Sweethearts: The Timeless Love Affair—On-Screen and Off—Between Jeanette MacDonald and Nelson Eddy*.

Rich's book was first published in 1994 and has been updated and supplemented as more revelations have come to light. She warns us, however, not to trust MacDonald's own autobiography. "Sometimes the manuscript is more telling in what it doesn't say (or leaves out) than what it says," she asserts. "She worked with a ghostwriter and also was deathly ill, didn't seem like she'd survive to finish the book. What you have is great detail on her childhood and sometimes the exact opposite of reality on facts in her life once she got to MGM."

As far as those facts go, through dogged, decades-long detective work, extensive interviews, and reading between the lines, Rich has concluded that Mayer was as infatuated with MacDonald as he was dismissive of Nelson Eddy (who he liked to refer to as "the chowderhead"). MacDonald does admit in her memoir that Mayer started to lose faith in her around 1937, but dances around the reason: an extramarital affair and unsuccessful pregnancy with Eddy. It is *Sweethearts* rather than MacDonald's own memoir that details Mayer's sexual advances and Eddy's physically assaulting Mayer in his office—after which Rich asserts that "the real reason Jeanette and Nelson never made a film together after leaving MGM in 1942 was that Mayer basically then blacklisted them in town as a screen team."[51]

Betty Garrett and Other Songs (1988) recounts, in a poking manner, the beloved character actress's numerous encounters with her boss, including the first one, which occurred backstage during the run of *Call Me Mister* on Broadway and which led her to a contract at the studio. She indicates in her memoir that she liked Mayer, overall, although she also found his melodramatics somewhat exasperating. Garrett is talking about another mogul, Harry Cohn, when she says, "He was awfully hard to like sometimes, but he certainly knew how to make movies."[52] But these words would also seem to apply, for her anyway, to Mayer.

Angela Lansbury, in an authorized biography (written by Martin Gottfried in 1999) is quoted as acknowledging Mayer's reputation as a tyrant, but she is also quoted as saying that he was "practically paternal" to her, "maybe because I was an English girl,"[53] she muses. This may sound superficial but might actually carry some psychological weight in that both Mayer and his films were always respectful and admiring of the UK and its people.

Lansbury's statement also brings up a near-constant in all of these autobiographies by female stars that might as well be addressed here. She and her contemporaries all tell us that *most* of the actresses who fell into Mayer's nets were eventually ground up into hamburger by Mayer and by his lustful minions. Then these actresses all tell us that fortunately that didn't happen to them and that they avoided this fate because *they* were of stronger character than their (usually unnamed) peers and possessed the character and moral strength to walk away from Hollywood's casting couch hedonism. The repeated scenario is reminiscent of those accounts by alleged witnesses to a crime who are absolutely certain that a suspect is the culprit because that suspect had been in a position to commit that crime. They all tell us that Mayer fit the stereotype, even if he never actually embodied or enacted that stereotype at least with them. But God help all those other actresses, who possessed less "character" than they.

This formula is more or less followed by one of the last MGM stars to tell her story, longtime holdout Esther Williams, whose biography is titled *Million Dollar Mermaid* (1999). Because she lived so long, dying in 2013, Williams's tale will presumably remain the last first-person star's perspective on the subject of life at MGM and on working for Mayer.

Williams's initial meeting with the man who would be her employer for a decade is described in a chapter self-servingly titled "L. B. Mayer Meets His Match," wherein she describes crossing to his desk across what she estimated to be "sixty feet of white

Esther Williams's tell-all from 1999 is candid and honest. We know this because she tells us that it is. *Author's collection*

carpet." When she first saw Mayer, across that carpet and behind that desk, he was sipping orange juice and surrounded by yes-men. Unperturbed, Esther flippantly asked for a glass herself, to which he offered her his. Being of high moral fiber, she naturally refused.

Williams overall describes Mayer as a being a "petulant child," because of those famous faked fits, his tantrums, of his chest-beating, and his hair-tearing. But that said, surprisingly, and despite all this, their relationship is, again, described as being one of warmth and of mutual respect—as though only with her and her alone did Mayer ever "meet his match."

Interestingly, it is worth noting that again, Schary, by modern standards, the more "waked" movie mogul, is described by Williams in her memoir as an "owlish intellectual"[54] and is criticized for possessing little innate feeling for the spectacles and musicals that had made the studio famous. She also notes that Schary, unlike that seeming luddite Mayer, possessed no idea whatsoever, no master plan as to how to run that studio after Mayer's departure.

Maybe, instead of Schary, Nicholas Schenck should have given Mayer's job to Esther Williams?

MAYER AND HIS STUDIO ON THE PAGE: FICTION

The influence of MGM as reflected in fiction is not as wide or diverse, aptly enough, as it is on-screen or in nonfiction writings. Although the quantity of these works has increased exponentially in the last decade, which perhaps illustrates as well as anything how, paradoxically, MGM seems to loom ever larger in popular culture as those that were there and qualified to speak about that era fade into the ethos.

In fiction, as in reality, Mayer is usually the symbolic avatar for MGM in novels about the studio in its salad days. Fitzgerald's *The Last Tycoon* and his overt connection to the studio has been mentioned already. Although his writings about Hollywood extend considerably beyond that famous, uncompleted work. As far back as 1932 Fitzgerald was already obsessed, in a literary sense, with the movie industry. His long short-story "Crazy Sunday," for example, had a movie milieu. And just before his death, but before the posthumous *Last Tycoon*—presumably to make some much-needed money—he published a series of shaggy dog short stories about a character he called "Pat Hobby," a failed Hollywood screenwriter, which along with being (at the time) a failed novelist, Fitzgerald himself also then very much was.

Late in his career, legendary novelist F. Scott Fitzgerald fell in love with Hollywood, or at least with the idea of Holly-wood, but the romance was decidedly one-sided. *Photofest*

The legendary author by that time had ventured into and lived amid the Hollywood crowd several times over several years. The studios there inevitably hired him for his illustrious, if faded, name and then continuously failed to use that name by awarding him screen credit. His only on-screen acknowledgment during his lifetime was for MGM's *Three Comrades* (1938).

The Pat Hobby stories consisted of a grimly humorous series of embarrassments and humiliations that Pat was inevitably forced to suffer through. These misadven-tures included degrading encounters with one "Harold Marcus," whom he floridly describes in "Pat Hobby and Orson Welles" as having a "great, overstuffed Roman face,"[55] and who is the head of the MGM-like studio where Pat works or, more often, wishes to work. Yet each time the mogul and the screenwriter come into contact with one another, Pat seems to be in the midst of some sort of personal calamity that will cast him in the worst possible light with the studio boss. The stories are funny and, although often sketchy, due perhaps to Fitzgerald's chronic alcoholism, are sadly apt in their wry observations of the movie colony, even today.

Ultimately, as can be imagined, the real Fitzgerald was probably never more than a minor blip on the mighty Mayer's radar, even if Mayer, by contrast, was a major force on the tide of Fitzgerald's fortunes at the time. Inevitably then, Harold Marcus is much less Mayer than Pat Hobby is Fitzgerald.

Fitzgerald's Hollywood writings naturally tend to attract a lot of attention and respect among serious readers, but ever since Harry Leon Wilson's *Merton of the Movies* (1919), the so-called Hollywood novel has been a source of popular fascination. Critics, however, usually choose to single out, along with *Last Tycoon*, Nathaniel West's *The Day of the Locust* (1939) as the two best Hollywood novels. Weirdly, Fitzgerald and West were acquaintances, and both died within hours of each other in 1940. Some of the same critics who have lavished praise on Fitzgerald and West often single out Horace McCoy's *They Shoot Horses Don't They?* (1935) and *What Makes Sammy Run?* (1941) by Bud Schulberg as "great" and "classic" Hollywood works in the field as well.

Unlike West's and McCoy's acidic tales, however, which are about the film industry's fringe dwellers, specifically, those who cannot even manage to achieve Pat Hobby's modest successes, *What Makes Sammy Run?* is about Hollywood's winners rather than its hangers on. Perhaps this is due to Schulberg's pedigree and upbringing because he was the son of former Paramount production chief B.P. Schulberg. Consequently, unlike McCoy, West, and even Fitzgerald, Schulberg looks at the industry from the inside out. His grasping, opportunistic protagonist, Sammy Glick, is repellent, but his slimy breed would have certainly been recognizable to Mayer, who hated the book's negative portrayal of his industry. Mayer even took out his rage on the author's father. Telling him that "I blame you for this. God damn it B.P. why didn't you stop him?" Mayer even suggested to the senior Schulberg that the boy should be "deported."

"Deported?" Where?" B.P. replied. "He was one of the few kids who came out of this place. Where are we going to deport him to? Catalina? Lake Helena? Louis, where do we send him?"[56]

What Makes Sammy Run? is also somewhat of a rarity among Hollywood fiction in that it does not contain a Mayer (or B.P. Schulberg?) inspired "studio executive." A relatively minor character, "Sidney Fineman," probably being this book's closest approximation to the archetype.

Most other Hollywood-set novels largely embrace and probably helped to create the powerful producer stereotype that has been perpetuated thereafter. Certainly, when classic Hollywood is evoked in literature, Mayer, and MGM, under whatever alias they are hiding, is usually in there as well.

But because the genre of Hollywood-set novels is so large, for the purposes of this discussion, only works that include them both, Mayer and MGM, by name, will hereafter be included. Therefore, vaguely Mayer-like characters like "Victor Milgrim" in Schulberg's *The Disenchanted*, "Mr. Chatsworth" in Christopher Isherwood's *Prater Violet*, "Jules Oppenheimer" in Raymond Chandler's *The Little Sister*, "Herman Teppis" in Norman Mailer's *The Deer Park*, "Abe Baum" in Kelly Durham's *Pacific Pictures* series of novels, and maybe a hundred more studio bosses with threads of Mayer DNA will not be further discussed here.

That said, Aldous Huxley's dystopian *Ape and Essence* (1948) is probably the first book in which Mayer appears as a character; although that character is here called "Lou Lublin," it is so obvious in this instance who Huxley is talking about that the alias is virtually unnecessary. Huxley had worked at MGM as a screenwriter later in the 1920s and early in the 1930s and characterizes his boss as the mogul purported to have denied Jesus Christ a pay raise! The story also contains a satiric version of Sam Goldwyn called, even more unsubtly, by his original name of Szmuel Gelbfisz.

Another MGM alumni, William Saroyan, published *Letters from 74 Rue Taitbout or Don't Go But If You Must Say Hello to Everybody* in 1969. Saroyan, who had already featured a pseudonymous Mayer caricature in his play *Get Away Old Man* (1944), uses an amusing, novelistic conceit involving short letters he had written but not sent to acquaintances and famous people, alive or dead, throughout history. His postmortem letter to his old boss was somehow both contemptuous and good-natured. Saroyan muses about how he never had learned what exactly the "B" stood for in L.B.'s name, while reminiscing that a fellow writer who felt Mayer had treated him badly had once offered a few censorable opinions on the subject of that "B" over drinks. Saroyan also notes with incredulity how he just couldn't believe or accept that Mayer had actually and in fact ever died. "For you to be dead didn't make sense," he reflects. "The fact is it was un-American. And if you stood for anything it was the simple dignity of not being un-American—ever." Saroyan concludes his correspondence by mentioning his preference for instead believing about Mayer that "you're still out there rounding up that patriotic money, as hale and hearty as ever."[57]

Almost ten years later, Stuart M. Kaminsky used Mayer much more fictitiously in his novel *Murder on the Yellow Brick Road* (1977), which was the second in a long-running series of books about the adventures of Toby Peters, a Hollywood private detective whose clients and suspects always included Hollywood luminaries.

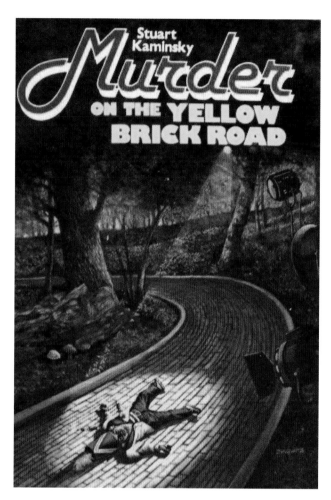

Stuart M. Kaminsky's long-running Toby Peters book series used actual Hollywood personalities fictitiously, which is common today, less so when *Murder on the Yellow Brick Road* (1977) was published. *Author's collection*

In *Yellow Brick Road*, as can be surmised by the title, Toby is hired to investigate the murder of a munchkin on the set of *The Wizard of Oz*. Mayer is presented as being gruff and powerful but not entirely unlikable. So, when he refers to Judy Garland as a "wonderful girl,"[58] the detective concedes that the executive is being as sincere as he is capable of. This rather benevolent characterization of Mayer continued on in the next book in the series *You Bet Your Life* (1978) in which the mogul hires Toby to protect the Marx Brothers.

After Kaminsky and Garson Kanin's novel *Moviola* (1979), there was little Mayer-related fiction published until the second decade of the twenty-first century, which marked a rich renaissance in Hollywood-set novels whose plots involved real people interacting with fictional ones.

Author Martin Turnbull almost single-handedly helped to instigate this trend in 2012 with *The Garden at Sunset: A Novel of Golden-Era Hollywood*, which was the first of a series of successful *Garden of Allah* novels that epically spanned the entire studio era. Mayer is a character in all of them save for one, in which he was still mentioned in conversation. "He was the Big Kahuna—how could he not be a regular?" Turnbull asserts and goes on to explain that he strived, over the course of his series to, above all else, humanize the cliché.

It's easy to lump together the movie moguls of Hollywood's golden era and see them all as big-talking, cigar-chomping, high-stakes-gambling, starlet-chasing egomaniacs. And certainly, some of them fit that bill. (I'm looking at you, Harry Cohn and Darryl F. Zanuck.) But running vast studios was a complex job that needed complex men who were up to the task. MGM's Louis B. Mayer held no more than a fifth-grade education, and yet he rose up to become the highest salaried man in America, a title he kept for years. You don't achieve that by being Mister Nice Guy. But you also don't get there by being completely heartless, either. You have to know which stories will appeal to the movie-going public. You have to know how to wrangle fragile and monstrous egos. You must be business savvy, have the fortitude to make million-dollar decisions, form policies that will affect thousands of employees. You have to be able to schmooze politicians and city officials and captains of industry to get what you want and need. But you also have to keep foremost in your mind the public's fickle tastes—or better yet, anticipate them. Mayer juggled all those balls every day of his professional life, and so I've strived to depict him in my books as a multi-faceted human being, who was a different sort of man to different sorts of people, because that's what it took to land atop the Hollywood heap.[59]

The success of Turnbull's *Garden of Allah* series also spawned a stand-alone novel, *The Heart of the Lion: A Novel of Irving Thalberg's Hollywood* (2020), in which the author placed Thalberg, with Mayer and MGM ever in tow, in an even more prominent position.

Following in the wake of the *Garden of Allah* books was a veritable plague of Hollywood novels in which Mayer always played a part. Sometimes, as Turnbull has strived to do, he is presented as an actual human with a human's feelings and failings, but most often he is again rather an omnipotent demagogue, pulling the strings from atop Mount Olympus and making those under him dance at his whims.

Often, the broad strokes that tend to define Mayer in literature are, as in films, dictated by the brevity of his appearances. It's hard to make someone who has everything

Author Martin Turnbull's *Garden of Allah* book series has used actual Hollywood personalities fictitiously since 2012. *City of Myths,* was the eighth in the series. "I picked the image of the back of the H in the HOLLY-WOODLAND sign as a signal to potential readers that they'll get a behind-the-scenes peak at what life was really like working and living in Hollywood," he has said.

Martin Turnbull (www.martinturnbull.com)

in the world into a protagonist or even into a character it is possible for audiences to relate to. So, all of his biographers in fiction and fantasy have struggled with the same issues. After all, Mayer is the "Wizard of Oz," so he can never be Dorothy. And like the Wizard, Merlin, Hannibal Lecter, or Shylock, his "character" works better, dramatically, when kept in the shadows and used only in measured doses, calling the shots, giving the orders, making the propositions and the pronouncements, and rounding up the patriotic money.

For example, *A Touch of Stardust* (2015) by Kate Alcott deals with the Clark Gable–Carole Lombard romance and is set specifically during the production of *Gone with the*

Wind. Mayer, true to form, is kept largely off-screen but is presented as boorish, predatory, and in fact, nearly illiterate, even trying to insist to a frustrated David O. Selznick that he change the book's downer resolution into a happier one for the film version.

All the Stars in the Heavens (2015), by Adriana Trigiani, dealt again with Gable but, this time, trysting with Loretta Young on the set of Fox's *The Call of the Wild* (1935). As such, Mayer has only a cameo and is given less to do than Ida Koverman!

Stewart O'Nan's *West of Sunset* (2015) and Sally Koslow's *Another Side of Paradise* (2018) both concerned themselves, again, with the last sad days of F. Scott Fitzgerald. O'Nan introduces Mayer holding court in the studio commissary and has his Fitzgerald describe his boss unflatteringly as "molelike."[60] Similarly, Koslow lets Fitzgerald pronounce Mayer as "a lout who represents everything money-grubbing and coarse about the movie business."[61] Both books are much more three-dimensional in describing the concurrent but doomed romance between Fitzgerald and gossip columnist Sheilah Graham, a literary device that had begun with Graham's own and, presumably, nonfiction memoir, *Beloved Infidel* (1958).

In *Stars over Sunset Boulevard* (2016) by Susan Meissner, the plot dealt, fictitiously, with the production of *Gone with the Wind*. But as with *A Touch of Stardust*, Mayer is little used, and Samuel Goldwyn is somehow represented as working at MGM during the film's production, which hardly lends the book credibility overall.

Platinum Doll (2016), written by Anne Girard, novelized the life of yet another of Mayer's stars, Jean Harlow. Although Irene Mayer, Mayer's daughter and Harlow's schoolmate, is featured more prominently than her old man, who Girard briefly describes in her text as portly, bespectacled, and intimidating, owing more to his immense power than to any direct interactions with Harlow.

A new crime series debuted in 2017, which like the previous Toby Peters mysteries, dealt with a world-weary detective shuffling down the mean streets of classic Hollywood. Author Guy Bolton, like Kaminsky before him, chose to center one of his mysteries around the production of *The Wizard of Oz*. The result was *The Pictures*, which follows police detective Jonathan Craine as he investigates the murder of one "Herbert Stanley," a (fictional) *Oz* producer. Mayer, of course, appears as a character. Mayer is, in this tale, among the most prominent real people stitched into the book's complex plot. The mogul is not presented here as being a sexual predator but, rather, as a dutiful, even hen-pecked husband. But by the tale's end, Mayer, like Craine, definitely does get dirty in trying to keep the studio's wholesome public reputation intact.

Incidentally, the Toby Peters and Jonathan Craine mysteries have not represented the only time the studio was the backdrop for a whodunit. Woodrow W. Walker's

Murder at MGM (2016) involved a homicide on the set of *Forbidden Planet*. But as the story is set in 1955, post-Mayer, it is therefore beyond the scope of this discussion.

A more amorous Mayer is on display in *The Girls in the Picture* (2019), by Melanie Benjamin. The subject being novelized is the friendship between director Francis Marion and superstar Mary Pickford. There are also several appearances by Mayer, who Benjamin amusingly describes as being "a short dumpling of a man with a beak of a nose, thinning black hair, and round glasses."[62] In one memorable scene, right after telling Marion how he only makes wholesome pictures, the executive pinches her in the fanny.

Margaret Porter's *Beautiful Invention* (2018) is one of many recent "biographical novels" concerning themselves with the lives of famous stars, such as Hedy Lamarr. *Author's collection*

Two novels about the life of screen goddess Hedy Lamarr followed. *Beautiful Invention* (2018), by Margaret Porter, appeared in bookstores first. Mayer is described by this Lamarr as being both a "horrid man" and a "monster,"[63] although, he is not portrayed overtly as being a sexual monster, at least not with her. But in *The Only Woman in the Room* (2019), author Marie Benedict does indeed include a scene in which the mogul propositions the star. But having fled Europe and an abusive husband, Benedict has her Lamarr conclude that she has "dealt with far worse than him,"[64] so she is quickly able to rebuke her boss's crude advances.

Author L. Frank Baum's widow Maud meets Judy Garland during the production of *The Wizard of Oz. Finding Dorothy* (2019) by Elizabeth Letts fleshed out the details of this meeting considerably. *Author's collection*

John W. Harding's *The Ben-Hur Murders* (2019) dealt with the production of MGM's 1925 epic and introduced Mayer uniquely dressed in a toga, aptly playing a Roman emperor at an extravagant production party on the set. It's the mogul's only significant appearance in the book.

Like *Murder on the Yellow Brick Road* and *The Pictures*, *Finding Dorothy* (2019), by Elizabeth Letts, also deals fictitiously with the production of *The Wizard of Oz* but in a less superficial way. The novel chronicles a visit to the set of *Oz* by Maud Baum, author L. Frank Baum's elderly widow in 1939. This visit did happen. Photographs exist of Maud and Garland together, presumably taken at the studio commissary. But, of course, most of the narrative is conjecture, including Maud's encounters with Mayer. This Mayer, wryly said to resemble "a prairie dog just emerging from his hole," somewhat echoes the Kamisky version, with Mayer again convincingly saying about Garland that "she's divine." Although Maud disapprovingly notes that a hug between Garland and the executive is "uncomfortably close," it is Arthur Freed, not Mayer, who turns out to be the book's villain. This assertion is apparently based on a passage in Shirley Temple's autobiography in which she alleges that Freed exposed himself to her when she was eleven. Mayer, by contrast, is ultimately depicted as being "a good man, deep down,"[65] at least in Ida Koverman's words, which is as good as the literary Mayer is ever allowed to be.

Rather outlandishly, at least at first glance, the notorious L.B. has also appeared as himself in several comic books and graphic novels, although not as a superhero or a romantic lead. Most of these cameos instead came in adaptations of the lives of stars in Mayer's stable, with the mogul somewhat tiresomely always presented as being a beneficent father figure. For example, in issue 2 of *Juke Box Comics* (dated May 1948) Mayer appears in support of MGM musical luminaries Frank Sinatra and Lena Horne. Later, in the first issue of *Famous Stars* (1950), Mayer again shows up in a brief, certainly sanitized adaptation of the life of Ava Gardner. Another comic book biography from the same period dramatized the life of Mario Lanza, and this time, in addition to Mayer, Koverman had a cameo too.

Even more surprising than the fact that Mayer has appeared in the comics at all is the fact that he still does so, even today, and in the same capacity as he was doing seventy years ago. Bill Griffith's acclaimed graphic novel *Nobody's Fool: The Life and Times of Schlitzie the Pinhead* (2018) featured Mayer visiting the troubled set of Tod Browning's *Freaks* and regretting it. Another graphic novel, *Femme Magnifique* (2018), features a biographical sketch of Lamarr and in a single panel included the star's

The adventures of Louis B. Mayer have been dramatized occasionally in comic book form. Here Mayer makes the acquaintance of Hedy Lamarr in the graphic novel *Femme Magnifique*, as written and illustrated by Gilbert Hernandez. Mayer's less genial introduction to the cast of *Freaks* has also been chronicled, here by Bill Griffith in *Nobody's Fool: The Life and Times of Schlitzie the Pinhead*. *Author's collection*

boss as well. Lamarr is also the subject of her own picture book for girls, *Hedy Lamarr and a Secret Communication System* (2006) by Trina Robbins, and several illustrated children's books and novels, all of which deal with the star's astonishing second life as an inventor and also, peripherally, with Mayer/MGM as well.

7

Influence of the Lion

The ebb and flow of popular culture makes it difficult to reliably discern where exactly a trend, a movement, a craze, or a fad first ignites and why it somehow finds favor with the populace, which for some reason then chooses to revere and copy aspects of it, sometimes fleetingly, and sometimes forever. MGM, it seems, has been the cause or the subject of many of these inexplicable wildfires over the years.

Most often, the MGM version of something, someplace, or someone tends to then become forevermore the defining and definitive version of that concept. David Copperfield, Sydney Carton, Mr. Chips, Dorothy Gale, Rhett Butler, Scaramouche, Ivanhoe, Judah Ben-Hur, Doctor Zhivago, and James Bond are all identifiable to us today, not from their literary versions, but from their cinematic ones.

There have been almost thirty actors who have played the character of Tarzan on the big screen. Yet when we regard the character, even readers of the original books tend to think only of MGM, or rather of Johnny Weissmuller's yodeling, inarticulate ape man and his best friend, Cheeta the Chimp. Both primatologist Jane Goodall and comic book writer Jerry Siegel have identified the character of Tarzan, specifically MGM's Tarzan, as an influence on their careers, Goodall in her game-changing study of chimpanzees in their natural habitat, and Siegel in the development of the character of Superman.

Likewise, many phrases or lines of dialogue uttered in MGM movies have entered the cultural lexicon. "I want to be alone," "gobble, gobble, we accept her, one of us," "Me Tarzan, you Jane" (or a variation), "let's put on a show" (or a variation),

The colossal and continuing influence of MGM worldwide is illustrated by these ads for *Gone with the Wind* (and its score) in French (1984) and in Romanian (2011)! *(top) Robert Lane ; (bottom) author's collection*

"nobody's perfect," "Bond. James Bond," "open the Pod Bay doors, HAL," "I'm as mad as hell and I'm not going to take this anymore," "Soylent Green is people," "yo, Adrian!" "I love the smell of napalm in the morning," "I'm a movie star, not an actor!" "they're heeere . . . " and "you'll shoot your eye out, kid," as well as just about anything that Scarlett, Rhett, or Dorothy ever said are still quotable and quoted today.

Occasionally, concepts expressed on the soundstages of MGM remain ever prescient today as well. The phrase "gaslighting," for example, means to manipulate a person or group into questioning their own sanity or beliefs. Although the prominence of that word in popular culture and political discussion today is entirely owed to the movie *Gaslight* (1944), rather than to a previous movie version or to the play from 1938 they were both based on. The recent film *Being the Ricardos* (2021), for example, depicted Lucille Ball, as played by Nicole Kidman, using the phrase.

The song "San Francisco," from the 1936 movie of the same name is widely associated with the city of San Francisco and the 1904 earthquake, although the song was written for the film.

Manhattan Melodrama (1934) is forever footnoted in history as the film public enemy number one, John Dillinger, ventured out of hiding to see, only to be gunned down by FBI agents outside the Biograph Theater in Chicago as he exited. Consequently, every media depiction, and there have been quite a few, of Dillinger's bullet-strewn demise have been forced to reference that particular MGM production.

Technology has miniaturized its computers in the twenty-first century, yet even scientists still reference the room-sized HAL 9000 from *2001: A Space Odyssey* (1968) as both accurate and quintessential. It should also be noted that rather ominously, Siri, Apple's virtual assistant, has been programmed, hopefully by her handlers, to respond when asked, that *2001* is her all-time favorite movie.

Another example is the Miniver Rose, introduced in 1944 and based on a like-named flower from *Mrs. Miniver* (1942). After decades thought lost, the rose has been rediscovered and is much praised by gardeners in the twenty-first century. Mrs. Miniver, if not her rose, has also been evoked by name in other movies, often made by other studios, including *Sherlock Holmes Faces Death* (1943), *A Raisin in the Sun* (1961), *The Americanization of Emily* (1964), and *One-Trick Pony* (1980). The Miniver Rose specifically did make an appearance in an episode of TV's *Downton Abby* (2010–2015), however.

Sometimes these echoes from the studio affect us on an individual basis too. Has any family dog, since 1943 at least, not been compared to that uber-collie, Lassie, and then found to be lacking? Has anyone taken a road trip, after 1991 at least, and not thought about the fates of the title characters in *Thelma & Louise*? Have any of us ever thought about the Old West, or old westerns, the same way after seeing *The Good, The Bad, and the Ugly* (1966)? And how many of us have walked down a rainy street at night and felt an urge to jump, Gene Kelly–like, onto a lamppost?

In the last case cited, at least, apparently a great many of us have. In *Coming to America* (1988), *Robots* (2005), *Brooklyn* (2015), *La La Land* (2016), and both a 1989 episode of *Columbo* and a 1995 episode of *The Simpsons*, a character actually does just that on a lamppost. In London's Lester Square, a statue of Kelly was erected in 2019, doing just that too, fifty-five hundred miles from Hollywood. Kelly's *Singin' in the Rain* title number, if not his specific dance moves, have also been evoked on-screen in films as diverse as *North by Northwest* (1959), *Crimes and Misdemeanors* (1989), *A Clockwork Orange* (1971), *The Last House on the Left* (1972), and *Leon: The Professional* (1994).

Gene Kelly isn't the only MGM star to be depicted on a statue, be it bronze or wax, either. John Wayne, for example, is the subject of *two* statues bearing his tall visage to be found in the Los Angeles area alone. Clark Gable, Elvis Presley, Judy Garland, Frank Sinatra, and Sylvester Stallone (as Rocky) also have statues, or in some cases, entire museums devoted to their exploits.

Singin' in the Rain and other golden-age Hollywood musicals are still constantly referenced by modern stars in conversations and in interviews too, maybe to show critics how knowledgeable they are about the history of their profession. Tom Hiddleston, for example, in an interview with fellow Marvel superhero star Benedict Cumberbatch in *Interview* magazine (2016), for example, told us that "I'm bowled over in awe and admiration by the uninterrupted takes of the dancing of Fred Astaire and Ginger Rogers and Gene Kelly. There's no 'we're going to fix it in post,'"[1] he asserted. Sadly, although modern Hollywood reliably makes statements like this, it doesn't often listen to them.

Many contemporary, or once-contemporary musicians, of course, have publicly acknowledged their debut to MGM musicals. None more so than Michael Jackson, however, whose music videos "Smooth Criminal" and "You Rock My World" were, he readily admitted, inspired by MGM's *The Band Wagon* (1953). It has also frequently been assumed that The Beatles' "Long and Winding Road" was inspired by *The Wizard of Oz*, although Paul McCartney seemingly refutes this in the documentary *The Beatles: Get Back* (2021).

Sometimes these disparate morse code connections to the studio bubble up in the strangest places though—and decades apart. One of the most memorable and roman-

Three versions of *Singin' in the Rain*'s legendary "lamppost" sequence, first as seen in the film and then as re-created in three dimensions at the Movieland Wax Museum in Buena Park, California, and at Disney-MGM Studios Theme Park in Orlando, Florida. *(top) Bison Archives; (middle) author's collection; (bottom) Werner Weiss (www.yesterland.com)*

tic scenes in *An American in Paris* (1951) involves, again, Gene Kelly, dancing with Leslie Caron along the Seine next to a moonlit bridge. The same scene would later be evoked in *Charade* (1963), made by Universal, although the previous film would be mentioned by name in dialogue between Cary Grant and Audrey Hepburn. Decades after that, in *Forget Paris* (1995), also by Universal, that scene would be name-dropped and location-checked one more time, but now by Billy Crystal and Debra Winger. *An American in Paris*, if not that romantic bridge, was also mentioned by name by former MGM star Judy Garland in *A Star Is Born* (1954), produced, not by Universal or by MGM, but by Warner Bros. The same beloved film, to use just one more example, was also name-dropped in an episode of the 1971–1979 TV series *All in the Family* in which Archie Bunker confuses its title with *Last Tango in Paris*!

Sometimes specific products from the studio go on to become wildly popular in ways and places they were never intended to. *A Christmas Story* (1983) was theatrically something of an underperformer. But in 1997, Ted Turner's TNT cable station, as a stunt, started running the film continuously for twenty-four hours every Christmas season. By 2002, it was estimated that almost a sixth of the country was watching at least some part of the marathon, making this little sleeper, unarguably and unexpectedly, one of the most beloved holiday films of all time. *A Christmas Story*'s massive popularity is rivaled perhaps only by MGM's *other* holiday perennial, *How the Grinch Stole Christmas* (1966).

As far as overall personal public affection for a movie though, nothing else in history compares to *The Wizard of Oz* and *Gone with the Wind*. *The Wizard of Oz* has been referenced in so many TV shows and movies that critic Danny Perry was once able to joke, maybe, that every film made since 1939 probably contained an *Oz* reference somewhere, which is possibly true even if the film did fail to inspire Paul McCartney. For many people, *Wizard* was the first live-action movie they ever saw, or remember seeing, and so it still holds a special, unassailable place in the hearts of millions—for whom it is still *the* classic Hollywood movie, and by marginalized groups like the LGBTQ+ community. In that context, perhaps it should also be mentioned here that the Stonewall riots in 1969, which are credited with triggering the modern gay rights movement, occurred, coincidentally or not, on the day of Judy Garland's funeral.

Gone with the Wind has likewise been beloved and in more ways and places than one might assume. For example, when the film was finally released in Japan, shortly after World War II, it found immediate and universal success there, which it has enjoyed ever since. And some of the undiluted affection that the Japanese people feel for Scarlett O'Hara and her world is undoubtedly because initially the Japanese people could relate to having their civilization and culture utterly destroyed by war. The film has also been evoked visually or referenced through dialogue in works as diverse as the sex comedy *Bob & Carol & Ted & Alice* (1969) or the gang melodrama, *The Outsiders* (1983). That said, under the clouds of cancel culture, which we now inhabit, one has to wonder how long *Gone with the Wind*'s reputation as history's great movie can continue. Indeed, in 2020, steaming service HBOMax took the precaution of adding an introductory disclaimer about the historical context of the film.

Ultimately, admittedly, MGM and MGM-created imagery is so pervasive in the real world that it is now hard to look anywhere and not see it—or to at least think that one sees it. In the following pages I will, however, restrict my search to a few key places where those three letters, in that order, have played a part in the world's cultural history.

ARCHITECTURE

MGM films in the 1920s and 1930s were well-known for their big white sets influenced by art deco, courtesy, of course, of Cedric Gibbons and his masterful art department. This style was introduced in *Our Dancing Daughters* (1928), which marked, according to author Howard Gutner, the "first overt attempt to use an art deco setting in order to underscore and support a narrative."[2]

Art deco had been officially introduced at the 1925 *Exposition International des Arts Decoratifs et Industriels*, the World's Fair from which the style took its name. But in 1928 it's curvy, distinctive look was still widely unknown to most Americans, who were about to be shaken from the Jazz Age and into the maelstrom of a devastating economic depression.

These traumatized audiences were initially impressed by the affluent and largely now-unobtainable world that the new style seemed to promise them. Therefore, it was the movies, and MGM movies specifically, that first exposed audiences and architects to a style that was to characterize the aspirations, if not the reality, of an era and at least one generation and to then represent that era for future generations evermore. Gibbons and MGM followed *Our Dancing Daughters* with many more deco-heavy hits, such as *A Woman of Affairs* (1928), *The Kiss* (1929), and *Our Modern Maidens* (1929), eventually fusing the style into the DNA of that time and ensuring its perpetuation.

As the Depression consumed all facets of US life, however, deco was increasingly used by Gibbons to signify 1920s "old-money," and to compare, or even condemn that affluence with the modern, stark realities of the world. Other studios at the time, like

RKO, flagrantly borrowed MGM's deco and moderne look and used it to then deny the existence of the Depression at all. There is not a single soup kitchen or flophouse to be found in a single Fred Astaire–Ginger Rogers RKO musical.

But contrary to its glamorous reputation, MGM in the 1930s was not only a place where audiences could flee to escape their real-world problems. Gritty alleys and tenements were never far away from the opulence in prominent Metro hits like *The Easiest Way* (1931), *Susan Lenox: Her Fall and Rise* (1931), and *the Secret Six* (1931). Incidentally, all three of these films featured Clark Gable, whose career would fire-cracker from bit parts to stardom over the course of this single, most eventful year. Gable's omnipotent prominence during this era was perhaps owed to the concept that, unlike anyone else on the lot at the time, here finally was a leading man who seemed equally comfortable and at ease in either setting.

More than once, sets designed on a soundstage or a backlot for a movie became the inspiration for real-world locations. For *When Ladies Meet* (1933), a rustic barn that had been sleekly converted into a house was called for in the script, giving Gibbons

Grand Hotel's (1932) art-deco influences and flourishes are readily visible in this preproduction view of its magnificent lobby set. *Author's collection*

and his artisans the chance to create just such a thing and that would then lead to a craze to create similar homes in real life. Reportedly the mailroom at the studio was inundated with requests for copies of the set drawings, which MGM dutifully copied and provided. The same craze for rustic, Connecticut-style homes would happen again in 1941 for a same-named remake. The standing backlot set for this second film, which now even included a surprisingly chic waterwheel, was destroyed in 1977, although, actual homes, inspired by these sets probably exist, somewhere, even today.

MGM's influence on architecture and interior design continues. Noted designer Susan Zises Green told *House Beautiful* in 2004 that *The Women* (1939) was one of her greatest influences. She praised the sets and costumes as being "stupendous, elegant and full of Old Guard chic."[3]

Often, a studio set based on a real location, in the mind of moviegoers, at least, became the definitive version of that place. The film *Paris* (1926) used the Atlantic Ocean as a backdrop, even though the titular city lacks any such body of water. Irving Thalberg defended the decision, claiming that "we can't cater to a handful of people who know Paris,"[4] and Gibbons admitted that he had received not a single letter pointing out the discrepancy.

Later, for the stupendous *Marie Antoinette* (1938), Gibbons added an elaborate ballroom to Versailles, re-created a grand staircase that was no longer there during the period, and designed stucco moldings for his sets that were either his own invention or reproduced more boldly than on the originals to register properly on film. One cannot help but wonder how many visitors to the real palace were subsequently disappointed.

MGM's longtime dominance over the motion picture industry ensured that their vision of the world would become the definitive one in their domestically set films as well. How many small US towns, for example, actually did resemble Andy Hardy's "Carvel?" and how many tried to? And which one really was the original influence on the other? Did nineteenth-century western cow towns, or cowboys, really look like Hollywood westerns told us they did, or do we believe so because those Hollywood westerns said it was so? The same is true of *most* historical eras, from the Stone Age to the Space Age.

There are many other examples along these lines. *Meet me in St. Louis* (1944) shows us a "Kensington Avenue" early in the twentieth century characterized by stately Victorian-era mansions and with hills in the background, neither of which the actual location could boast—yet even Missourians probably assume that's how their St. Louis must have looked in 1904.

And sometimes a movie will inspire a real-world place to become more like Hollywood's notion of that place. Because of *The Wizard of Oz*, the Kansas prairie will forever be characterized as flat, barren, and sepia, although it really isn't. But because of the movie, Kansas really does now have an actual farmhouse for the fictional character of Dorothy Gale.

In 1978, a Kansas businessman named Max Zimmerman noticed that when he was working out of state and told people where he was from, they would almost always immediately ask him about "Dorothy's home." As neither the movie nor its source novel ever specified where specifically in Kansas its heroine hailed from, Zimmerman decided that his own hometown, Liberal (population of twenty thousand) would be just perfect. The resultant farmhouse and museum includes interactive displays, costumed characters, and naturally, its own yellow brick road. Incidentally, Ray Bolger, that movie's beloved Scarecrow, had, in 1970, attempted to get a similar attraction off the ground, but that one ultimately had come to naught.

The Southern Mansion set on the MGM backlot in happier days. *Bison Archives*

Perhaps the strangest funhouse mirror instance of an MGM set inspiring real-world architecture occurred in Pasadena, California, in 1978 when William and Lola Holland saw a picture in the *Los Angeles Times* of what was identified as the Twelve Oaks mansion from *Gone with the Wind* being demolished on the MGM backlot. They both fell in love with the set's picture-book plantation architecture and decided to build their own home as a tribute. To this day, their resultant house is often identified in city guidebooks and in architectural surveys as actually having played Twelve Oaks in the film, which it hadn't.

Unfortunately, the picture of the set that had inspired the Holland's home was not really of Twelve Oaks either!

In 1994 David Bowen, who had once worked as a tour guide for MGM, told the *Times* that the facade in the photograph they had published had not appeared in *Gone with the Wind* at all. "MGM guides were trained to say that a Southern mansion that existed for years on the old MGM backlot was Twelve Oaks—the Ashley Wilkes homestead from *Gone with the Wind*, although it wasn't. . . . I think they just did it for the tourists," Bowen said. "They wanted to have something interesting to show them."[5]

FASHION

The studio was slow to notice how much money could be made marketing items seen in their products. But that does not mean that other people did not step forward to fill in that gap.

The most copied star of the 1930s, fashion-wise, was arguably, Greta Garbo. Garbo's favorite designer, Gilbert Adrian, designed dozens of hats for her, including the famous "slouch cloche," which teasingly almost covered one of her beautiful eyes, as well as assorted berets, pillboxes, turbans, and, most notably of all, the "Empress Eugenie." The latter was named after a French empress, who Garbo never played, but whose hats, again often worn tilted over one eye, both the movie star and the designer appropriated. The trend started in Europe but when Garbo first wore one such hat in *Romance* (1930), the style became outrageously popular in the US as well.

Another notable example of MGM, and Adrian, influencing popular taste came on the occasion of the Joan Crawford vehicle *Letty Lynton* (1932). It has been claimed that half a million copies of the organdy gown with ruffled sleeves she memorably wore in the film were eventually sold. Yet because MGM did not then bother to license copies of their film's fashions, it fell to the Macy's Cinema Fashions Department (yes, there was such a thing) and other manufacturers to flood the market with fashion inspired by "Letty Lynton." Author and historian Richard Adkins tells us that "there were Letty Lynton hats, coats, negligees, girls' pajamas and aprons as well. Remarkably, this trend lasted for three years."[6]

Adkins further notes that this "is even more remarkable when you realize the film was pulled from exhibition due to a lawsuit that claimed M-G-M had failed to obtain the permission to use the real-life story. The studio had to pay a fine and the film has never been re-released since 1932."[7]

Greta Garbo models a prototype of her soon-to-be famous "slouch cloche" look for *Flesh and the Devil* (1927). *Author's collection*

Examples of fashion crazes based on MGM-designed costumes continued. *It Happened One Night* (1934) was a Columbia film but top-billed MGM mainstay Clark Gable, who in the film revealed that he wore no undershirt, reportedly decimated the bottom line for companies that made such garments. Gable influenced men's fashions again when he started wearing a sports coat over a turtleneck sweater, causing millions of male fans to do likewise. Garbo and Katharine Hepburn's pants and Crawford's shoulder pads were also widely copied.

These fashion trends were charted, and sometimes created, by fan magazines and fashion magazines into which the studios poured an unending supply of fashion and gossip. These magazines, like the movies and the movie stars they fawned over, were widely popular, and they could be purchased for about the same price as a movie ticket—about twenty-five cents in the mid-1930s.

While all of this was going on, Adrian himself noticed, even if MGM did not, how much money others were making off his designs. He had been approached to license his MGM styles several times but had been concerned that he would not be able to control the quality of the product. In 1941, he left MGM, however. Slyly realizing that no new fashions would come out of Paris for the duration of the war, he saw the perfect opportunity. Adrian thus entered the retail market and became a leading designer for a public craving a French look inbred with a Hollywood pedigree. His successful and influential business lasted until 1952.

Joan Wears Her Newest

And designed by Adrian for her picture "Today We Live," they give you advanced ideas for a new season. A fashion scoop!

Photos By
Clarence Sinclair Bull

A new Crawford dress of the "Letty Lynton" type—but Adrian has made it distinctively different by using fluted ruffles. They curve up across the shoulders in the back and I ruffle down the skirt. Black velvet bows on white

It's crisp and tailored, this brown tweed dress, just the type of thing Joan likes so much. Starched linen gives a side lapel accent, under cuffs are starched, too. The round neckline is youthful, as is the fabric belt

Who but Adrian would think of putting myriad little white cotton pique bows on a crinkle crepe silk gown? And what you can't see is the slit skirt—a daring touch for a demure gown! Isn't Joan's hairdress charming?

Photoplay's issue from June 1933 paid particular attention to Joan Crawford's frilly gowns inspired by *Letty Lynton* (1932). Women worldwide did too. *Author's collection*

Fashion trends instigated by MGM included female hairstyles, and hair colors, as well. The white set in *Dinner at Eight* (1933), which Adkins tells us contained seven individual and identifiable shades of white, also incorporated an eighth—star Jean Harlow's hair. Harlow's follow-up, *Bombshell* (1933), again featured similarly monochromatic boudoirs and coiffures.

A (briefly) platinum blonde Garbo is admired (or maybe not?) by Albert Conti in *As You Desire Me* (1932). *Author's collection*

Cumulatively, these platinum blonde sets inhabited by this platinum blonde star led to both being, again, widely imitated. Sales of peroxide for lightening hair skyrocketed and the term "bottled blonde" became widely used for the first time. And other MGM stars copied the platinum look as fervently as MGM audiences did. Joan Crawford, Marion Davies, Paulette Goddard, Alice Faye, Lucille Ball, and even Greta Garbo all, at least briefly, tried the platinum look, as did millions of starstruck shopgirls and housewives around the world.

MUSIC

In comparison with other studios, particularly Warner Bros., MGM was rather late to the piano in the production of musical films. But they more than made up for their tardiness by becoming the world's preeminent creator of that type of film, which today remains the genre the company is best remembered for. In *That's Entertainment!* Frank Sinatra even acknowledges this publicly, telling us that "some studios can claim they made the finest gangster films or the greatest horror movies, but when it came to musicals, MGM, they were the champions."

The music in these champion musicals was written by the greatest musical talents of all time. Setting aside contributions from deceased classical composers, whose

MGM's iconic Scoring Stage is where countless legendary songs and scores have been recorded. Here, four-time Academy Award–winner Johnny Green is on the podium. Note the movable acoustic panels behind the vocalists, which provided a degree of acoustic separation from the orchestra, circa 1954. *Bison Archives*

works and lives the studio often both exploited and perpetuated, legendary musicians who actually worked at the studio include Cole Porter, Irving Berlin, José Iturbi, and Jerome Kern, as well as longtime and in-house composers like Arthur Freed, Nacio Herb Brown, Roger Edens, Harry Warren, and Bronislau Kaper.

The famous duo of Richard Rodgers and Oscar Hammerstein II both worked at Metro too, but not as a team. Rodgers and his partner Lorenz Hart produced a song for the studio back in the 1930s that was rejected and ultimately got rewritten as "Blue Moon." Hammerstein had extensive Metro connections through his friendship with Arthur Freed, who brought in their one-off hit, "The Last Time I Saw Paris," for the film *Lady Be Good* (1941). It won the Academy Award and also caused a big flap because it hadn't been created specifically for that film, which led to some eligibility restructuring at the Academy.

Musicologist Greg Gormick, who has studied Hollywood's musicals, tells us that those that originated specifically at MGM possess a distinctive sound, a sound that fans can distinguish from that which originated any place else. "In classic Hollywood there were really only three major and distinctive producers of musicals," he states. Going on to say that:

> The sound in a Warner Bros. musical, like their movies, was very much in-your-face. In theater terms the Warner sound could perhaps be equated to high-end vaudeville, with an aural quality similar to what you would hear from the larger orchestras at New York's Palace Theater or in other big presentation houses, as enjoyed by a patron seated somewhere in the fifth row, center section. Incidentally, this type of theater is exactly where Ray Heindorf, Warner Bros. longtime composer/conductor had cut his musical teeth while arranging for composers on Tin Pan Alley.

> 20th Century Fox, by contrast, featured an audio experience comparable to that found in a Broadway showplace pit orchestra, which, again is where their house composer Alfred Newman had honed his own talents.

> And then there was MGM. The MGM sound was the most refined of all, comparable perhaps to listening to classical music from one of the best balcony seats of a great concert a hall; a symphonic, pops, or promenade concert maybe—and exactly what their longtime in-house composer/arranger Johnny Green's inspiration and aspiration was in creating that sound for that studio.

> I like and I appreciate all three sounds, but I'm sure you can guess which one I think worked best and set the highest musical standards.

Gormick goes on to tell us that

> Metro was already on its way to creating that very sophisticated sound before Johnny arrived, thanks to the orchestrators they began hiring in the mid-1930s, especially Leo Arnaud. Another strategic move was the hiring of Conrad Salinger, who from 1939 until his death in 1962 set the high standards of the arrangements and the orchestrations for much of the studio's output, along with composer Roger Edens. Ironically, Salinger had been recruited from Johnny's own arranging stable in New York. It had been at Arthur Freed and Roger Edens' urging that Green had followed him to Metro in 1942, giving up the chance to serve as the musical director on Broadway's *Oklahoma!* for Rodgers & Hammerstein and the Theatre Guild to do so.[8]

To perpetuate these musical standards, MGM actually and intentionally "flattened" their music out, as a part of an overall attempt to create a subdued and, largely nondirectional, large concert-style experience. Consequently, the songs, orchestrations, and backgrounds were all recorded loudly and clearly but with little "space" between the vocals and the instruments on their tracks.

This consistent overall aural effect was probably owed to Douglas Shearer, the seven-time Oscar-winning brother of actress Norma Shearer and the head of the studio's Sound Department from its inception. The "MGM sound" did get more spacious, if perhaps less distinctive, when Green largely repositioned and replenished the MGM orchestra in 1949 as it was recorded on the scoring stage and brought in Fred McAlpine as a music mixer. Green also started allowing outside techniques and outside sound designers to influence and infiltrate the famous "studio sound."

A consistent problem in creating this sound was the need to separate the vocalists from the orchestra, so as to isolate their tracks as much as possible while still keeping them out on the floor of the scoring stage with everyone else. Placing baffles around the singer tended to help, although the vocalists themselves found these partitions understandably distracting. Green eventually discovered that another partial solution was to put those vocalists up on the podium and right next to the conductor. For *Raintree County* (1957), for example, he ended up placing Nat King Cole alongside him on the conductor's platform to record his vocals for the main and end titles. Eventually the development of better and more directional microphones would go a long way toward minimizing this consistent dilemma.

Also responsible for what is now regarded as that sound was Roger Edens, who came in the early 1930s as a musical supervisor, arranger, composer, and associate producer and, for the next twenty-five years, contributed to the scores of much of the

DAILY MUSIC REPORT

PROD: WORDS AND MUSIC

PROD: 1427

FROM: RICHARD POWERS

The following recordings were made today:

DATE: 5/28/48

SCENE No.	COMPOSITION	COMPOSER	TIME	DISC. NUMBER	REMARKS	LIBRARY NUMBER	CLASS.	USED IN PRODUCTION
2029	The Blue Room	Rodgers-Hart Salinger t 1 t 5	4:42 4:46		Orch. Perry Como & Chorus Hayton Cond.			
2030	Blue Moon	do t 7	2:08		Orch. Mel Torme Vocal Hayton Cond.			
2031	I Wish I Were In Love Again	Rodgers-Hart Hayton t 5	2:29		Orch. Judy Garland & Mickey Rooney Vocal - Hayton Cond.			
					Time 9:23			

A song is born: "I Wish I Were in Love Again" as represented by the internal daily music report, by Mickey Rooney and Judy Garland recording it, and, finally, by the finished album label. *Scott Brogan (www.thejudyroom.com)*

studio's output, musical or not, and who Gormick credits with being "a bigger part of the Arthur Freed musical unit than Arthur Freed was."[9]

The MGM studio sound, distinctive, bold, and familiar as it was to audiences for decades, still eventually became impossible to differentiate from the sound that emerged from any other studio or from any other recording of any other orchestra, which perhaps begs the question whether MGM's Sound Department was eventually infiltrated by outsiders—or whether the rest of the world just started to sound more like MGM.

HUMOR

MGM is innately a rather pompous company. Its release slate in the early years was full of classics by literary lions like Charles Dickens, Jane Austen, and William Shakespeare and its in-house lion, who has been spoofed so many times that I am according him his own chapter, roars under a pretentious moto—printed in Latin for heaven's (and art's?) sake. Therefore, comedians, authors, and intellectuals, actual and would-be, have always found it to be a target worthy of lobbing their satiric harpoons at.

More often than not, Hollywood in general rather than MGM in particular is their target. Although sometimes one can use the clues to figure out what or who these uber-wits are so scornfully talking about. J. D. Salinger, for example, in his masterpiece *Catcher in the Rye* (1951) has Holden Caufield say, "If there's one thing I hate, it's the movies. Don't even mention them to me,"[10] on the first page. Although the objects of Caufield's scorn specifically seem to be Hitchcock's *The 39 Steps* (1935), *The Baker's Wife* (1938), and assorted Warner Bros.–type gangster films.

Famous wit Dorothy Parker, though, was indeed referring to MGM in 1952 when she described a musical version of *Huckleberry Finn* then being made at what she only refers to as a "great studio. . . . They can't let anything alone. They have to 'fix' up *Huckleberry Finn*. They have to do it! So that voyage down the river, and the raft. Do you think they could leave one of the greatest characters in American literature on it? No. There was a little blond girl with no brassiere."[11] Incidentally, the musical Parker was here acidly referring to would not be made at the great studio until 1960, and by which point, it had been entirely shorn of both its music and its uninhibited blonde.

As far as MGM parodies in print go, forget Parker, because the literary and respected *Mad* magazine has long taken it on itself as its divine duty to skewer, puncture, and eviscerate any pretentions that Hollywood has ever imposed on our world. Their

Safe, company-approved humor at MGM as represented by this a 1940 "studio lot map" and a 1929 Photoplay cartoon. *Author's collection*

MGM film parodies have sported deathless titles like "Blackboard Jumble," "Mutiny on the Bouncy," "Throw-Up" (a spoof of *Blow-Up*, if you aren't hip enough to get it), "Dirtier by the Dozen," "Where Vultures Fare," "201 Minutes of a Space Idiocy," "Nutwork," and a hundred others.

This issue of *Mad* from June 1975, written by Frank Jacobs and illustrated by Mort Drucker, offered one of the more perceptive reviews of *That's Entertainment! Author's collection*

In particular, *Mad* has delighted in parodying the James Bond franchise, perhaps because the advent of that series was roughly concurrent with the magazine's biggest flash of popularity. Their Bond satires, titled "Dr. No-No," "From Russia with Lunacy," "Goldfingerbowl," "Thunderblahh," "You Only Live Nice," "On His Majesty's Secret Shamus," "Dollars Are Forever," "Live and Let Suffer," "The Spy Who Glubbed Me," "Moneyraker," "For Her Thighs Only," "Spyfail," "Cash-in Royale," and "Quantum of Silliness," have now been quoted, hopefully, without the teacher hearing it happening, in classrooms and on playgrounds for decades.

A particular favorite among *Mad*'s self-named "usual gang of idiots" has been, unsurprisingly, *The Wizard of Oz*, which they have mocked as "The Guru of Ours" (July 1969), "The Wizard of Odds" (January 1991), and "The Wizard of O" (October 2010). The 1991 article was, incidentally, also the self same immortal issue in which they finally got around to parodying both *Gone with the Wind* and *Casablanca* (1943).

Of particular interest is *Mad*'s satire of *That's Entertainment!* as "What's Entertainment?" in June 1975, which effectively eviscerated the original film, its stars, and its studio. Herein James Stewart is mocked for his conservatism, Gene Kelly is mocked for his ego, and Frank Sinatra is mocked for his toupee and for his mob connections. Likewise, the audience itself is mocked for paying to see clips from movies they could see uncut and for free at home, and Peter Lawford is mockingly made to say that "I was never a big star at MGM, which is why Frank Sinatra allowed me to appear here, I'm no threat."[12] Louis B. Mayer also gets his due, in a parody of "Ole Man River" in which his beleaguered stars sing that:

> Life gets weary –
> It's really stinkin' –
> We don't need unions –
> We need Abe Lincoln!
> 'Cause L.B. Mayer
> He keeps on ownin' us all![13]

All of these articles assumed that *Mad*'s young readers would be in on the joke and would thus understand myriad references to movies made before they were born. In truth, many of those readers *did* get the jokes, at least some of them, because there were still only three major broadcast networks. And each of those networks was still running the same decades-old movies every night, sometimes creating new fans for MGM. Just as, in its way, *Mad* magazine was doing.

Radio and later television have consistently mocked their big brother in Hollywood. In 1932, Jack Benny, early in the run of his popular radio series, featured a multi-episode running gag spoofing that year's big hit *Grand Hotel*, which led Benny to many other riffs on current films; others on radio and later television followed suit as well. In 1955, Sid Caesar did a TV sketch on *Caesar's Hour* called "Boardrooms of Hollywood," which specifically referenced, among other things, *Gone with the Wind* by name. Caesar also pioneered the art of spoofing individual movies, a formula that would be adapted later by variety shows featuring everyone from Bob Hope to the Muppets.

Carol Burnett, in particular, having grown up in Hollywood and possessing her generation's abiding love for old movies and old movie studios, made sure that her long-running (1967–1978) variety show eventually featured specific "salutes" to all of the major corporations in Hollywood. MGM, however, was the only one that received this treatment twice. Burnett also spoofed specific MGM movies and musical numbers, including, once again, *Gone with the Wind*, first as "Gone with the Breeze" (1967), and most infamously as "Went with the Wind" (1976). Her other MGM film parodies, incidentally, also all sported their own amusing names like "Rancid Harvest," "Babes in Barns," and That's Entertainment 86."

And there have been other comedic TV variety shows that, for whatever reasons, have visited Culver City. These include but are not restricted to: *Rowan & Martin's Laugh-In* (1967–1973), which deadpanned in one episode that MGM was remaking *Gone with the Wind* with comedian Flip Wilson signed to play Scarlett O'Hara. Incidentally, as a character, O'Hara, or at least a comic version of her, also has appeared on *MadTV* (1995–2016), *The Bonnie Hunt Show* (2008–2010), a 1970s cat food commercial, thousands of fan-made online videos, and even in a much wind-centric episode of Sesame *Street* (1969–).

Elsewhere, Canada's *SCTV* (1976–1981) once somehow imagined *Ben-Hur* as an Abbott and Costello vehicle, and *The Simpsons* (1989–) used a family swimming pool as the location for an Esther Williams musical. And by all means, don't forget that *Saturday Night Live* (1975–apocalypse) has parodied *The Wizard of Oz, Singin' in the Rain*, Andy Hardy, and, of course, *Gone with the Wind*—and sometimes more than once.

TV commercials have long used MGM iconography, recently giving us Fred Astaire, in altered footage from *Royal Wedding* (1951) and *Easter Parade* (1948) dancing with a

It's 1977, and Mickey Rooney and his wife Jan are standing-in for Jeanette MacDonald and Nelson Eddy for the purposes of hawking beer—laughing yet? *Krista Christofferson (www. spokaneviking.org)*

RALPH

"Here's a contract from MGM for $10,000 a week to never ask to be in one of their pictures."

From the collection of Rob Gold

Dirt Devil vacuum cleaner, and Jane Krakowski as (again) Scarlett O'Hara, now seemingly interacting with the real Clark Gable and even more passionately with a fattening bowl of Breyers Ice Cream.

This is a recent trend only in its level of sophistication. In 1977, Mickey Rooney and his wife Jan made two amusing commercials for Rainier Beer in costume as Nelson Eddy and Jeanette MacDonald and singing "Indian Love Song" from *Rose Marie* (1936). Rooney also made money and commercials in his golden years (and evoked his MGM persona) for Valueguard Insurance, Kellogg's Corn Flakes, and Braniff Airlines. Likewise, Van Johnson at the same time was shilling for Post Oat Flakes, Peter Lawford for Andy Capp Liquor, and Ann Miller was feverishly tap dancing for Great American Soup.

Most horrifyingly memorably of all, June Allyson was long the official spokesperson for Depend adult diapers. Allyson was also memorably impersonated on *Saturday Night Live* as fictitiously and unforgettably saying in those commercials that "I'm a former MGM star, and right now I'm taking a dump."

8
The MGM People

As the undisputed industry leader in its first decades in existence, MGM was a source of envy to its peers. Darryl F. Zanuck at 20th Century Fox in particular seemed to pattern his studio's business model, operations, and product after that of his larger rival up Motor Avenue, as did, to a greater or lesser degree, other studios during that era. Although this rivalry, if that word can be used, was, at the end of the day, only business. It is an overstatement to say that Zanuck or, for that matter, Jack Warner or Harry Cohn were "obsessed" with MGM, although they were perhaps obsessed with MGM's dominance over them and with someday eclipsing that dominance. Cohn, for one, for some reason did actively pursue a relationship with Louis B. Mayer, who for his part once owned some Columbia Pictures stock.

Obsession, however, is not an inadequate word to use in describing some people's feelings about MGM inside or even outside of Hollywood. Yes, this personal connection with the studio exists even among many who have no financial or personal involvement with the entertainment industry at all.

Whether this reverence and passion over MGM or, for that matter, over any soulless corporate entity is deserved is, perhaps, a moot point. Film historian David J. Hogan once wrote that, at the end of the day, "MGM was just another business; unsentimental, self-absorbed, intimidating. And like other businesses, its life was finite."[1] Although Hogan also readily admits that none of this would have mattered to those who had bought into the dream.

Those that bought into the dream are a varied lot indeed. This group could reasonably be said to include several world leaders. Mayer enjoyed a warm relationship with

A group of priests visit the lot and Louis B. Mayer, who would once flirt with converting to Catholicism, poses with them in the back row. In the front row are Antonio Moreno, Roman Novarro, Norman Kerry, Lillian Gish, Mae Murray, Fred Niblo, Pauline Starke, Mae Busch, Conrad Nagel, and Lon Chaney. Marion Davies's palatial bungalow is the backdrop, 1926. *Michael F. Blake*

President Herbert Hoover and lunched with him in the White House in 1932. During World War II, Winston Churchill reportedly refused to be interrupted from his screening of *The Big Store* (1941), even when summoned for a conference by German second-in-command Rudolf Hess, although some sources claim that the Marx Brothers movie Churchill was apparently enjoying so much was actually *Go West* (1940) or perhaps even (Paramount's) *Monkey Business* (1931).

Both Churchill and President Franklin D. Roosevelt also publicly praised *Mrs. Miniver* (1942), as did, and more ominously, Joseph Goebbels, the Nazi Minister of Propaganda. Adolf Hitler, whose favorite actress was reportedly Greta Garbo, was able to privately view *Gone with the Wind* in 1940 because he apparently had his officials seize a print that the studio had recently shipped to Paris for subtitling. When Germany refused to return the movie to its rightful owners, it briefly caused an international incident. Der führer, though, reportedly liked what he saw so much that consequently he ordered Goebbels to make him a Teutonic-Technicolor equivalent, *Kolberg* (1945).

Official state visits to the lot were not at all uncommon. Gathered here in June 1926 are John Gilbert, Prince Erik of Denmark, Ramon Novarro, Louis B. Mayer, Princess Louise of Sweden, Princess Lois of Denmark, Lon Chaney, and Prince Gustav Adolph of Sweden. *Michael F. Blake*

Celebrities from all walks of life always seemed to gravitate to MGM. One of the more unlikely lunches there involved Charlie Chaplin, George Bernard Shaw, Marion Davies, Louis B. Mayer, and Clark Gable. One cannot help but wonder what they all discussed that day in 1933. *Author's collection*

The first recorded case of royalty actually visiting the lot occurred in June 1926 when Prince Gustav Adolph of Sweden and Prince Erik of Denmark arrived for a royal visit and were dutifully escorted across the grounds and, with due pomp, were introduced to their nearest US equivalent, MGM movie stars. King Alphonso XIII of Spain, however, on his own state visit later surprised everyone by instead requesting an audience with Irving Thalberg!

Recent world leaders have not been immune to the MGM effect either. President Dwight D. Eisenhower was a big fan of *Rose Marie* (1936) and counted "Indian Love Song" among his favorites. President Ronald Reagan, having long been under contract there was, unsurprisingly, a Warner Bros. man, but President Jimmy Carter, again unsurprisingly, was profoundly affected by *Gone with the Wind*. "I went to a lot of movies when I was young, whenever I could. In the South, we date life as either before *Gone with the Wind* and after *Gone with the Wind,* as you know," he told the American Film Institute on its tenth anniversary. "When *Gone with the Wind* first came out, every school in Georgia was closed, and all the students were hauled to the theaters on the school buses. And it made a great impact on our lives." Carter did wonder, however, if "perhaps we saw a different version from what was seen in the rest of the country?"[2]

Carter has not been the most recent president to respond to the studio's siren call either. Movie buffs Bill and Hillary Clinton reportedly enjoyed *The Wizard of Oz* while in the White House—among a great many other films.

But maybe, most tellingly of all, Donald Trump, was once, in 1990, specifically quoted as saying that "I've always thought that Louis B. Mayer led the ultimate life, that Flo Ziegfeld led the ultimate life, that men like Darryl Zanuck and Harry Cohn did some creative and beautiful things." The future president concluded his deep ruminations by saying that "the ultimate job for me would have been running MGM in the '30s and '40s—pre-television."[3]

Some cases of the studio's omnipotence could be said to involve a mass, rather than individual, interest in the studio or its stars. One only has to look at the top-ten box office attractions of the late 1920s and early 1930s and beyond, which MGM stars routinely and overwhelmingly dominated, to realize the impact that MGM had on individuals and on the larger moviegoing public.

And even those stars themselves were not immune to MGM's mystique. There is hardly a memoir, autobiography, or ghostwritten fan magazine article that does not mention the glamour of MGM as those stars experienced it. Although much of this material was probably generated by studio hacks in the stars' names, the sentiment, in some cases at least, was real.

Debbie Reynolds is the star name that comes up first when discussing the studio. Unlike, someone like Elizabeth Taylor, who became a celebrity as a child, and had no basis for comparison, so would not have seen the place as at all remarkable, Reynolds came to the studio at nineteen after an exceedingly banal childhood, and so could appreciate the sublime oddness and wonder of what was going on all around her. As fans know, her obsession for the place led to her buying up everything she could afford at the 1970 auctions and elsewhere. She valiantly tried to save the studio backlots from destruction too, pleading unsuccessfully with the current management not to sell land they stood on for development. Reynolds then tried for decades to establish a movie-related museum in which to display her treasures, failing at this worthy task time and again, usually due to short sighted apathy on the part of MGM, the six other studios, the Motion Picture Academy, and the city of Los Angeles itself.

Consequently, near the end of her, life Reynolds was forced to sell off her beloved collection to pay off her debts. For example, a pair of *Wizard of Oz* ruby slippers, not even worn in the film, which she had once reportedly paid $300 for, sold in 2011 for $690,000. She probably would have happily donated those shoes to any museum willing to take them before having to sell them.

Reynolds ultimately got the last laugh for her foresight—but it was a bitter one.

Not all performers with an interest in the studio took it that far. Two-time Oscar-winner Jessica Lange once told her hometown paper, "Growing up in Cloquet [Minnesota], we didn't even have a movie theater, so it was really about watching old movies on TV. That was my whole encounter with acting in the beginning. When I went up for my first screen test at MGM, I remember driving through those gates and walking the Andy Hardy streets. Esther Williams' swimming pool was still there. I was in awe."[4]

On the other side of the employee spectrum from the star power of Reynolds and Lange are those who worked in the trenches, sometimes literally toiling in the cata-combs of the studio, who were wiser as to the values of the studio's heirlooms than management was.

In 1970, Kent Warner was a twenty-six-year-old costumer at MGM who was specif-ically tasked with finding *The Wizard of Oz*'s screen-worn ruby slippers for the studio auction. Like Reynolds, Warner was obsessed with movies and with *Oz* in particular. Unlike her though, he was in no position, either politically or financially, to acquire his own pair. So, he took this random assignment as a divinely appointed crusade.

But where to look? Any sort of MGM asset inventory system had recently been dumped, leaving Warner with literally hundreds of buildings on the lot, each with hundreds of potential hiding spots, to search in.

So, Warner became a ghost in a city of ghosts. He spent weeks crawling through catacombs and basements and into attics above empty production offices and castle towers on the backlots—making him, perhaps, the last person ever to explore the place thoroughly and systematically while it was still entirely intact. It is fascinating to imagine what he must have seen on his quest, what he salvaged, and what he left behind.

John Raymond Lebold, another coworker and collector also on the lot at the time, was later interviewed by author Rhys Thomas and remembered the day Warner's efforts came to fruition, however:

> He said they [the shoes] were in an old soundstage called "the barn," which was used for storage. It was an old building, missing its roof, three or four levels. MGM stored a lot of older wardrobe on the upper levels. One lady thought they might be up there, but said, "I wouldn't go up there, it's a very, very dangerous building. Rat infested." He found the *Marie Antoinette* costumes up there, found a whole storage for shoes. He started going through everything up there. Everything was covered with dust. The only light was sunlight bleeding through the roof. He found himself in a sea of green shoes. Something caught his eye. He blew away the dust, and there were the ruby slippers.[5]

Warner himself enjoyed telling and, doubtless, embellishing this admittedly dramatic, nearly Indiana Jones–esque story. But he wasn't telling the whole tale at all. Apparently that pair of slippers, the one that he gave to his bosses and that subsequently and famously sold at auction for an astonishing and now comical $15,000, was not the only shoes he found in that dusty attic that day. And Warner, after setting one pair aside for his employer, allegedly spirited these other ruby slipper(s) home with him.

How many more were there? Again, the facts differ dramatically here. Everyone agrees, though, that Warner (who died in 1984) was not merely a burglar looking to sack the studio of its holy relics. Instead, romantically, he saw himself as a Robin Hood figure who had liberated the shoes from a studio that was then shortsightedly selling them.

Perhaps. Although Warner apparently did try to sell a pair, or pairs, of shoes several times over the years, especially after he was diagnosed with AIDS and realized that he himself would soon be gone. But because he did not own them legally, Warner was unable to make the money that the studio-sanctioned and better provenanced (and by him!) auction shoes had generated previously. Many today believe that it was proba-

The Wizard of Oz's legendary ruby slippers, as scavenged from the attics and catacombs of the Property Department and sold (for a then astonishing $15,000) in 1970. *Bison Archives*

bly a Warner pair of shoes that Christie's sold at auction for a meager $12,000 in 1981. Today, if the same slippers were to come onto the market it is estimated that they could easily fetch $2 million or more!

Warner's story in many ways parallels that of Vincenzo Perugia, who stole the *Mona Lisa* in 1911. Because of its worldwide fame, he was then unable to show the thing to anyone. Warner, like Perugia, could instead only spend his remaining evenings at home, alone in cheap, badly lit apartments, privately admiring a prize that he could not share. Warner at least continued to obsess over his treasure, even while he was dying, staring into the red-beaded light of a trophy that he had acquired but could never really find a way to own.

Yet another pair of *Oz*-used ruby slippers were stolen from the Judy Garland Museum in Grand Rapids, Minnesota, in August 2005. Local resident Rob Feeney ended up almost inadvertently investigating the case for a local private detective agency. Although the pursuit of those shoes for Feeney, ended up becoming a five-year obsession and included authorizing a $1 million bounty for their recovery (put up by an anonymous fan) and organizing a scuba dive expedition into the nearby Tioga Mine Pit when rumors surfaced that the thief had hidden or ditched the shoes there.

Feeney, who also has tracked down *Oz*'s "horse of a different color" carriage and (in a barn in Kentucky) the "Metro-Goldwyn-Mayer" sign, which once stood above the Madison Avenue studio gate, once presided over a press conference in which John Kelsch, the museum's executive director, told the press, and with more insight than he probably realized, that "France has the *Mona Lisa*, America has *The Wizard of Oz.* Both equally important national treasures."[6]

That statement ultimately proved to be as true for Feeney as it had been for Warner and for Perugia. In 2018, thirteen years after their theft, this pair of ruby slippers were finally recovered, although legal issues kept him from revealing the details to me.

But like Dorothy, and like the Wicked Witch of the West too, Feeney had already paid the price. "I had become obsessed by then. I had faced down death threats, risked my life, made enemies and interacted with dangerous criminals. And I ruined my marriage. I'm divorced now."[7]

One wonders if, after all that, the result was worth the price.

For some fans, however, an MGM obsession is more benevolent. One of those fans, Tommy Hines, explains how he has carried and fed that obsession over a lifetime and is the better for it:

> One Christmas, when I was about eight years old, my paternal grandmother sat down beside me on the couch and began to tell me a story. She was a great weaver of tales

MGM's legendary East Gate as it looked in its heyday, and its original signage today, as preserved in a warehouse in Kentucky. *(top) Bison Archives; (bottom) Rob Feeney*

and her descriptive narrative mesmerized me as she recounted the plot of a movie called *Gone with the Wind*. Even at this age, the few movies that my family saw at the local theater seemed to have a profound effect on me. I loved going to the movies and the sights and sound on the big screen stayed with me for weeks afterward. I knew I wanted to see *Gone with the Wind,* but really had no hope of doing so in those days.

My other grandmother was a high school librarian. She expanded my world with books and records, giving me free [rein] after hours to read or listen to anything I wanted. True to form, I was drawn to books about the past and to recordings of old music. My grandmother often gifted me with books. For Christmas, 1971 she gave me something that charted my course for a love of old movies: the first three volumes of *This Fabulous Century*, a Time-Life series that highlighted social history from 1870 to 1970. She eventually bought me the entire set, but I always went back to one book more than the rest, *Volume V, 1930–1939*.

In that volume highlighting the 1930s there was a chapter simply called "The Movies." It gave me glimpses of a world I had never seen before. There were full page, black & white, crystal clear images of Jean Harlow, Clark Gable, Eleanor Powell, and Gary Cooper, a compilation of photos of

Tommy Hines's lifetime interest in MGM began when he was eight years old. *Tommy Hines*

Bette Davis in her broad range of 1930s roles, and a graph of top-ten stars throughout the decade. At the time, we had only one television station available and there was no way for me to actually see any of these films, so the photos were all I had.

Two things soon happened that changed all of that: being able to watch Dick Cavett's *Hollywood: The Dream Factory* at the house of a neighbor who had better television reception than we did, and the discovery of the Movie Book Club in *TV Guide*. The Cavett documentary allowed me to see, for the first time, moving images from the films I had only read about. I also saved my money and began buying books from the Movie Book Club. Lots of books. One of my favorites was Griffith and Mayer's *The Movies*, a massive volume that covered the history of film from the beginning to the early 70s. The photos were all black & white, but I didn't care. I poured over the volume time and time again.

A pivotal experience toward my focus on MGM took place at The Bard, a movie theater in Louisville, Kentucky, when my grandfather took my brother and me to see *That's Entertainment!* in the summer of 1974. While my grandfather slept and my twelve-year-old brother fidgeted, I was spellbound from start to finish. Seeing clips of MGM musicals in shimmering black & white and brilliant Technicolor was a sensory experience I will never forget. It decidedly cemented an obsession with MGM that has only grown stronger over the years.

My MGM collecting began in earnest with the discovery of a series of soundtrack albums called *Those Glorious MGM Musicals*. Each album contained music from either two or three films, and I scoured the record stores to see what I could find. In the days before Amazon, you had to constantly be on the lookout for what might show up in the record bins. I eventually collected all twelve double albums, representing soundtracks from twenty-nine different musicals.

In the mid-1970s the luxury of cable television finally afforded me the opportunity to see classic films at home. Old movies were usually broadcast after midnight and the prints were often poor, but I watched faithfully in the dark. I had no way to record the movies that I liked but would turn on my portable cassette recorder and tape the audio. You do what you have to do!

In 1975 I saved my money and purchased *The MGM Story*. I read the book from cover to cover, digesting the information about every film and somehow committing to memory release dates and the cast lists. This book was soon be supplemented with two other important works on MGM history, Hugh Fordin's *The World of Entertainment: Hollywood's Greatest Musicals* and James Robert Parish and Ronald Bowers's *The MGM Stock Company*. All three volumes became sources of great pleasure, but also supplied invaluable information about the people who worked at the studio. The books are still on my shelf, showing more signs of wear than anything else in my collection.

It was during the 1980s that I started purchasing classic films on VHS and eventually amassed a large collection, with an emphasis on the MGM product. As other, better formats became available, I moved on to laser discs, then DVDs, and eventually to Blu-ray. I am certain that there are many films that I have purchased in every one of these formats. It didn't matter, because the desire to be able to experience old movies that looked and sounded their absolute best has been, to be honest, insatiable. Today my DVD and Blu-ray library numbers over 1,000 films and about 350 were originally produced by MGM. Obviously, watching these beautifully restored prints today is quite a different experience than listening to my scratchy cassette recordings.

From the standpoint of a collector, nothing has impacted me more than the arrival of eBay. Beginning in the mid-1990s, I discovered things in greater numbers online than I would have found in local antique shops in a lifetime. I branched out into vintage sheet music, purchasing examples that were originally produced to capitalize on the MGM musicals of the 1930s, 40s, and 50s. Then it became photographs, period portraits of MGM stars and contract players, production stills, and costume tests. I also became fascinated with studio portraits by Eric Carpenter, Russell Ball, and George Hurrell and was especially interested in examples that included autographs contemporary with the period. Most recently, my obsession has been a quest to acquire a complete collection of MGM's in-house trade publication, *The Lion's Roar*. Thirty-two large-format, lushly produced issues were released between 1941 and 1947. I now own all but six of them.

After 50 years of collecting, from the black and white pages of 1970s movie books to meticulously restored Technicolor MGM movies on Blu-ray, I have no desire to stop. Resources that I would never have even dreamed of in my youth are readily available today. The advent of TCM, where MGM films are shown twenty-four hours a day, is a constant source of pleasure. The availability of information online continues to astound me. New books continue to be made available, adding fresh insight, knowledge, and scholarship to the subject.

Sometimes it is difficult to explain my fascination. I admit that there is still a sense of excitement when I hear the lion roar at the beginning of an MGM film. The distinctive sound of the studio orchestra in the mid-1930s or the lush arrangements heard in the background of films in the 1940s are unmistakably unique to MGM. The consistency of unequaled production values, from the costume dramas of the [19]30s to the romantic comedies of the [19]40s, is always recognizable and still awe-inspiring. The plethora of talent, both on the screen and behind the scenes, is unmatched. The costumes, the glamour, and, admittedly, the sheer beauty of the studio's "stable of stars" draws me again and again to the MGM product.

I often catch myself being sad that the MGM of old is gone, that the artistry and magic took place so long ago. But I am happy that most of the films have survived and thankful for the curators and caretakers of MGM's legacy. After all this time, I still can't get enough of it.

Richard Kingcott's interest in Hollywood and with MGM in particular led him into to a career in the entertainment industry. Although until recently, he had never actually made the pilgrimage to the lot from his home in the UK.

My name is Richard Kingcott. My love of Hollywood history, and especially MGM history, started a very long time ago.

Richard Kingcott, finally on the lot, 2020.
Richard Kingcot

In 1988, as a child, I was lucky enough to get to see Mickey Rooney and Ann Miller live in the musical *Sugar Babies* at the Savoy Theatre in London. Their obvious talent and exuberance made me interested in where all that talent had come from. It had come from a place named MGM.

Around ten years ago I decided that I was going to collect all of producer Arthur Freed's MGM Musicals on DVD—although I have since expanded into Blu-ray and digital downloads. Whatever the format, Arthur Freed was just the start. I then determined to collect films by other MGM producers like Joe Pasternak and Jack Cummings, and on and on. My collection now also includes MGM movies and related documentaries spanning from the 30's all the way through to the late 1950's. Sadly, here in the UK, imported films have become more and more expensive owing to a tax which they charge on imports at the border. Fortunately, I was able to amass some 175 MGM titles before this happened!

My obsession with the studio also includes books about it. I have spent many hours searching many second-hand book sites and buying anything I could about the place and its times. I'm particularly interested in collecting older books which are now out of print and so harder to find. My private Library on MGM and on Hollywood history is now well over 150 volumes, and it's still growing.

One of my prized possessions is an original set of auction programs from the 1970 sale. I find it wonderful looking through them and marveling at the volume of stuff which was sold then. No wonder the sale went on for days. I am saddened that although Debbie Reynolds was able to rescue such a large amount of studio history during the auction, (she reportedly spent over $180,000 on props and costumes) she was never able to realize her ambition of opening a permanent Hollywood museum. The closest she came was a hotel in Vegas, which finally closed too. It must have been very upsetting for her when, in 2011, her collection was broken up and itself sold at auction.

For many years I thought and fantasized and dreamed about actually going to MGM. In these dreams I'd imagine I was there, at the studio, transported back in time, walking her streets and exploring her vast backlots. Maybe this is why I became so fascinated with discovering where exactly on those backlots specific scenes in specific films had been shot. I'd spend hours obsessing over photographs with a magnifying glass. I'd try to match up current and vintage Aeriel pictures. I'd watch a single movie, again and again with those photographs, or a book, or a dozen books, spread out on the floor around me. I'd keep one finger ever on the remote, freezing the images on the screen, moving them back or forth a frame at a time, until I knew, or thought I knew, where exactly on the lot a specific scene had been shot.

Yes, I know this is certainly not how these movies were intended to be seen. For me the result has been that sometimes now I think I know perhaps *too* much about how these films were made. And I do grieve, just a little, over no longer being able to enjoy these movies for what they are, rather than *where* they are. But, for me, that's just the way it is!

One thing which has been very useful in my research is the truly wonderful *That's Entertainment* series. I am so glad that these three films were made, as there is something quite wonderful in seeing the likes of Mickey Rooney for the last time walking down the backlot New England Street set where he had made sixteen Andy Hardy movies. I wish I could have walked there with him.

A much sadder experience is the 1974 film *The Phantom of Hollywood*, which documents the destruction of MGM's backlots. It's very unsettling to see on-screen JCB tractors and wrecking balls knocking over and eviscerating these familiar, beloved sets. These sets also appear, for the only time, flimsy and temporary here, not at all like the great stone structures they had portrayed in countless movies. It's all made even worse because these backlots being destroyed here look like they hadn't been maintained in years. What had MGM been thinking? The first time I saw this film I was heartbroken, and very upset to think that all this could have actually happened. Even all these years later it's still hard for me to watch such needless destruction of something which should have been, which could so easily have been saved. On recollection, I guess that the film is at least a valuable record for future generations to see—as something which should never have been allowed to occur.

This is all the more tragic because if only these iconic sets had been saved, I know they would have made for the greatest studio tour in Hollywood. Especially since other studios have done exactly that. You can take a tour of these other studios and step back in time and walk their legendary backlots. But, tragically, achingly, you can't do this at MGM.

Regardless, when I finally got to make my first visit to Los Angeles in 2014, a pilgrimage to MGM, of course, was the first thing I wanted to do. By then I had explored every corner of the lot so many times in my dreams that actually, physically going there, and seeing whatever was left, was certain to be an emotional experience for me.

Unfortunately, by that time, MGM no longer occupied the property. But thankfully Sony, the current owner of Columbia Pictures does. And they conduct a public tour of Lot One, as it used to be called.

As I walked through the gates and onto the lot, it was for me both the first and the thousandth time I had done so. Inside I imagined all the people I had seen in all those movies for all those years. I thought about the stars and the directors whose careers I had studied and charted walking those same streets, but lifetimes ago, going about their daily business.

I was in awe.

Upsettingly, Sony really glosses over the fact they are operating out of one of the greatest movie lots that ever existed. They hardly mention anything about the MGM days. Thankfully, I have learnt so much, that, as I wandered around with the tour group, off to visit the latest game show or sitcom set, I could still marvel at what we were passing, and snap photos of such places as the towering Stage 6.

The interior of this stage, I knew, had long ago been turned into an office complex, but as we walked by, I wondered if any of the people working in those offices knew, or cared, that the famous scene in *Singin' in the Rain*, the one where Debbie Reynolds is singing for Jean Hagen at Grauman's Chinese Theater, had been shot on that stage? Fortunately, the exterior of the building still looks similar, although "Columbia Pictures" is now the name on the big sign on that tall roof. To have gone back in time to that day in 1951, when they shot that scene, even for just a minute, would have been just so incredible.

Since that first trip I have been back to Los Angeles yearly. I've now taken the Sony tour a total of six times. Each time on each visit I see new stuff. Being there I feel a living link to the past. I would love it if Sony Pictures could design a second tour that focuses specifically on the history of MGM. That would be, for me, and for others too, I think, the next best thing to actually, really, going back in time. That would be the icing on the cake.

I've also visited the MGM backlot! No, I haven't built that time machine, yet. But I have been to those vast suburbs around Sony Pictures where decades ago, the backlot magic happened. Some of the streets in those complexes have been named after MGM stars, so to be actually standing at the Junction of Garland Drive and Lamarr Avenue, and to think that I was then standing exactly where, seventy-odd years ago, Gene Kelly had Roller-skated on the streets of New York in the movie *It's Always Fair Weather* is just wonderful. I get such a thrill out of being there. It is magical. I really do feel all of the ghosts from the past around me when I do this.

I am sure many people must think I'm slightly mad, but to be there, on such hallowed ground is incredible. It's also nice to think that, in a way I have finally now been able to take that walk with Mickey Rooney on New England Street!

I'm now a Stage Manager in London's West End. You probably don't need me to draw a line from my seeing Mickey Rooney and Ann Miller on stage and my subsequent interest in MGM, and then back to the West End. But that is exactly the course my life has followed.

You could certainly argue about MGM's overall effect on the world. All I know is that it certainly has affected my world.

Like Kingcott, Woolsey Ackerman found himself almost cosmically attracted to the entertainment industry, but Ackerman's interest would eventually pull him quite literally into the very epicenter of Hollywood itself.

My grandparents ran a movie/vaudeville theatre in a small town in upstate New York for some fifty years. It was torn down before I was born, but I grew up with stories about the grand old days of the vaudeville acts which came in on the train, and about the movies—the golden age of movies.

My grandmother told me stories of climbing up a ladder into the projection booth where her father was hand turning nitrate print film, sparks flying everywhere. Later they put in sound equipment. The chairs could also be taken out for the town masquerade ball, variety shows and even basketball games.

My grandparents would go to Albany, NY once a month and select the films they would show from all the different studios. They were even once awarded an exhibitor's trip to Hollywood where they visited several movie lots, including Warner Brothers and witnessed James Cagney in action.

The legendary MGM Dressing Room building as visited by Woolsey Ackerman, and the same building as it looked in 1926. *(top) Woolsey Ackerman; (bottom) Bison Archives*

That was my inspiration. From the age of five, I told my mother that when I grew up, I was going to Hollywood to be an actor and meet Shirley Temple. I grew up watching, and studying the classics, *The Wizard of Oz* being my favorite film. The films of MGM, Warner Brothers, RKO and Disney intrigued me. Later I would work on projects associated with the history and films at all of these studios.

I came to Los Angeles, green, not knowing a soul. My interest was film history and at the time, there was a growing interest in archiving that film history, and even jobs in the area. It was fairly easy to get interviews then, you just called or wrote a letter—and people got back to you. That's how I met Ron Haver, who had recently produced a lavish book on David O. Selznick. Ron sent me to David Shepard at the Director's Guild of America, and I got a job. For three years I worked on the DGA's history project and on publishing oral histories there.

I was plunged into an incredible and surreal rabbit hole my first week on the job because that first week was also the Guild's fiftieth [a]nniversary. For the celebration, the parking lot of the building was tented over and a huge party was held. Saul Bass designed a special poster for the event, and my job was to sit at a table and ask each guest to sign it. So, I met Billy Wilder, John Huston, Frank Capra, Vincente Minelli, and Ruben Mamoulian, just to name a few!

Soon after I was sent to all of the archives and to the actual studio lots to gather information on the DGA's history. I also got to visit the estate of Cecil B. DeMille, which was a trip. The house was an archival shrine to him, it looked exactly as it had in the 1920's. It felt like the home of Norma Desmond. My job was to access his personal archive regarding his career, and it was a real eye-opening view of what working in the Hollywood studio system had once been all about.

I went on to work with George Sidney (His house was full of original works by Renoir, Monet, Pissarro and many other great artists—thanks, I learned, to fellow collector Edward G. Robinson.), Arthur Jacobson (who told me stories about Clara Bow), and Norman Lloyd (who I had ice cream for lunch with along with his wife Peggy). Visiting these fascinating characters in their homes I learned about their lives within the studio system and after.

After this remarkable apprenticeship in the industries history, I moved on to Ted Turner's company. Ted had just bought the MGM film library. At first no one was sure what to do with the studio outputs of MGM, RKO and pre-1950 Warner Brothers films which made up this library, but after about a year creativity flowed.

First up was a fiftieth [a]nniversary tribute to *The Wizard of Oz*. I was assigned to assist Jack Haley Jr. in making a documentary. That project took me deep into the archive—the contents of which had come from the MGM Studio lot. I also got to venture onto that lot to retrieve and discover artifacts which would go into that show, as well as, eventually, into books, video presentations, press releases and various celebrations of that great, classic film.

At the time Turner also had a publishing division, so it occurred to us that with all of the vintage photography and art we had, why not produce coffee table movie-themed books too? So, we did. I was the text and art researcher on these books, and I was also allowed to do some of the writing.

Our biggest project was the award-winning book *MGM: When the Lion Roars*, which then inspired a same-named mini-series. We conducted interviews with anyone and everyone willing to speak to us about their time working at what everyone called the Cadillac of studios, MGM. Visiting Vincente Minnelli's home and working with his widow Lee was a treat, as were all of the wonderful experiences we had in putting that show together. We all worked very hard to present a very detailed look at the workings of a classic-era Hollywood studio. To this day, TCM still uses pieces from the interviews we did for their interstitials.

The popularity of *When the Lion Roars* [led] the company to the conclusion that an entire network showing classic films of the golden age and running them 24/7 might be possible. That's how in 1994, TCM, Turner Classic Movies, was born.

For the first ten years TCM delved into every aspect of studio history. We made many more archival interviews with many more then still-living great actors, directors, producers, musicians, make-up artists, dancers and technicians, all telling us their life-career stories. These sequences were then used for broadcast, in part and whole on the network. In association with Turner Home Video, MGM Home Video and TCM, we also made full documentaries in-house, including ones about Warner Bros.' *Casablanca*, MGM's *Meet Me in St. Louis* and *Ben-Hur*, and RKO's *King Kong*.

During the production of the 1989 Oz show, we had discovered that MGM had had the foresight to save and preserve all of the raw soundstage recordings of their music and sound effects. And Turner had the sense to keep key persons on staff who had been there in the old MGM days, including editors who had started working there in the 1940s, to assist us in accessing this material. Therefore, a contract with Rhino Records eventually allowed us to release dozens of CD's created using these priceless original sound elements.

Every Tuesday night, the Los Angeles TCM staff would go over to the MGM (Sony) lot to see a movie. The movies were projected for us in one of the old studio screening rooms where the dailies for classic MGM film had first been screened! We could invite guests too, so with a friend or two I'd arrive early, and we would run around the lot to see what was going on in the stages. The feeling of being in one of the mammoth studio soundstages is amazing. There were still signs of the old MGM everywhere too, literally, as make-up tables and lighting equipment still then had MGM's name stenciled on them.

One memorable day I spent exploring studio attics with David Niven Jr., who was working on the *Oz* show with us. We didn't find anything, but it was an exciting adventure. Another time I was allowed into the bowels of the costume area, still stashed away back then were bolts of fabric, bows removed from shoes and dress dummies with the names of Ava Gardner and Elizabeth Taylor!

During the first ten years of TCM, the operation was similar to the old studio contract days. On-staff were the researchers, writers, producers, directors and talent needed to create the original programming. There was also an entire public relations department and a separate marketing department just for us. TCM also boasted both [E]ast [C]oast (Atlanta) and [W]est [C]oast (mostly myself) units. Yes, there was the usual corporate tinkering, but we also had a work environment with a real sense of creativity.

In 1996, Turner merged with Warner Brothers, and I moved over to Burbank where I was allowed access to the lot every day. Being on that lot gave me the sense that this great studio was still being utilized to its full potential.

One day at the old Turner archives, Debbie Reynolds came in. She had worked for years to gather a collection of Hollywood memorabilia for which she had long wanted to build a museum. I had watched her start her collection at the MGM auction when I was a kid, and twenty-years later, I found myself assigned to assist her in researching photography for what would become her finally realized museum in Las Vegas. Sadly, that museum would be short lived. She unfortunately could not sustain it, and another twenty years later I watched as she sold her collection off, piece by piece. Things had come around.

Fortunately, Debbie Reynolds' selling of her treasures has stimulated a growing appreciation of the history of the movies. So, I'm very gratified to see increasing institutional, library and museum interest in preserving and presenting Hollywood history.

The private collecting market is strong too. Building on my past work in film history, research, archives, studios and auctions I currently work with college libraries, universities and museums in creating collections of film ephemera for their study archives. The new Academy of Motion Picture Arts and Sciences Museum will certainly perpetuate and stimulate more interest in this field as well.

I did meet Shirley Temple! And for the past few years I have assisted her family in curating her vast career memorabilia for auction and for museum display. An early pioneer of costume preservation, Shirley's mother Gertrude requested that one hundred of Shirley's costumes from her 20th Century Fox films come home with them when she terminated their contract in 1940. Fortunately, Shirley kept those costumes in pristine condition too.

I have a great many memories about my working days in Hollywood. Many are stories which were told to me and some are my own experiences; I remember, for example, the former MGM dancing ladies telling me how cold the body make-up was first thing in the morning, and how rough the make-up girls slathering it on them were. Those same dancers also told me that costume designer Irene Scharaff had insisted that they wear corsets, which after one day of fainting while filming they abandoned; Roger Mayer's assistant June once told me that she had started as a mail girl on the MGM lot during World War II when all the boys were away, and how she had to assert herself to keep working once they returned; then there was being told first-hand what it was really like to work on-set with Welles, Chaplin, Renoir and Hitchcock by Norman Lloyd; or watching Shelley Winters tell a make-up girl that she did not want to use face pulls on camera because she liked to eat and did not mind that it showed; or Eleanor Keaton talking about how Buster taught her to play bridge on the set of *Bathing Beauty*; or Fay Wray rifling about through her purse while sitting next to me at Claudette Colbert's auction, and turning to me and promising to be quiet . . . in a minute; or Roddy McDowall and Stanley Kubrick visiting the archive to borrow prints; and Jane Fonda coming in to make a show on Katharine Hepburn. I also remember discovering star wardrobe at the Warner Bros. Archive where their studio history was being preserved. It has been a surreal journey. A journey of exploring and presenting, to those who care, the whole gamut of the history of movies, and of movie studios.

I've also made a few films as an actor, fulfilling the other part of my five-year old's long-ago proclamation to my mother. One film I acted in was made at the Triangle Studio in Silver Lake, which is one of Los Angeles's first film studios. The feeling of history is overwhelming in the well-maintained studio, which today is mostly used for commercials, music videos and independent film shoots. Old equipment and lights still line the walls, making it feel like it must have felt like in the days of Mabel Normand, which was appropriate because the movie we were making was a sort of mockumentary about classic studio days, and about how Orson Welles could never finish a movie.

Today, like at the Triangle Studio, the main lots of most of the historic studios still stand. They are landmarks and they are also, like Warner Bros. still utilized to the fullest. Just as in the days of old, they are still factories. Factories making movies. There will be many more stories to tell!

There were others who revealed their obsessive nature regarding MGM while, like Kent Warner, they explored that studio even as it toppled around them. But unlike the sanctioned-yet-devious Warner, some of those last studio archaeologists were trespassers who had climbed over the fence, or under it, to look around.

In some cases, in some ways, some of these interlopers never returned.

Donnie Norden's obsession regarding MGM goes back fifty years. But it all started the day he found a hole in a fence.

My attachment to MGM does not connect to a specific moment. It was more like a slowly developing love affair. . . .

Growing up a block away from MGM Studios, the sounds of machine gun fire on the backlot sometimes seemed endless. World War II was being refought in the early 60's at MGM for the TV series' *Combat!*, *Garrison's Gorillas*, *Jericho*, and *Rat Patrol*. So, the noise and smoke from those staged battles were frequent side effects in my neighborhood.

The place where all of this sound and fury came from refused to be contained by the old fences surrounding it either. As a curious kid I could see sets there intriguingly towering high above its green fence line. For years, tiny holes in those fences tried to seduce me with tantalizing views of . . . just what? "*C'mon in*" they whispered! "*I dare ya!*"

One day in 1970, when I was ten, nature finally allowed me to satisfy my old curiosity by felling a eucalyptus tree into that fence, creating a boy-sized hole. My best friend Jimmy and I decided to use this magic portal to finally and at last, sneak inside the studio and become *explorers*! We knew that we would have to be careful though. Bigger, braver kids were already secretly prowling the place and had found out that the studio security department happened to have a different word for our explorations. *Trespassers*!

Donald Norden (www.phantomofthebacklots.com)

But explore, or *trespass*, we did! On that first day when we climbed through to the other side of that fence, we immediately found ourselves in the middle of a graveyard set. Perfect, since we were scared to death. Tantalizingly, we also saw what looked like an entire German village ahead of us—of which we had only seen the tops of over those fences before. But we also saw that we were going to need to cross a wide and open field to get to it. Frightened, we hesitated, wanting to stay close to the security of the fence line. So instead of venturing into that beckoning village, as we very much wanted to do, we crept, very cautiously, along the wall instead.

Eventually we ended up at a swimming pool. This is the weird thing part. Understand that we'd never been there, to that old, empty and decaying pool before. Yet, immediately, it was somehow . . . familiar. It took us a minute to figure it out. We'd just seen it, that very spot, in an episode of *The Twilight Zone* called "The Bewitching Pool." The fuse of my soul had been lit.

A teenage Donnie Norden leaps out of a backlot window. *Donald Norden, taken by Danny Hancock (www.phantomofthebacklots.com)*

Our horizons thus expanded, we numbly crept back along the wall, through our opening and home to the real world. But, of course, we knew that this hole-in-the-fence portal would present itself to us again, first in our dreams that night, and the following day in reality. How could we, how could anyone, then fail to answer to its siren's call?

Jimmy and I promised ourselves that getting all the way out to that German village would be our goal this time, and that no open area was going to scare us away. So, the second time we ducked through our hole in the fence, feeling like Alice through the looking glass, we immediately ran past the cemetery and across that scary open space, ducking briefly behind a crushed army vehicle on the way. But to our relief, we saw not a single armed-security guard or Nazi stormtrooper as we did so. At the village we moved like *Combat*'s liberating soldiers ourselves, building to building, door to door. But aside from us, the only thing moving there that Sunday morning was some tattered drapes fluttering in the windows of the façades.

And that word. "façades," couldn't do this place justice. Instead, this was a fully detailed replica of an entire and complete European town, from the church steeple to the cobblestone streets. And that town was as shell-shocked as the two of us were that day. There were bullet holes everywhere, bomb craters, shell casings, debris, blown up sides of buildings. Whatever the last battle fought there here had been, it had been a good one. How could any red-blooded boy not have been completely enthralled by such a spectacle?

And we quickly found out that the backlot wasn't confined to being just a grave-yard, a swimming pool and that crazy, wonderful village. The sets on the MGM back-lot were endless. They rolled on for acres. They represented every form and style of architecture and every era in human history. There were city streets and small towns and French courtyards and gardens and jungles and artificial lakes. And the best thing about it all was, merely by climbing through a fence, it could all be ours.

Fast forward, these explorations quickly became the norm, first with Jimmy or with other kids, and as I got older, solo. I returned again and again to this backlot. I came to play and explore, and for entertainment of course. But it was deeper, more profound than that. Over the next years I haunted, and was haunted by, these sets, that place. I was like a phantom there. And the backlot was my own personal and singular sanctuary.

I need to point something out here. There's a movie called *The Phantom of Hollywood.* It's about a masked actor, played by Jack Cassidy, who haunts a movie studio. But before that film was made MGM security used to call me "the phantom," because like the character in the film, I was always there, haunting the place. Other kids climbed through that hole in the fence. They came in, played there for a while, grew up, went away. But the backlot was mine. I was constant.

When they were filming *The Phantom of Hollywood*, MGM hired Gene Levitt, a director who had long-toiled on *Combat!* So, he probably knew the place almost as well as l did. For that film they shot a scene of a teenage trespasser falling from a building. This was interesting because I had built a fort inside that very building. The

The New York dock set as it looked in its heyday . . . and when Donnie played there. *(top) Bison Archives; (bottom) Donald Norden* *(www.phantomofthebacklots. com)*

studio knew it was there, both MGM Security and the Culver City Police Department had raided it twice trying to catch me, but magically, I'd escaped both times. And I was still using it even when they were shooting outside. But seeing this scene in which that teenager's chalked body is laid out at the base of my fort was weird—after all, in a very real way, I was both the phantom, and I was also his victim!

So, in this scene, Broderick Crawford, who played the studio security chief in the movie, has dialogue here about the backlot being trespassed by those "long-haired teenage punks" as he puts it. To which his boss says "that's what we put up fences for, to keep things like this from happening." Well, John Ireland, who plays a cop in on the powwow then says, "It's curiosity, you can't fence it in!" Those words not only summed up part of the romantic appeal of the lot, but more precisely, my presence there too.

Later on, during that same film, I came face to face with Jack Cassidy during a scene. We made eye contact. He waved at me. The two phantoms, reality and fiction intersecting. *That's why I'll forever feel that I'm part of the narrative of that film.*

Filming did not need be taking place to have fun at MGM either. Trust me, for a kid, an empty studio is a very fun place to be. It's one large, if sometimes ancient,

Jack Cassidy played the "other" *Phantom of Hollywood. Bison Archives*

toy-chest. Props were stored there that had last been used sometimes decades ago, now aged and layered with dust, waiting for a next role which probably would never come. Cannons and guns and bazookas and even whole tanks could be found rotting away out there in the uncut grass. Think about it, could there ever have been anything cooler for a romantic, imaginative ten-year old boy? I mean, *Disneyland with weapons!*

I went to the studio every day, or every night. Sometimes I climbed through my hole in the fence every day *and* every night. And, trust me, once you start to scratch this itch, you just can't stop. Even if I wasn't on the lot, my heart was. Watching television didn't help either. By this time, I knew MGM so well that I recognized every set in every scene on every channel—which just made me wish I was there playing on the lot instead of watching actors do it.

Other kids recreated things they had seen on TV; battles and brawls and bombings, in their backyards, right? My friends and I played the same games, but in the *actual spots* where those scenes had been shot. *Combat!* for example? Well, we lived it in the form of [BB gun] fights and dramatic recreations of scenes that we had sometimes just watched, or just watched filmed. In our games we could even die in exactly the area, in the actual spot, where a filmed death had earlier been shot. It was almost as if we were somehow going back in time. Looking back now, in a way, maybe we were.

I lived my life as if MGM was my home. Louis B. Mayer was never able to say as much. My pals and I made our forts inside some of the most iconic sets in Hollywood. We built one of our best clubhouses in an old, probably long dead, caretaker's hut, but which was still outfitted with electricity, carpet, even hot-and-cold running water. We eventually carried in an old rabbit-ear-equipped TV set, and if we extended the antenna at just the right angle, we could sometimes catch *The Twilight Zone* on it. Even while we lived there.

Yes, my parents knew what I was doing. How could they not? They knew that, unlike other, *bad* kids who were also climbing the fences of the studio, my friends and I weren't (usually) concerned with stealing from or vandalizing the property. I loved it too much to do that. But over the years Dad still ultimately had to pick me up at the security offices of two different, but equally indulgent MGM watch commanders.

Mom was more pragmatic. Her only rule was *"Donnie, be careful!"* To her credit, Mom also helped me by getting me a fancy camera with a telescopic lens to document my on-lot criminal adventures.

And I was careful, for the most part. But hazards exist everywhere, especially in a war and poverty-ravaged movie studio. But I found out early on that I was apparently protected by some Hollywood-guardian angel. If that had not been the case, I most certainly would not be here to write this now.

As my studio, and as I, aged up though, MGM could no longer bother, or no longer afford, to pay those ever-indulgent watch commanders to patrol the place solely in order to keep me out of it. So private companies took over. The good news was that without those pesky security guards around, MGM was now officially mine.

Or should I say, Dino De Laurentiis's and mine? It seems that the mega-producer then had a grand plan for this studio in decline. Over the next year, our backlot would become a 24/7 operation for his big budget 1976 *King Kong* remake. First Dino built an impressive Skull Island set, Kong-proof wall, and native village. Then, he constructed a full-size Kong-robot and converted those earlier sets to play New York's Shea stadium. *King Kong* proved to Hollywood that the property was still a viable location and brought other big-budget films like *Sgt. Pepper's Lonely Hearts Club Band* and *The Stunt Man* to my backlot during this period.

In 1979 I was, in the greatest irony in the history of Hollywood, hired by one of those outside companies using the lot to guard the very place I had been a thousand-time trespasser on. Yes me—Donnie, the kid that security had then chased around for most of the decade, now had a badge! I probably even chased around a few 10-year-old trespassers myself during that time.

But the lot, finally, was winding down, Debbie Reynolds kept trying desperately to save New York Street, that was about the only section left then. But in spite of what people say about the backlot not being used during that sad era, the cameras just never stopped rolling. Those cameras were turning on both *Hero at Large* and *Being There* even as the last of my old fantasyland itself finally itself became a fantasy.

October 1980, the final blows are delivered. There was no fanfare. Just me and some bulldozers.

I've learned the hard way to appreciate that nothing lasts forever. But in some ways that doesn't apply here. Movies and TV reruns magically can pump life back into times long gone. Hence, it makes me happy that my backlot can never really die, can never truly disappear.

In case you are wondering, I didn't disappear either. I've had a long and wonderful career in Hollywood. But nothing for me will ever equal the adventures that that hole in the fence opened up for me.

Not all interactions by outsiders with the studio have been so benign, however. In 1937, Patricia Douglas was a twenty-year-old who lived with her mother and occasionally did extra work, not because she had any particular dreams of stardom, but "just for something to do,"[8] when she received a summons for a casting call at MGM. She regretted going for the rest of her life.

This casting call turned out to be no such thing. Instead, her services, along with 120 other pretty aspirants were being sought for a private party the studio was throwing for 282 MGM sales executives from all over the country. Douglas and her companions were paid $7.50 and a meal to dress in skimpy cowgirl outfits and told to "be nice" to the attendees. "You'd never think they'd pull anything like that," she remembered decades later. "You're trusting with the studios. You're not expecting anything except to work in a movie. That's what you're *there* for."⁹

One of those attendees was thirty-six-year-old David Ross from the Chicago sales office. Ross targeted Douglas for his most unwanted attention. Although she repeatedly rebuked his crude advances and fled to the ladies' room to escape, he and some other conventioneers physically held her down and then poured a whole glass of scotch and champagne down her throat. Again, she escaped, but Ross followed her out into the parking lot, where he pulled her into a parked car, threatened her life, and then raped her.

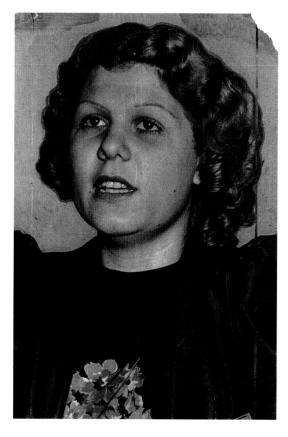

In 1937 Patricia Douglas was a twenty-year-old occasional movie extra when she attended an MGM-sponsored party that would effectively ruin her life. *Photofest*

Douglas was taken to a hospital across the street from, and largely under the finger of, the studio, where she received little treatment and little sympathy. She eventually swore out a legal complaint against Ross, who had by then returned to Chicago. Because Douglas was still a minor, her mother had to sign the complaint. But the Los Angeles District Attorney, Buron Fitts, was also then firmly under the finger of MGM. "The power MGM had is unimaginable today," Bud Schulberg has said. "They owned everyone—the D.A., the L.A.P.D. They ran this place."[10]

But Douglas would not let MGM run her. Her lawyers went to the press, which published her allegations but were unable or afraid to even identify the name of the studio involved, which for its part wholeheartedly denied the accusations against it and Ross and hired Pinkerton detectives to besmear Douglas's reputation and find witnesses to refute her claims.

Eventually, a parking lot attendant, who later became a strangely well-compensated chauffeur at MGM, mysteriously changed his testimony under oath. Consequently, the grand jury refused to indict Ross. Undaunted, Douglas's lawyers filed a civil suit against both he and the studio for $500,000, which was mysteriously dismissed. Another, this time federal, lawsuit quickly came to nothing as well.

Ross, who never paid for his crimes, died of rectal cancer in 1962. Douglas, whose story would be buried until historian and writer David Stenn discovered her in 2003, died later that same year.

It should be noted that not all MGM studio parties were nearly so debaucherous. Producer Pandro Berman told author Neil Gabler that a studio guest from Europe specially requested from Mayer a "Hollywood party"—fully expecting sex and show-girls and drugs. Mayer, wanting to show his guest how refined Americans were, instead threw him the same sort of classy and deadly dull affair which the visitor had hoped to avoid.

9
Shadows of the Lion

IN THE LION'S DEN

MGM's longtime feline mascot is arguably the most recognized corporate symbol in the world.

The studio became keenly aware early on of the potency inherent in the image of a roaring lion. Luise Rainer, who despite winning two Academy Awards there did not have a happy experience at MGM, once wistfully said that, "I think the best of it is still that lion. That roaring lion."[1] Rainer today, like most stars of her era is not well-remembered, whereas the lion, although diminished, somehow still reigns and roars.

In an undated press release, probably from the 1930s, MGM once trumpeted that "the studio decided to find out just how well-known the trademark was, and in a public opinion poll conducted around the world and involving every prominent trademark in the universe, it was determined that Leo the Lion and the *Ars Gratia Artis* was far and away the best known."

Of course, this sort of material, from this sort of source, should always be taken with a grain of salt, but in this case, well, these admittedly authoritative-sounding words may even have been accurate.

This opinion is perhaps borne out by the footnote that decades and generations of studio executives and studio publicists later, such possible hyperbole was still being spouted and in weirdly similar statements by the same lion's handlers. For example, in 2000, Michael Nathanson, MGM's chief operating officer, confidently told *Variety* that "next to Coca-Cola, MGM's logo is the most famous in the world."[2] Maybe so.

Bison Archives

If all of this all still sounds like studio ballyhoo, and it does, isn't it also true, in a John Ford sort of way, that when repeated often enough, the legend eventually does become the reality?

There are actually statistics to support these words too. In 2000, as part of the company's seventy-fifth anniversary, MGM's Consumer Products Division hired an outside branding consultation firm, Landor Associates, to rate the company's physical image in terms of what they annoyingly then called "brand freshness." This survey was intended to quantify a broad cross section of the public's "differentiation, relevance, esteem and familiarity toward famous branded products."[3]

Remarkably, considering the company's many-decades-long apparent slide toward oblivion, MGM was, somehow and against all odds, then still rated one of only four corporations, among the 150 surveyed, that had routinely increased *in all four* categories!

The lion's only peers, at least according to this probably arbitrary measurement, were judged to be Adidas, Revlon, and Lego. And it should be noted that the studio logo is older, therefore less "fresh," in some cases by decades, than any of these three rivals—making the lion's world dominance and age-defying appeal all the more stunning and head-scratching.

The only explanation for the longevity and appeal of this lion, overall, worldwide, is that Leo has apparently become a symbol—a symbol not only for his studio but for the movies at-large and for the US film industry in general and the people in it, to the point that he is now a sort of generic avatar for Hollywood, and especially for classic Hollywood—whatever that word now means.

It is odd, it is bittersweet, and it is ironic, that as MGM's market share and influence in Hollywood decline, its mascot's recognizability factor tends to increase annually to the point that the lion and Hollywood itself are now seen as interchangeable. And no embarrassing public indignity perpetuated on the company by Nicholas Schenck, James Aubrey, or Giancarlo Parretti seems to be able to besmirch this image either. It is perhaps also worth noting that the industry trade papers still constantly refer to MGM simply as the "lion," which is most interesting in an era in which one of MGM's rival mini-majors is a company tellingly called Lionsgate.

Thanks to Kirk Kerkorian, part of Leo the Lion's high recognizability, of course, comes from his prominence as a brand even outside of his appearances in nearly every MGM movie. And even outside of that he has also been the subject of fanciful biographies, advertisements, political cartoons, animated films, urban legends, myths, parodies, poetry, satire, fan fiction, and documentaries. He has been portrayed on-screen by at least seven actual lions and impersonated in live events, exhibitor conferences, tours, premieres, and Las Vegas floorshows by countless dozens more. He has starred in TV series, been portrayed by human actors in ill-fitting costumes, and been mass-produced as a saccharine-adorable plush toy. He has greeted guests in casinos and resorts and theme parks. His regal profile once even adorned an airline. He was once the mascot of a (studio-sponsored) sandlot baseball team called, of course, the MGM Lions. He's been evoked in the title of several studio-made promotional

Leo the Lion's image has been spotted woven into the carpets at the Las Vegas MGM Grand, 2004. *Rob Gold*

shorts like *Lionpower from MGM* (1967). His visage has been reproduced on countless products, from wristwatches to liquor cabinets, from T-shirts to training bras for more than a hundred years.

The sum total of all of this class, kitsch, and ephemera is that Leo the Lion now exists, now lives, quite apart from the companies he obstinately represents.

For example, let's look at publishing. Almost every book ever published about the studio, and we have discussed many of them, of course, features the logo/lion somewhere on its cover. Although any actual, unaltered version of that apparently indelible image is allowed only to adorn works specifically licensed or written about internally by the company itself. Peter Bart's book about MGM in twilight, *Fade Out*, for example, featured Leo getting stepped on for its cover, which Kirk Kerkorian certainly would not have sanctioned if given the opportunity. Weirdly, completely unrelated to the company and about the company, books, including largely unrelated novels, like Gore Vidal's *Myron*, have also featured the same logo iconography, even if these variations were again not photo-finish close enough to attract the studio's lawyers.

Sometimes in art, the studio's founders are referred to as lions themselves. Director John Huston, for example, was once vividly quoted as saying that "L. B. Mayer is one of the rulers of the jungle,"[4] which seems to evoke Mayer as a king of beasts, symbolically, if not specifically. Interestingly, actor Buddy Ebsen's memoir later used almost the exact same phraseology to describe the same man.

More recently, Scott Eyman's book *Lion of Hollywood*, about Mayer, and Martin Turnbull's novel *Heart of the Lion*, about Thalberg, have also evoked two of the studio's founders with lion analogies in their titles.

Despite the remarkable consistency of all of this "lionization," it should be noted that the company's own on-screen and lawyer-sanctioned lion, although viewers will surely assume otherwise, has itself been altered, rethought, reimagined, parodied, and generally screwed with many times over many decades. These internal changes have been a result of variances in lions, technology, and audience tastes. Therefore, a roll call of the different lions and different logos those stalwart kings of the jungle have appeared in might be useful in this discussion.

Hold tight to your whip and to your chair.

A Goldwyn Pictures advertising director and lyricist, Howard Dietz, is credited with coming up with the idea of using a lion as its company's mascot. Dietz, who would himself reside at the future MGM for decades, also came up with the Latin-sounding phrase *Ars Gratia Artis*, which, sort of, means "art for art's sake"—although the actual phrase and sentiment are actually French.

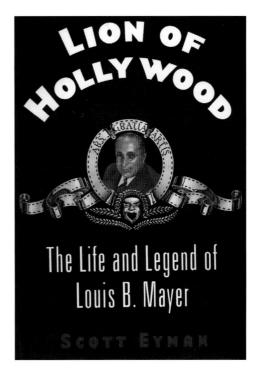

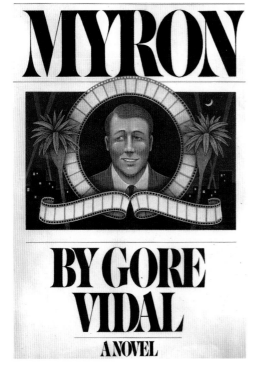

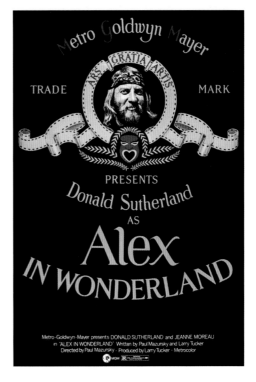

Sometimes, often for legal reasons, Leo does not need to be seen at all, only suggested. Gore Vidal's novel *Myron* (1974), Hugh Fordin's *The World of Entertainment* (1975), and Scott Eyman's Mayer biography, *Lion of Hollywood* (2005), took this tack, as did MGM's own movie *Alex in Wonderland* (1970). *Author's collection*

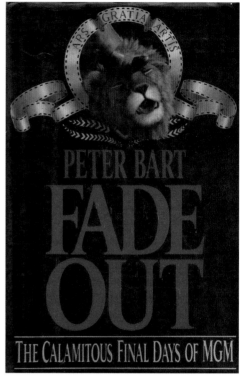

Sometimes Leo is treated respectfully in the media—and sometimes not so much. *Author's collection*

The first Goldwyn Leo was reportedly not Jackie, the Selig Zoo resident who, after all, would be there for Mayer and Thalberg's first handshake, but was reportedly another big cat, born in Ireland with the name Cairbre, but usually called Slats. This feline confusion, if nothing else, begs the question as to just how many male lions there were working in the movies in Los Angeles during this era. Whatever his identity, this lion is the one who opened the first Goldwyn film, *Polly of the Circus* (1917). He did not, of course, yet roar but instead looked sternly at the camera.

The Goldwyn lion, Slats, was adapted into the subsequent MGM logo for *He Who Gets Slapped* (1924). The lion, of the three available logos, was chosen for the new company because it was more dynamic than that of Metro Pictures, which featured a bird who looked like a peacock, and Louis B. Mayer Productions, which was represented by an eagle. The apparent but charming coincidence that the German word for "lion" is "Lowe" probably didn't hurt either. No one remembers where the obvious, if apt, "Leo" moniker—Leo being the name of a lion-shaped constellation in the zodiac—for this cat first came from either.

The original Goldwyn-era lion was much more sedate than he would become after the merger and sound. *Bison Archives*

The figure and form of a lion, of course, has also long held a proud tradition of prominence in religions and nations all over the world as a suitable representation of honor, faith, majesty, fertility, and chivalry. Lion imagery is, in fact, so prevalent and so potent, that these big cats are weirdly well-represented even in lands where the animal could have never actually have prowled, namely, in Southeast Asia, Europe, and the Americas.

Lion imagery can also be observed worldwide in fine art, in heraldry, music, sports, currency, and literature. Even today, venerated and sometimes centuries-old lion statues can be found silently guarding the entrance to the Forbidden City in Beijing, at the site of the battle of Chaeronea in Greece, at London's Trafalgar Square, the New York Public Library, Ulysses S. Grant's tomb, the William McKinley Monument, and, lest we forget, at assorted MGM hotel properties worldwide.

Although lions had a then already millenniums-long history in art and culture, MGM's first prototype feline, Slats, telegraphed to us just how unimpressed he was by all of this by dying in 1936. Although by then, a second lion, the familiar Selig

Zoo animal, Jackie, had already assumed, as early as 1928 (accounts vary), the official on-screen Leo moniker.

Jackie was the first lion to audibly roar for sound film, indicating that Slats, perhaps, possessed the same problems vocalizing for the microphone as some other silent stars did. It is also Jackie who is most identified with MGM, having been a resident of both the Selig Zoo and later of the studio's own on-lot menagerie. Known for his amenable personality, Jackie also reliably played any other lion needed in any MGM picture during this era. It was also Jackie who reliably appeared as Leo for publicity events, in still shoots with stars, on newsreels, and, of course, those hundreds of times on-screen.

The studio constructed a special airplane, a single-engine Ryan Brougham, just for Jackie's transport around the world, allowing delighted MGM publicists to anoint the feline as "Leo, the MGM Flying Lion," which was even painted onto that plane's fuselage. In 1927, this fuselage crashed in the Arizona desert, although remarkably,

Martin Jensen poses with his copilot shortly before their 1927 incident in the Arizona desert. *Bison Archives*

both Jackie and the pilot, if not the fuselage, were unharmed. That pilot, however, pioneer aviator Martin Jensen, after crawling from that crumpled wreck, realized that he would then have to leave Jackie behind to hike back to civilization for assistance. When Jensen got to a telephone and called the studio, reportedly their first question was, "How's the lion?"

Fortunately, when Jensen and the rescuers returned to the site, the lion was fine and was waiting patiently there for them to return with his lunch. The happy outcome to this unexpected publicity bonanza would lead to yet another new nickname for Jackie: "Leo the Lucky."

Although he went to a well-earned feline heaven in 1935, Jackie's name would be carried on by his trainer Melvin Koontz, using two other, apparently unrelated, lions. The records indicate that neither Jackie the second nor Jackie the third, as they were called, ever portrayed Leo on-screen, however. But the last Jackie did book the title role in MGM's lion-centric comic adventure *Fearless Fagan* (1952).

Perhaps the most beloved of MGM's mascots, Jackie the Lion, spawned a dynasty that was still going strong at the time of this 1954 trade ad. *Bison Archives*

The original Jackie, Jackie the Lucky's image, however, continued to be used intermittently by the studio in its logo and in accompanying publicity for decades. Most recently to date, it was Jackie who nostalgically roared on-screen at the beginning of the 1930s set *Hearts of the West* (1975)—a very long reign indeed.

Two other lions also portrayed Leo during this era. A lion named Telly roared in two-strip color shorts until 1932 and another, named Coffee, also did so until 1935. Tanner, a third lion, was selected for three-strip technicolor films, starting with *Sweethearts* (1938), and was the go-to Leo for all new logo footage in all new film formats until 1956. He also was the studio's acting lion in films like *No Place like Rome* (1936) and essentially for any lion role not played by Bert Lahr during this era. However, some MGM experts, Leo the Lion experts, and conspiracy theorists have suggested these three animals may actually have been the same lion, using an alias or two.

During this period, the logo was also represented by an animated lion for cartoons and in new formats like 3D and CinemaScope as they came along, although sometimes older prefilmed intros were retained and tinted or reformatted during this era, meaning that it would then be another lion, most often Jackie, who would actually roar on-screen.

Yet another king of beasts, this one not-so-inspiringly christened George, started appearing around 1956. George was distinguished by his fluffy, afro-like mane, which makes him stand out among the MGM lions, even if nothing else about him, his inconsistent roar, or his demeaner does. In addition to the unsatisfactory work contributed by George's hairstylist, he was also usually lit and positioned badly inside the circlet of film around his head, making him appear somewhat kittenish, despite his sometimes-full-throated roar. Unsurprisingly, George last roared that roar in 1958.

The logo surrounding Leo was also modified about this time, although few noticed. Until June 1959, the name "Metro Goldwyn Mayer" (again without hyphens) was printed in an ornate box underneath Leo. But starting with the December release of the film *Never so Few*, the logo was redesigned so that the studio's name now wrapped around the loop of curling celluloid framing Leo's head. Overall, this rejiggering was an improvement, however, because it allowed the roaring lion to be represented larger than it had before, and the new stereophonic processes made his roar larger as well.

A new, larger lion was apparently called for to embody this new, larger logo, and poor George, despite his hyperactive mane, was just not up to the task. This last actual (to date) lion was finally and officially named Leo. Leo first roared in *Jailhouse Rock* (1957). But his color debut came in *Cat on a Hot Tin Roof* (1958), and it would be this version, with this particular roar with this particular lion, that would be used until

2021. Although several films circa 1950 and beyond used a freeze-frame version, and late in the 1960s, a horrible, stylized lion graphic would briefly replace the live Leo. This last version would be so unpopular that the live Leo returned after just a couple on-screen absences, although that artist's rendition continues to be used even today to promote various nonfilm MGM endeavors.

All things considered, the MGM studio logo has remained one of the few and one of the more consistent aspects of its corporate history, although there have been other variations. A full-body profile sculpture of the lion appeared in many films and was, particularly in the late 1930s, used as the default background for opening or for closing credits, although the last instance of its appearing on-screen was as late as *Nothing Lasts Forever* (1984). Additionally, the inexplicable, except to the lawyers, words "Trade Mark" have usually appeared to the left and to the right of Leo's head. And the usually black background behind the opening roar has been tinted blue, green, or red occasionally to freshen things up. A television version, an MGM Kids home-video version, and variations on the main logo reflecting assorted anniversaries, mergers, divisions, and web addresses have also been added, removed, tweaked, or deleted during assorted brief or permanent regimes over the decades as well.

On-screen, sometimes Leo also remains in his familiar place, but the audio instead is manipulated. For the opening of their dire remake of *Tarzan the Ape Man* (1981), the lion roars, but it is instead Tarzan's famous yodel that issues from his jaws. *Poltergeist* (1982) changed the timbre of the roar just enough to unnerve audiences. And if these audiences chose to sit through the end credits, under Leo's closing wail, the laughter of ghostly children could also be heard. Similarly, for its 2015 remake of that property, the studio digitized and briefly broke up the same logo, as though it were now being manipulated by supernatural elements.

In 2008 the original footage of Leo was digitized and remastered; this new version of this old version made its debut in the James Bond film *Quantum of Solace*. In 2012 the image was further tinkered with to start with a close-up of a lion's eye and then pull back to reveal the familiar iconography, but the lion, once seen, still then remained the same king of the jungle.

. . . until 2021, when MGM announced that this Leo, originally shot on film sixty-four years previously, was finally starting to look its nondigital age. Consequently, the company hired an outside effects house called We are Baked Studios to create an all new, all CGI lion.

The latest Leo looks and roars almost exactly like his live-action predecessors, although the familiar imagery and lettering around his head is now all gold, and the *Ars*

Gratia Artis motto is now also shown in English as *Art for Art's Sake* first, as though untranslated Latin might intimidate modern audiences.

The first film to feature the new logo was originally intended to be another James Bond film, *No Time to Die*, but when coronavirus (COVID-19) restrictions repeatedly pushed that film's release date forward, the Channing Tatum comedy *Dog*, in February 2022 instead became the first film to introduce a new MGM canine to a new generation.

Considering that Dietz and, certainly, Goldwyn intended their lion logo and the accompanying *Ars Gratia Artis* to be a symbol of solemnity and class, it must be said that MGM has sometimes been a good sport about having some fun at Leo's, and at its own, expense.

The lion was first allowed to look less than dignified in trade ads in the early 1930s, which sometimes depicted him, for the first time, anthropomorphized into a (usually) tuxedo-wearing human with a lion's head and paws. This humorous lion-man characterization would, decades later, and perhaps unintentionally become King Looey, the mascot for the MGM Grand's theme park ventures.

Also, during this era, specifically in 1932, an on-screen live lion crashed a film called *The Chimp*, causing Stan Laurel to blubber to Oliver Hardy that "I just saw MGM." Another Laurel & Hardy project, *That's That* (1937), comically substituted a shrieking cat for Leo's roar in its logo, although because that short was created internally for Stan Laurel's birthday party and never intended to be seen by the public, it doesn't really count.

Sometimes fan magazines, surely with the studio's blessing, poked a little fun at that mascot as well. In a *Photoplay* article Sheilah Graham in 1949, writing under Leo's byline, made a startling confession and dished dirt on fellow animal star Lassie at the same time. "You know, lions can't stay young forever, like certain lady stars and dogs who will be nameless. So, I'm the fifth Leo the Lion. Wanna make something of it?"[5]

But these rare comic escapades were the exception. For many years, the on-screen Leo was considered sacrosanct. For example, the Marx Brothers irreverently shot a parody logo for their MGM debut, *A Night at the Opera* (1935), featuring them rather than Leo roaring (Harpo approximated by tooting his horn) under the words *Marx Gratia Marxes*. But perhaps because of this hesitation on the studio's part to lampoon itself, this amusing gag was characteristically not used in the film, although it did sneak into some of the trailers.

MGM's long-standing reluctance to trample sacred ground was still partially intact as late as 1970 when some of the promotional materials for *Alex in Wonderland*

An anthropized version of Leo started appearing in trade ads in the 1930s. His dapper appearance perhaps coincidentally anticipated the studio's later King Looey character. Here he toasts the new year in an issue of *The Motion Picture Herald* (1952). *Author's collection*

One of the more memorable variations of the studio's trademark came to us via none other than Harpo Marx in 1935. *Author's collection*

depicted a hirsute Donald Sutherland instead of Leo inside the logo, although, again, this would still not be the case in the movie itself.

It would not be until the 1960s that the on-screen Leo was allowed to be the subject of parody inside of an MGM film itself. Perhaps the first example of this self-lampooning of the lion would arrive in a *Tom and Jerry* cartoon, *Switchin' Kitten* (1961), which features Jerry the mouse, and not Tom the cat, roaring from out of a mouse hole with *Ars Gratia Artis* printed above it.

Director Chuck Jones must have found this gag amusing because beginning with his own first cat and mouse short, *Pent-house Mouse* (1963), he would segue from Leo inside the logo to Tom's less than inspiring yelps. Additionally, in the short *Much Ado about Mousing* (1964), Jones menaced the duo by dubbing Leo's roar into the mouth of an animated shark.

Apparently reasoning that if Jones could get away with it, director Robert Youngson audaciously opened his *Big Parade of Comedy* (1964) compilation feature with an "out to lunch" sign superimposed over the lion's head, which turns out to be literal because when the sign is removed, Leo with animated human arms and legs flailing from his jaws is seen. Two years later, for *The Fearless Vampire Killers*, this rather grand *guignol* theme is continued when Leo morphs into a cartoon vampire—fangs dripping with blood.

Since then, the variations have been even more audacious. *Strange Brew* (1983) featured perhaps the most elaborate logo variation of all. Instead of roaring, this Leo belches, whereupon the stars of the film, Dave Thomas and Rick Moranis, most intriguingly walk behind him into a cluttered soundstage and pull on the big cat's tail. *Crocodile Hunter: Collision Course* (2002) replaced Leo entirely with a crocodile, although his roar is still familiar. In *The Pink Panther* (2006), the feline is interrupted midroar by an animated Inspector Clouseau, and then by the Pink Panther himself, who slams a door and makes this king of beast's eyes comically bug out. Most recently, in *The Addams Family* (2019), the big yellow cat sees a big red ball and jumps off-screen to chase it.

Leo, meaning the character rather than the lion portraying him, has also appeared in other studio-sponsored media and in real life. In 1955, as part of their debut TV series *The MGM Parade*, the studio occasionally featured either an animated or live-action plush lion toy, again in a tuxedo, now named "Little Leo."

In 1993, MGM introduced the world to King Looey and his feline family with the opening of their MGM Grand Adventure theme park. Looey, who exactly resembled Leo in many of those early print-ad appearances, was most certainly intended to evoke the famous lion in the logo, so why he was rechristened here, in defiance of decades of consistent branding is somewhat mysterious. King Looey was represented in the park by costumed actors and in gift shops by assorted plush toys, gaming tokens, print cartoons, and souvenirs. But like the park that he was created to promote, King Looey never really caught on, not with children and not with their parents, who probably only wanted to drag those children away from those gift shops and rides to get to the gaming rooms.

Perhaps having learned from their mistake, the company tried again with a TV show, *The Lionhearts*. This animated series premiered in 1998 and concerned itself with the adventures of one "Leo Lionheart." Apparently unlike the perhaps now dethroned and disgraced King Looey, this lion really *is*, apparently, the official and actual MGM mascot.

Leo and Lana Lionheart pose for an official studio portrait at the time of their 1998 TV series. *Author's collection*

This Leo, as voiced by William H. Macy, is specifically depicted as working at MGM Studios in Hollywood. His on-lot adventures are contrasted with his chaotic home life. It seems that Leo has a wife and three cubs, all of whom are aptly named after former MGM stars, although this unexpected facet of the series must have confused the too-many 1990s children who had never heard of Lana Turner, Spencer Tracy, or even of Judy Garland, who was specifically here the namesake of the pride's youngest daughter. Father Lionheart also has a father himself, "Leo Sr." (voiced by occasional MGM star Harve Presnell) who perhaps represents Jackie to Leo's "Leo?" Maybe we're putting more thought into this than the writers did?

Despite, or perhaps because of, the series' welcome hat tips to the company's past, *The Lionhearts* only lasted for thirteen episodes. More recently, the current MGM Kids home-video line, depicting adorable baby lions, has marked the only subsequent child-friendly variation on the traditional logo and fanfare.

As noted, Leo has been represented by many lions over many years in personal appearances. Jackie, in particular, because of his good luck and amiable nature was a past master in this capacity. Another particularly notable Leo stand-in was a lion named Joseph, trained by Charlie Sammut, who appeared extensively opposite Patrick Stewart in the epic documentary *MGM: When the Lion Roars* in 1992.

Leo's most prestigious live personal appearances came on January 22, 2014, on the occasion of the studio's ninetieth anniversary, when he placed his big paws in cement in the forecourt of Grauman's Chinese Theater on Hollywood Boulevard. Sylvester Stallone, who

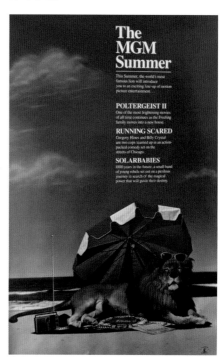

Leo (here portrayed by a magnificent animal named Zamba) relaxes at the beach to celebrate his studio's 1986 summer releases. *Nicholas Toth*

has admitted to owing his career to MGM (or, more accurately, to United Artists), was also there, alongside Leo, for the event. "We may have had the eye of the tiger," he (Stallone, not Leo) admitted to the crowd, "but it was the lion who put us on the map, he made it all happen."[6] Then Leo, here portrayed by a magnificent animal named Major, obediently stepped onto that cement slab and left his mark for the ages. Steve

Leo, now played by a lion named Major, was afforded the greatest single honor in the motion picture industry on January 22, 2014, when he placed his paws in cement in the forecourt of Grauman's Chinese Theater. MGM Chairman and CEO Gary Barber and Sylvester Stallone were among the attendees. Trainer Steve Martin holds the leash. *Steve Martin (www.workingwildlife.com)*

Martin, Major's trainer, tells us that they rehearsed the move in advance to get it just right. Even Jackie would have been proud of the resultant performance.

When that performance was over, Martin looked up to Stallone and quipped, "You're not going to beat up my lion, are you?" To which the two-legged superstar replied, "Very funny."[7]

LEO UNCAGED

Internally, and despite these sometimes comic examples, the studio's logo, and by extension, its self-image has largely remained publicly consistent, even reverential. But that has not been the case, to say the least, in other, outside media in the real world.

Perhaps the first outside-the-gates parodies of the studio logo were to be found in cartoons like Warner Bros.'s *Bosko's Picture Show* (1933), which featured a lion with laryngitis as the mascot of "TNT Pictures," anticipating the name of a Ted Turner cable network by sixty-five years.

Warner Bros.'s cartoon unit struck again in *She Was an Acrobat's Daughter* (1937), which depicted the "Warmer Bros." lion, who crows like a chicken and introduces a film within a film called "Petrified Florist."

Another cartoon, *Mother Goose Goes Hollywood*, appeared the following year. This one was distributed by RKO but produced by Walt Disney. Numerous MGM stars were caricatured, none more prominently than Leo the Lion, who was replaced in the opening gag by a roaring goose! The familiar banner above the bird's scrawny head replaces *Ars Gratia Artis* with *nuts to you*—and in pig Latin. Ouch.

Bob Clampett's manically animated Warner Bros. cartoon *Bacall to Arms* (1946) featured a scrawny lion again roaring under a "Warmer News" banner, although here it turns out that a lion cub is actually biting his tail even while setting it on fire. Some pertinent stock footage from *She Was an Acrobat's Daughter* is also reused here.

Outside of animation, jokes about MGM continued to show up in outside media during this period and beyond. Abbott and Costello, Jack Benny, and Jimmy Durante in their popular radio shows often referenced the logo and the lion on the air. Film and television comics, from Sid Caesar to *Family Guy* later did the same thing. For example, Mel Brooks, in *Silent Movie* (1976), rewrote Leo's motto to read *Ars est Pecunia* (*Art Is Money*). And the gonzo blockbuster *National Lampoon's Animal House* (1978) includes a three-fingered nod to MGM in the person of the unkempt Delta fraternity's unlikely and familiar logo, *Ars Gratia Artis*.

The internet is full of hundreds of homemade parody MGM logos. Some of these are clever indeed, and some are crude. Some are even pornographic. The web is also the home of baseless, long-debunked rumors regarding Leo allegedly killing his trainer and, depending on where you read about it, two hapless burglars as well—and all right after his big scene had been shot. Then there are those grisly and widely reproduced pictures of an Israeli lion named Samson, drugged-up and strapped to a table for a CT scan—which have then been digitally doctored to make him look like MGM's Leo, tied down and abused, presumably, to get him to roar on camera.

Perhaps the most visible and consistent parody of the logo on television has turned out to be Mary Tyler Moore's hyper-successful MTM Enterprises. MTM was a TV production company that was so successful that for almost thirty years it became its own studio. The MTM name was indeed originally intended to be a gentle satire of the older company, although they surely never dreamed in 1969 when they first used it that they would be using that spoof logo for so long. Accordingly, Moore's version features a gold ribbon similar to the original, but encircling a much smaller cat, a house kitten named Mimsy. But rather than roaring into the rafters, Mimsy instead meekly

Mimsy was Mary Tyler Moore's venerable kitten mascot, and she was cute too. *Author's collection*

meows. Mimsy herself, who would live from 1968 to 1998 eventually "costarred" with Leo himself when MGM acquired the Orion Pictures catalog, including MTM's *Just Between Friends* (1986).

With time, the MTM spoof logo also began to spoof itself. For example, the kitty was memorably replaced by the star herself in a 1973 *Mary Tyler Moore Show* episode in which she stutters "that's all folks." For MTM Christmas episodes, a holiday wreath would also be substituted for the loop around the cat's head, and she would sometimes be depicted meowing while wearing glasses or holding a TV remote. Finally, shortly after Mimsy's passing, the last episode of *St. Elsewhere* featured the pussycat rather poignantly on life support . . . and then flatlining.

Aptly enough, the MTM-MGM connection would also be evoked in a 1971 episode of Mary's show in which Leo's familiar roar is heard in a movie theater, causing a character watching the film to groan and say, "I saw this already."

Another beloved sitcom *The Dick Van Dyke Show* (1961–1966) had a Leo the Lion shout-out too. In one episode, Rose Marie tells a joke about two drunks in a zoo who are roared at by a caged lion. "Let's get out of here," the first one says. "We can't leave now," his friend slurs, "the movie's starting."

For its annual telecast of *The Wizard of Oz*, CBS hired entertainer Danny Kaye to host the program in 1964. And Kaye made certain to warn younger viewers, for some of whom this would be the first movie they had ever seen, not to be afraid when Leo roars at the beginning. His warm persona, and his commentary before the movie, was so liked by audiences that the network would rerun the movie and Kaye's introduction for the next three years.

On her variety show, and as noted previously, comedienne Carol Burnett occasionally took playful jabs at MGM and at the MGM lion. For example, in one episode Carol is positioned in Leo's traditional spot, letting rip a Tarzan yell for "Metro Goldwyn Mouth Studios." And in a studio salute episode she tells her audience that "of course, any tribute to MGM would not be complete without showing that magnificent creature that made MGM what it is today"—and then cutting to a picture of Elizabeth Taylor inside the logo.

Children's spoofs of Leo are oddly plentiful, considering that young demographic's presumed unfamiliarity with what exactly is being mocked. MGM lion references can be found in *Sesame Street*, *Pokémon*, *My Little Pony: Friendship Is Magic*, and, of course, *The Lionhearts*.

The feature cartoon *Cats Don't Dance* (1997) was set at the fictional Mammoth Pictures, whose familiar logo, instead of *Ars Gratia Artis* is *Optimum Est Maximum*.

Television's *Tiny Toon Adventures* (1990–1995) continued Warner Bros. Animation's long tradition of not-too-gently ribbing their rival by once featuring their popular character Furrball, a protégé of Sylvester the Cat, standing in for Leo. Elsewhere in kiddie entertainment, the Muppets, not at all surprisingly, have been particularly keen on the dissing on the lion, replacing him with the character of Animal or with Fozzie Bear (*Metro Goldwyn Bear*), as well as with assorted felt chickens, sheep, and Muppet Babies in various features and TV episodes documenting those beloved characters' adventures.

All these riffs on Leo's fragile dignity are by no means restricted to the US either. The British Monty Python feature *And Now for Something Completely Different* (1971) parodied the lion by substituting him with a less-than-majestic roaring . . . bunny. Likewise, a British TV show, *The Goodies* (1970–1982) once replaced the lion with a chicken. Farther afield, a 1978 Soviet film *Ograblenie po . . .* (which translates, kind of, as "Robbery . . . Style") featured a more-apt roaring lion, who then morphs into a famous Russian cartoon star named Cheburashka. There are also, it should be mentioned, reports of at least two Swedish features and a TV show all with comedic references to Leo the Lion. None of these reported comedies, it probably doesn't need to be noted, were directed by Ingmar Bergman.

Despite this love and derision, ultimately, Leo the Lion, like cinema itself, is finally an ephemeral thing. Outside of his lairs in Vegas and elsewhere and outside of cinema and souvenirs, there is no permanent, physical place to visit and commemorate this most famous feline's time on earth. That having been said, a museum in McPherson, Kansas, does have a lion skin on display, which was, allegedly, once sported by one of the actual on-screen Leos. This hide's provenance, however, is as moth-eaten as it itself is. The curators there won't even commit to which MGM cat this pelt once supposedly covered. Slats is the most likely candidate. Surely it wasn't Jackie the lucky?

Another tangible trace of our feline icon is to be found behind the Culver Hotel and just blocks away from Leo's old lair. "The Lion's Fountain" was commissioned by the city in 2004 and sculpted by Minneapolis artist Douglas Olmsted Freeman. But maybe this lion isn't a tribute to art for its own sake either. Culver City's official website takes pains to duly inform us that "although the theme for this art work is inspired by other lions associated with Culver City's movie studio history (MGM's Leo the Lion and the Cowardly Lion from *The Wizard of Oz*), this lion is neither a representation nor direct interpretation of either of these felines."[8] Okay then.

But take heart, another equally physical and authorized remnant of the lion and his times still exists nearby as well. In the dark and perpetual twilight of a cavernous

Douglas Olmsted Freeman's "The Lion's Fountain" sculpture in Culver City isn't based on any particular Culver City lion, right? *Author's collection*

warehouse in downtown Los Angeles for many years sat the big MGM sign—in fact, it was the biggest MGM sign ever made—fifteen tons in all, 21 feet high, 105 feet long, and complete with the 3000-pound, 32-feet-wide lion emblem that once majestically surveyed his vast kingdom from the top of Stage 6 on the lot, and which, on clear days, brave employees could once climb to the pinnacle of and look east from—all the way to the Hollywood sign.

It was this mighty edifice, at least in part, which was eventually disassembled, salvaged, and then finally rebuilt across the street when the studio retreated there in November 1986. On June 11, 1987, there was an official unveiling of the sign in its new location, with fireworks, a live lion, and Gene Kelly in attendance as the guest of honor.

And this Leo's travels were not yet over. In 1991, when MGM relocated yet again, this behemoth alpha-lion was, sadly, found to be too large and too heavy for its studio's new office complexes in Beverly Hills and then in Santa Monica. Culver City officials had originally thought the sign too large for its previous home too but had been inclined, eventually, to look the other way, but Santa Monica, ultimately, could

The big sign in its longtime home on the roof of Stage 6. *Bison Archives*

Even in its earliest incarnation, the sign attracted studio employees, such as Robert Florey (left), in search of a photo op (1920s). *Bison Archives*

The addition of neon to the big sign, although not long lasting, was a nice touch. *Bison Archives*

A rare look inside the sign in the early 1970s. *Donald Norden (www.phantomofthebacklots.com)*

Leo the Lion vacates the lot forever in November, 1986 . . . *Bison Archives*

likewise not be bribed to allow MGM to assemble this veritable Hollywood sphinx on one of its single-story cinderblock-supported rooftops there. Therefore, Leo and his accompanying signage was unceremoniously warehoused.

It needn't have been a life sentence. Several years ago, Hollywood Heritage, a notable Los Angeles preservation organization, inquired as to borrowing and displaying this largest, and heaviest, of all of Hollywood's seemingly lost artifacts in some place where the public could appreciate and gawk at it. And MGM management, to its credit, was not really averse to the idea (think of the publicity!) either. On the initial call, the company only asked when the organization wanted to come and pick it up! Unfortunately, on the second meeting studio lawyers got involved and produced a draconian list of admittedly sometimes reasonable requirements about where actually their sign would be displayed and how and who exactly would maintain it while it was. Ultimately, it turned out that the DeMille-sized costs to meet such requirements

…and moves across the street (1989 photo). *Rob Gold*

would have been cosmically, breathtakingly prohibitive. And so, the idea, most reluctantly by everyone, was ultimately, regrettably, scrapped.

A few years later, sadly, as part of yet another cost-cutting measure, it was decided to only retain the center circlet piece containing Leo himself for posterity and so the vast "Metro-Goldwyn-Mayer" panels were reportedly destroyed.

Thus, this largest of all the MGM lions in all the world, at least outside of Las Vegas, presumably still waits, still crouches in a dark warehouse—a battered, faded, feral star, waiting to roar again.

Appendix

Lords of the Lion

When I undertook this book, I was dismayed to discover that no one, in all of the research undertaken and books written about MGM, had ever attempted to compile any sort of comprehensive listing of either the CEOs or the heads of production at the studio from its founding to the present day. It's pretty easy to chart the company's first quarter-century, when the ying-and-yang duo of Louis B. Mayer and Nicholas Schenck ruled supreme. But after that, well, a person would have to be slightly crazy to attempt to chart movements of the executive musical chairs, which, largely from then on, have ensued.

Fortunately, in 2004, on the occasion of the studio's eightieth anniversary, some anonymous researcher at *Variety*, bless his or her heart, was just crazy enough to attempt to solve just such a Rubik's cube of conflicting titles and overlapping corporate responsibilities. To this obviously slightly daft individual then, we all owe our thanks and our gratitude for the following list.

Unfortunately, and yes, unsurprisingly, when I attempted to verify all the rotating names on this MGM Rosetta Stone I discovered a few forgivable omissions and errors, however. Several musical chair corporate shuffles had been omitted entirely. And there had been even more Machiavellian shake-ups, shankings, coups, corporate takeovers, and outmaneuvering since the list had been published, which, the brave author of that list, again whoever he or she was, surely cannot be held responsible for, right?

I too might well have missed a head of production or a chief operating officer or two in the following text. Although, please note that I have not tried to track parallel

Succession of presidents and studio heads
Metro-Goldwyn-Mayer:

Presidents:

Nicholas M. Schenck

Arthur Loew

Joseph Vogel

Robert O'Brien

Louis Polk

James Aubrey *1969 - 1973*

FRANK Rosenfelt

Studio heads:

Louis B. Mayer

Dore Schary *1948 - 1956*

Benjamin Thau *1956 - 1958*

Sol C. Siegel *1958 -*

Robert Weitman *1962*

Clark Ramsey *1967*

Herbert F. Solow *1969*

DAVID MELNICK
DICK SHEPHARD *1973*

DAVE BEGELMAN *1980*

An internal studio document from 1980 honeycombed with annotations, cross outs, and erasures, written by an unnamed employee who was apparently trying to keep track of who his (or her) boss was on that particular day. *Author's collection* and concurrent (post-1981) United Artist management teams. I did this to try to avoid confusion, a well-meaning if naive assumption, which has occasionally backfired on me because it turns out MGM/UA CEOs and presidents sometimes tended to hop back and forth between the two companies, making the timeline of their employment sometimes even more problematic.

Specific titles and responsibilities have also obviously changed over the years, sometimes making it difficult to fathom who the modern-day equivalent of a boss like Mayer or Schenck really is anymore. After all, does anyone really understand the difference between a motion picture group chair and a motion picture group president? I sure don't.

Daniel Melnick, who was a head of production in the 1970s once reportedly admitted that he took the job "because one does not often get the chance to climb into the shoes of an Irving Thalberg."[1] True enough, but the truth is that, although Thalberg undisputedly headed production at MGM, he never officially did hold that title. Instead, the boy wonder was actually, usually referred to instead as the "vice president in charge of production." Therefore, Melnick has a key spot on this list, but Thalberg, strange as it seems, is here relegated to the status of an also-ran.

I've also avoided overlords who might have had power in the boardroom, or even owned the company, or part of it, outright but were never officially titled as a CEO of MGM itself. Therefore, Kirk Kerkorian, in this one section at least, fails to make an appearance, as does, more recently Kevin Ulrich, and presumably soon, Jeff Bezos.

Despite all of this minutia, maybe *because* of all of this minutia, I hope you find the following information helpful. Both for its own sake and as crib notes in digesting the rest of this volume, if only because these names, both legendary and obscure, represent a first-ever, confounding, sad, and reasonably comprehensive (at least as of 2022) rap sheet regarding the tenures of all of the "official" lords of the lion.

CEO	Head of Production
Nicholas Schenck (1924–1955)	Louis B. Mayer (1924–1951)
	and Irving Thalberg (1924–1936)
	and Dore Schary (1948–1951)
Arthur M. Loew (1955–1956)	Dore Schary (1951–1956)
Joseph Vogel (1956–1963)	Ben Thau (1956–1958)
	Sol C. Siegel (1958–1962)
Robert H. O'Brien (1963–1969)	Robert M. Weitman (1962–1967)

CEO	Head of Production
Edgar Bronfman Sr. (1969) and Louis F. "Bo" Polk Jr. (1969)	G. Clark Ramsay (1967–1969)
James Aubrey (1969–1973)	Herbert Solow (1969–1970)
	and Douglas Netter (1970–1975)
	and Jack Haley Jr. (1972)
Frank Rosenfelt (1973–1981)	Daniel Melnick (1972–1978)
	Richard Shepherd (1978–1980)
	David Begelman (1980–1981)
Donald Sipes (1981–1982)	Freddie Fields (1981–1982)
Frank Rothman (1982–1986)	Frank Yablans (1983–1984)
	Jay Kanter (1984)
Lee Rich (1986–1988)	Alan Ladd Jr. (1985–1988)
Stephen Silbert (1988)	
Jeffrey Barbakow (1988–1990)	Richard Berger (1988–1990)
Giancarlo Parretti (1990–1991)	Alan Ladd Jr. (1990–1991)
Alan Ladd Jr. (1992–1993) and Dennis Stanfill (1992)	Jay Kanter (1991–1993)
Frank Mancuso Sr. (1993–1999)	Mike Marcus (1993–1997)
	Michael Nathanson (1997–2004)
Alex Yemenidjian (1999–2005) and Chris McGurk (1999–2005)	
Harry E. Sloan (2005–2009)	Daniel Taylor (2006)
	Rick Sands (2006–2008)
Stephen Cooper (2009)	Mary Parent (2008–2010)
Roger Birnbaum (2010–2012) and Gary Barber (2010–2012)	Jonathan Glickman (2011–2020)
Gary Barber (2012–2018)	
Christopher Brearton (2018–)	Pamela Abdy (2020–)

Acknowledgments

During this book's gestation, I kept wishing I could talk again to so many of the writers and performers and historians and executives who were so kind to myself and to my coauthors Michael Troyan and Stephen X. Sylvester, during the writing of our first studio book, *MGM: Hollywood's Ultimate Backlot* and who returned to assist on many of my/our subsequent books as well. Sadly, so many of them have since passed away, which makes me conscious indeed of both the passing of time and of the importance of sometimes asking questions beyond the scope of whatever one's current project may then be.

Fortunately, in a few instances I did just that. In 2010, executive Roger Mayer and his charming wife Pauline invited me to their home in Beverly Hills for what turned out to be a wide-ranging but MGM-centric talk over coffee and cake. Roger was not related to Louis B. Mayer, but he was an influential force for good at Mayer's old studio for decades. We are all in his debt for the countless vital restoration and preservation decisions he cajoled or charmed his sometimes-coldhearted bosses into financing. I wish I could thank him again for that, for that day, and for some of his stories and opinions that I've then been able to pilfer here.

Likewise, there have been, most regrettably, many other late historians or studio veterans who in the past were helpful and generous in sharing their memories or perspectives with me regarding MGM. I so wish I could talk to them again now for that reason, as well as for others. Although reading this manuscript, I've noticed that, in many cases, their opinions, either duly credited or appropriated by me, have still found their way into this text. So, due thanks to you again: Richard Anderson, Rudy Behlmer, Robert S. Birchard, Billy Blackburn, Earl Hamner Jr., Brainard Miller, Robert W. Nudelman, Debbie Reynolds, Walter Seltzer, and to many others too.

Fortunately, there are a lot of MGM people still out there. As belabored in the text, there has been a lot of consistently worthwhile writing about the studio in recent decades. I've relied on this material for both facts and personal opinions, probably more than I sometimes should have, due to the inaccessibility of archives and private collections and primary research during the last year of this book's preparation during a worldwide pandemic. In some ways, I suppose this is apt because a central tenant of *The MGM Effect*, after all, has been the studio's outside contributions to our larger world.

I've tried to credit all of this material in the bibliography, but the work of three authors, none of whom I know personally, was particularly useful. Scott Eyman's *Lion of Hollywood: The Life and Legend of Louis B. Mayer* is both well-researched and sympathetic and is a good read as well. William C. Rempel's *The Gambler: How Penniless Dropout Kirk Kerkorian Became the Greatest Deal Maker in Capitalist History* was useful in helping me navigate the corridors of big business outside of Hollywood's thirty-mile zone. And Peter Bart, both in his book *Fade Out* and his long-running *Variety* columns, consistently offered a bemused, boots-on-the-ground perspective on both the enigma that was Kerkorian and on the lion's long winter. Bart is such a consummate Hollywood insider that I never could get him to agree to an interview.

Those I did interview, usually over the phone, via Zoom, or email are also dutifully listed in the bibliography and here. I've tried to date our conversations, but some of those conversations, to the subject's probable horror, ebbed or flowed over days or even months. I want to thank all the participants for dealing with me and answering my questions. Any mistakes I made in transcribing your answers are mine—although I'm afraid you'll now forever have to answer for them.

In particular, Greg Gormick was helpful in untangling MGM's musical history—some of which we shamelessly pillaged from his own upcoming book *The Lion's Serenade*.

I'd also like to thank my essayists, Woolsey Ackerman, Tommy Hines, Richard Kingcott, and Donnie Norden, for writing down their personal stories about their life-long relationship to the studio and what that relationship has meant to them. Donnie recently published his own unique book on the subject, *Phantom of the Backlots Present: Hole in the Fence*, which, trust me, you are going to want to read.

Additionally, I'd like to thank the following and acknowledge their support and encouragement and willingness to share their materials over the long gestation process of this book, namely, Richard Adkins, Marilyn Allen, Ron Barbagallo, John Bengston, Michael Benson, John Bertram, Michael F. Blake, David Bowen, Scott Brogan, Krista Christofferson, Ned Comstock, David English, Mike Escarzaga, John Escobar, Christian Esquevin, Rob Feeney, Robert Florczak, Rob Gold, Darryl M. Haase, Danny Hancock, Jon Heitland, Carl Hymans, Rob Klein, Kristine Krueger (of the AMPAS Margaret Herrick Library), Robert Lane, Steve Martin, Alicia Mayer, John Mcelwee, Naomi Minkoff, Scott Moore, Larry McQueen, Les Perkins, Ana Maria Quintana, Sharon Rich, Rick Rinehart, Richard W. Smith, Steven C. Smith, E. J. Stephens, William Stillman, Stephen X. Sylvester, Stan Taffel, Karl Thiede, Frank Thompson, Nicholas Toth, Michael Troyan, Martin Turnbull, Gary Wayne, Werner Weiss, Robert Welch, Josh Young, Charles Ziarko, and Deana Zvara.

Many of the photographs reproduced here come to me via Marc Wanamaker and the Bison Archives. I've never written a book without Marc's assistance. I hope I never have to.

This book is for my parents, and for Beth and Zoe.

Notes

CHAPTER 1

1. Eyman, *Lion of Hollywood.*
2. Ibid.
3. Marx, *Mayer and Thalberg.*
4. Kanin, *Hollywood.*
5. Higham, *Merchant of Dreams.*

CHAPTER 2

1. Thompson, "The House that Mr. Mayer Built."
2. Schwartz, with Schwartz, *The Hollywood Writers' Wars.*
3. Epstein, *Essays in Biography.*
4. Fitzgerald, *The Last Tycoon.*
5. "Screen Genius' Death Stuns Industry's Heads."
6. Flamini, *Thalberg.*
7. Eyman, *Lion of Hollywood.*
8. Marx, *Mayer and Thalberg.*
9. Eyman, *Lion of Hollywood.*
10. "Trust Everyone, but Cut the Cards."

11. Wellman, *A Short Time for Insanity.*
12. Hay, *MGM.*
13. Powell, *The Girl Next Door . . . and How She Grew.*
14. Reynolds, with Columbia, *Debbie.*
15. Higham, *Merchant of Dreams.*
16. Davies, *The Times We Had.*

CHAPTER 3

1. Minnelli, *I Remember It Well.*
2. Higham, *Merchant of Dreams.*
3. Knepper, *Sodom and Gomorrah.*
4. Crowther, *Hollywood Rajah.*
5. Schary, *Heyday.*
6. *MGM: When the Lion Roars*, 1992 documentary miniseries.
7. Jarman, *My Life and the Final Days of Hollywood.*
8. Eyman, *Lion of Hollywood.*
9. *MGM: When the Lion Roars.*
10. Hamilton and Stadiem, *Don't Mind If I Do.*
11. Roger Mayer, interview with author, 2010.

CHAPTER 4

1. Rempel, *The Gambler.*
2. Roger Mayer, interview with author, 2010.
3. Rempel, *The Gambler.*
4. "The Lion and the Cobra."
5. Douglas, *The Ragman's Son.*
6. Rempel, *The Gambler.*
7. Greg Gormick, interview with author, July 2020.
8. Rempel, *The Gambler.*
9. Harwood, "Just What Has Kerkorian Sold? MGM's Not What It Used to Be."
10. Bart, *Fade Out.*
11. "Kerkorian: The Man vs. the Myths."

12. Di Stefano, *The MGM Connection*.
13. Nicholas Toth, interview with author, June 2021.
14. Di Stefano, *The MGM Connection*.
15. Bart, "Enigmatic Krikorian and MGM Were Never a Good Fit."
16. Di Stefano, *The MGM Connection*.
17. Ibid.
18. Bart, "Sometimes a Roaring Silence Is Best."
19. Brennan, "CAA Prods Bank to Feed Its Pet Lion."
20. Vincent and Eller, "MGM to Move from Luxurious Century City Offices."
21. "UA Started with Artists in Lead Role."
22. Bart, "Enigmatic Kerkorian and MGM Were Never a Good Fit."
23. Vincent and Eller, "MGM to Move from Luxurious Century City Offices."
24. Lang and Spangler, "Amazon Buys MGM, Studio behind James Bond, for $8.45 Billion."

CHAPTER 5

1. Pykett, *MGM British Studios*.
2. Ibid.
3. Ibid.
4. "Paul Mills Last to Go."
5. Roger Mayer, interview with author, 2010.
6. James Spada, *The Secret Life of a Princess: An Intimate Biography of Grace Kelly*.
7. Bart, *Fade Out*.
8. Richard, "It's Official: New Biloxi Ballpark to be MGM Park."
9. Svetkey, "The Tonight Show's Greenroom at 30,000 Feet."
10. Stephen X. Sylvester, interview with author, May 2021.
11. *MGM: When the Lion Roars*, 1992 documentary miniseries.
12. Bart, *Fade Out*.
13. Grover, *The Disney Touch*.
14. *Echo in the Canyon*, 2018 documentary.
15. Morse, "MGM Theater of the Air."
16. Zicree, *The Twilight Zone Companion*.
17. "MGM Lionizes Versatile New Video Tape System."
18. Riedel, "The Lion that Ruled 42nd Street."

19. Cox and Rooney, "B'way Opens Screen Door."
20. Hofler, "Lion Goes Legit."
21. "Blown Away."
22. Stalter, "MGM Plans Pilots for Net."
23. Hanna, *A Cast of Friends.*

CHAPTER 6

1. Capra, *The Name above the Title.*
2. Picker, "All in the Family."
3. Murphy, *Say. . . Didn't You Used to Be George Murphy?*
4. MGM 90th Year Anniversary: Paw Print Ceremony Sizzle Reel—YouTube
5. Guber, *Tell to Win.*
6. Winkler, *A Life in Movies.*
7. Clarke, *Get Happy.*
8. Alicia Mayer, interview with author, December 2020, supplemented by comments on her blog, "The film Colony," at hollywoodessays.com.
9. Ibid.
10. Ibid.
11. Ibid.
12. Ibid.
13. Ibid.
14. Silver, "Mr. Film Noir Stays at the Table."
15. Zinnemann, *Fred Zinnemann.*
16. Crowther, *Hollywood Rajah.*
17. "NY Times' Bosley Crowther Discusses 'What You Don't Know about the Movies.'"
18. Loy and Kotsilibas-Davis, *Myrna Loy.*
19. Marx, *Mayer and Thalberg.*
20. Carey, *All the Stars in Heaven.*
21. Ibid.
22. Selznick, *A Private View.*
23. Altman, *Hollywood East.*
24. Ibid.
25. Carey, *All the Stars in Heaven.*

26. Marx, *The Grouchophile.*
27. Marx, *Harpo Speaks!*
28. Barrymore, as told to Shipp, *We Barrymores.*
29. Ibid.
30. Ardmore, *The Self-Enchanted.*
31. Rooney, *I.E.*
32. *MGM: When the Lion Roars*, 1992 documentary miniseries.
33. Horne with Schickel, *Lena.*
34. Lamarr, *Ecstasy and Me.*
35. Ibid.
36. Gish with Pinchot, *Lillian Gish.*
37. Murphy, *Say . . . Didn't You Used to Be George Murphy?*
38. Miller with Browning, *Miller's High Life.*
39. Davies, *The Times We Had.*
40. Ibid.
41. Turner, *Lana.*
42. Loy and Kotsilibas-Davis, *Myrna Loy.*
43. Ibid.
44. Powell, *The Girl Next Door . . . and How She Grew.*
45. Reynolds with Columbia, *Debbie.*
46. Douglas, *The Ragman's Son.*
47. Gardner, *Ava.*
48. Hepburn, *Me.*
49. Welles and Bogdanovich, *This Is Orson Wells.*
50. Ebsen, *The Other Side of Oz.*
51. Rich, *Sweethearts*, supplemented by interview with author, May 2021.
52. Garrett with Rapoport, *Betty Garrett, and Other Songs.*
53. Gottfried, *Balancing Act.*
54. Williams with Diehl, *The Million Dollar Mermaid.*
55. Fitzgerald, *The Pat Hobby Stories.*
56. Schwartz with Schwartz, *The Hollywood Writers' Wars.*
57. Saroyan, *Letters from 74 Rue Taitbout or Don't Go But If You Must Say Hello to Everybody.*
58. Kaminsky, *Murder on the Yellow Brick Road.*
59. Martin Turnbull, interview with author, October 2020.
60. O'Nan, *West of Sunset.*

61. Koslow, *Another Side of Paradise*.
62. Benjamin, *The Girls in the Picture*.
63. Porter, *Beautiful Invention*.
64. Benedict, *The Only Woman in the Room*.
65. Letts, *Finding Dorothy*.

CHAPTER 7

1. Cumberbatch, "Tom Hiddleston."
2. Gutner, *MGM Style*.
3. "I Love *The Women* . . .".
4. Marx, *Mayer and Thalberg*.
5. Welkos, "The Case of the Missing Mansion."
6. Matukonis-Adkins, *Adrian*.
7. Ibid.
8. Greg Gormick, interview with the author, July 2020.
9. Ibid.
10. Salinger, *The Catcher in the Rye*.
11. Puma, *7 Arts Number Three*.
12. Jacobs with illustrations by Drucker, "What's Entertainment?"
13. Ibid.

CHAPTER 8

1. Hogan, "MGM."
2. https://www.presidency.ucsb.edu/documents/american-film-institute-remarks-reception-the-occasion-the-loth-anniversary-the-institute.
3. "Playboy Interview: Donald Trump."
4. Justin, "Why Jessica Lange Is Minnesota's Greatest Actor."
5. Thomas, *The Ruby Slippers of Oz*.
6. https://www.youtube.com/watch?v=JB6K1PHb5tM.
7. Rob Feeney, interview with author, April 2021.
8. Stenn, "It Happened One Night . . . at MGM."

9. Ibid.
10. Ibid.

CHAPTER 9

1. Bingen, Sylvester, and Troyan, *M-G-M*.
2. Kilday, "Beyond Nine Lives."
3. Phillips, "Creating $ in Its Own Image."
4. Ross, *Picture*.
5. Graham, "Confessions of Leo the Lion."
6. https://www.youtube.com/watch?v=OIfsb7paSnI&t=12s.
7. Steve Martin, interview with author, June 2021.
8. https://www.culvercity.org/Public-Art/The-Lion%E2%80%99s-Fountain.

APPENDIX

1. Bart, *Fade Out*.

Bibliography

BOOKS: NONFICTION

Allyson, June, with Francis Spatz Leighton. *June Allyson*. New York: G. P. Putnam's Sons, 1982.

Altman, Diana. *Hollywood East: Louis B. Mayer and the Origins of the Studio System*. New York: Birch Lane Press, 1992.

Anger Kenneth. *Hollywood Babylon*. San Francisco: Straight Arrow Books, 1975 (originally published in 1959).

Ardmore, Jane Kesner. *The Self-Enchanted: Mae Murray, Image of an Era*. New York: McGraw-Hill, 1959.

Astaire, Fred. *Steps in Time*. New York: Harper & Brothers, 1959.

Aylesworth, Thomas G. *The Best of MGM*. New York: Gallery Nooks, 1986.

Balio, Tino. *MGM: Routledge Hollywood Centenary Series*. Abingdon-on-Thames, UK: Routledge, 2018.

Barber, Bill. *The Best Is Yet to Come: A Life that Went from the Lion of Metro Goldwyn Mayer to the Lion of Judah*. Shippensburg, PA: Relate to God Ministries, 2017.

Barbera, Joseph. *My Life in Toons: From Flatbush to Bedrock in Under a Century*. Atlanta: Turner Publishing, 1994.

Barrymore, Lionel, as told to Cameron Shipp. *We Barrymores*. New York: Appleton-Century-Crofts, Inc., 1951.

Bart, Peter. *Fade Out*. New York: HarperCollins, 1990.

Baxter, John. *King Vidor*. New York: Monarch Press, 1976.

Benson, Michael. *Space Odyssey: Stanley Kubrick, Arthur C. Clark and the Making of a Masterpiece*. New York: Simon & Schuster, 2018.

Bergen, Ronald. *The United Artists Story*. New York: Crown Publishers, 1986.

Billecci, Frank. *Irene: A Designer from the Golden Age of Hollywood: The MGM Years (1942–1949)*. Atglen, PA: Schiffer, 2014.

Bingen, Steven, Stephen X. Sylvester, and Michael Troyan. *M-G-M: Hollywood's Greatest Backlot*. Solana Beach, CA: Santa Monica Press, 2011.

Bizony, Piers. *The Making of Kubrick's 2001: A Space Odyssey*. Cologne, Germany: Taschen, 2020.

Blake, Michael F. *Lon Chaney: The Man Behind the Thousand Faces*. Lanham, MD: Vestal Press, 1997.

Braitman, Jacqueline R. *She Damn Near Ran the Studio: The Extraordinary Lives of Ida R. Koverman*. Jackson: University Press of Mississippi, 2020.

Brown, Peter H., and Pamela Brown. *MGM Girls: Behind the Velvet Curtain*. New York: St. Martin's Press, 1983.

Canemaker, John. *Tex Avery: The MGM Years*. Atlanta: Turner Publishing, 1996.

Capra, Frank. *The Name above the Title*. Boston: Da Capo Press, 1997 (originally published in 1971).

Carey, Gary. *All the Stars in Heaven: Louis B. Mayer's MGM*. New York: E. P. Dutton, 1981.

Carrol, Willard. *I Toto: The Autobiography of Terry, the Dog Who Was Toto*. New York: Harry N. Abrams, 2013.

Clarke, Gerald. *Get Happy: The Life of Judy Garland*. New York: Random House, 2000.

Coakley, Deirdre, with Hank Greenspun and Gary G. Gerard. *The Day the MGM Grand Hotel Burned*. Secaucus, NJ: Lyle Stuart Inc., 1982.

Cooper, Jackie, with Dick Kleiner. *Please Don't Shoot My Dog*. New York: William Morrow & Company, 1981.

Crawford, Joan. *A Portrait of Joan: The Autobiography of Joan Crawford*. Los Angeles: Graymallkin Media, 2017 (originally published in 1962).

Crowther, Bosley. *Hollywood Rajah: The Life and Times of Louis B. Mayer*. New York: Dell Publishing Company, 1961.

——. *The Lion's Share: The Story of an Entertainment Empire*. New York: E. P. Dutton, 1957.

Davies, Marion. *The Times We Had*. Edited by Pamela Pfau and Kenneth S. Marx. New York: Ballantine Books, 1975.

Denkert, Darcie. *A Fine Romance: Hollywood/Broadway (The Magic. The Mayhem. The Musicals.)*. New York: Billboard Books, 2005.

Di Stefano, Giovanni. *The MGM Connection*. Independently published, 2013.

Douglas, Kirk. *The Ragman's Son*. New York: Simon & Schuster, 1988.

Eames, John Douglas. *The MGM Story*. New York: Crown Publishers, 1990 (originally published in 1975).

Ebsen, Buddy. *The Other Side of Oz*. Newport Beach, CA: Donovan Publishing, 1993.

Eells, George. *Hedda and Louella*. New York: G. P. Putnam's Sons, 1972.

Eyman, Scott. *Lion of Hollywood: The Life and Legend of Louis B. Mayer*. New York: Simon & Schuster, 2005.

Fawell, John W. *The Student Prince in Old Heidelberg: The Art of Classical Hollywood*. Lanham, MD: Lexington Books, 2018.

Flamini, Roland. *Thalberg: The Last Tycoon and the World of M-G-M*. New York: Crown Publishers, Inc., 1994.

Fleming, E. J. *Paul Bern: The Life and Famous Death of the MGM Director and Husband of Harlow*. Jefferson, NC: McFarland, 2009.

——. *The Fixers: Eddie Mannix, Howard Strickling and the MGM Publicity Machine*. Jefferson, NC: McFarland, 2015.

Fordin, Hugh. *M-G-M's Greatest Musicals: The Arthur Freed Unit*. Boston: Da Capo Press, 1996 (originally published in 1975 as *The World of Entertainment! Hollywood's Greatest Musicals*).

Friedrich, Otto. *City of Nets: A Portrait of Hollywood in the 1940's*. New York: Harper & Row, 1986.

Gabler, Neil. *An Empire of Their Own: How the Jews Invented Hollywood*. New York: Doubleday & Company, 1988.

Gallagher, John Andrew, and Frank Thompson. *Nothing Sacred: The Cinema of William Wellman*. Asheville, NC: Men with Wings Press, 2018.

Gardner, Ava. *Ava: My Story*. New York: Bantam Books, 1990.

Garrett, Betty, with Ron Rapoport. *Betty Garrett, and Other Songs: A Life on Stage and Screen*. Lanham, MD: Madison Books, 1998.

Gillespie, A. Arnold. Edited by Robert Welch. *The Wizard of MGM*. Orlando: BearManor Media, 2012.

Gish, Lillian, with Ann Pinchot. *Lillian Gish: The Movies, Mr. Griffith, and Me*. Englewood Cliffs, NJ: Prentice Hall, Inc., 1969.

Gottfried, Martin. *Balancing Act: The Authorized Biography of Angela Lansbury*. Boston: Little Brown & Company, 1999.

Graham, Sheilah. *Beloved Infidel: The Education of a Woman*. New York: Henry Holt and Company, 1958.

Griffin, Nancy, and Kim Masters. *Hit and Run: How Jon Peters and Peter Guber Took Sony for a Ride in Hollywood*. New York: Simon & Schuster, 1997.

Griffith, Richard, and Arthur Mayer. *The Movies: The Sixty-Year Story of the World of Hollywood and Its Effect on America*. New York: Bonanza, 1957.

Grover, Ron. *The Disney Touch: How a Daring Management Team Revived an Entertainment Empire*. Homewood, IL: Business One Irwin, 1991.

Guber, Peter. *Tell to Win*. New York: Currency Publishers, 2011.

Gutner, Howard. *MGM Style*. Guilford, CT: Lyons Press, 2019.

——. *Gowns by Adrian: The MGM Years (1928–1941)*. New York: Harry N. Abrams, 2001.

Hamilton, George, and William Stadiem. *Don't Mind If I Do*. New York: Touchstone, Simon & Schuster, 2008.

Hanna, William. *A Cast of Friends*. Dallas: Taylor Publishing, 1996.

Harmetz, Aljean. *The Making of* The Wizard of Oz, *75th Anniversary Edition*. Chicago: Chicago Review Press, 2013 (originally published in 1989).

Haver, Ronald. *David O. Selznick's Hollywood*. New York: Alfred A. Knopf, 1980.

Hay, Peter. *MGM: When the Lion Roars*. Atlanta: Turner Publishing, 1991.

Hepburn, Katharine. *Me: Stories of My Life*. New York: Ballantine Books, 1991.

Hess, Earl J. *Singin' in the Rain: The Making of an American Masterpiece*. Lawrence: University Press of Kansas, 2009.

Higham, Charles. *Merchant of Dreams: Louis B. Mayer, M.G.M and the Secret Hollywood*. New York: Donald J. Fine, Inc., 1993.

Horne, Lena, with Richard Schickel. *Lena*. New York: Doubleday & Company, 1965.

Huston, John. *An Open Book*. New York: Alfred A. Knopf, 1980.

Isackes, Richard, and Karen Maness. *The Art of the Hollywood Backdrop*. Cypress, CA: Regan Arts, 2016.

Jarman, Claude Jr. *My Life and the Final Days of Hollywood*. Murrells Inlet, SC: Covenant Books, Inc., 2018.

Kanin, Garson. *Hollywood*. New York: Viking Press, 1974.

Keaton, Buster, with Charles Samuels. *My Wonderful World of Slapstick*. New York: Doubleday & Company, 1960.

Knepper, Max. *Sodom and Gomorrah: The Story of Hollywood*. Los Angeles: self-published, 1935.

Knowles, Eleanor. *The Films of Jeanette MacDonald and Nelson Eddy*. Lancaster, Lancashire, UK: Gazelle Book Services Ltd., 1976.

Knox, Donald. *The Magic Factory: How MGM Made an American in Paris*. Westport, CT: Praeger Publishers, 1973.

Koszarski, Richard. *The Man You Loved to Hate: Erich von Stroheim and Hollywood.* Oxford: Oxford University Press, 1983.

Lamarr, Hedy. *Ecstasy and Me: My Life as a Woman.* New York: Bartholomew House, 1966.

Larkin, T. Lawrence. *In Search of Marie-Antoinette in the 1930's: Stefan Zweig, Irving Thalberg, and Norma Shearer.* London: Palgrave Macmillan, 2019.

Lever, James, and Cheeta. *Me Cheeta: My Life in Hollywood.* New York: Ecco, 2010.

Loy, Myrna, and James Kotsilibas-Davis. *Myrna Loy: Being and Becoming.* New York: Alfred A. Knopf, 1987.

Maltin, Leonard, ed. *Hollywood: The Movie Factory.* New York: Popular Library, 1976.

Marx, Groucho. *The Grouchophile: An Illustrated Life.* New York: Pocket Books, 1977.

Marx, Harpo. *Harpo Speaks!* Lanham, MI: Limelight, 2004 (originally published in 1961).

Marx, Samuel. *Mayer and Thalberg: The Make-Believe Saints.* New York: Random House, 1975.

Matukonis-Adkins, Richard. *Adrian: American Designer, Hollywood Original.* Independently published, 2020.

Miller, Ann, with Norma Lee Browning. *Miller's High Life.* New York: Doubleday & Company, 1972.

Miller, Frank. *MGM Posters: The Golden Years.* Atlanta, GA: Turner Publishing, 1994.

Minnelli, Vincente. *I Remember It Well.* New York: Doubleday & Company, 1974.

Montgomery, Elizabeth Miles. *The Best of MGM.* Darby, PA: Bison Books Corporation, 1994.

Moreno, Rita. *Rita Moreno: A Memoir.* New York: Celebra, 2013.

Murphy, George. *Say . . . Didn't You Used to Be George Murphy?* New York: Bartholomew House Ltd., 1970.

Nixon, Marni, with Stephen Cole. *I Could Have Sung All Night.* New York: Billboard Books, 2006.

Norden, Donald. *Phantom of the Backlots Present: Hole in the Fence.* Independently published, 2021.

Novitsky, Edward, and Michael Ruppli. *The MGM Labels [3 volumes]: A Discography.* Santa Barbara, CA: ABC-CLIO LLC, 1998.

Parish James Robert, and Ronald L. Bowers. *The MGM Stock Company: The Golden Era.* New York: Arlington House Publishers, 1974.

Parish, James Robert and Gregory W. Mank. *The Best of M-G-M: The Golden Years (1928–1959).* New York: Arlington House Publishers, 1981.

Parish, James Robert, Michael R. Pitts, and Gregory W. Mank. *Hollywood on Hollywood.* Metuchen, NJ: Scarecrow Press, 1978.

Peary, Danny. *Cult Movies.* New York: Delacorte Press, 1981.

Ponedel, Dorothy, Meredith Ponedel, and Danny Miller. *About Face: The Life and Times of Dottie Ponedel, Make-up Artist to the Stars.* Orlando: BearManor Media, 2018.

Powell, Jane. *The Girl Next Door . . . and How She Grew.* New York: William Morrow & Company, 1988.

Pykett, Derek. *MGM British Studios: Hollywood in Borehamwood.* Orlando: BearManor Media, 2015.

Rempel, William C. *The Gambler: How Penniless Dropout Kirk Kerkorian Became the Greatest Deal Maker in Capitalist History.* New York: Dey Street Books, 2018.

Reynolds, Debbie, with David Patrick Columbia. *Debbie: My Life.* New York: William Morrow & Company, 1988.

Rich, Sharon. *Sweethearts: The Timeless Love Affair—On-Screen and Off—Between Jeanette MacDonald and Nelson Eddy—Updated 20th Anniversary Edition.* New York: Bell Harbour Press, 2014 (originally published in 1994).

——. *Jeanette MacDonald Autobiography: The Lost Manuscript.* New York: Bell Harbour Press, 2004.

Rooney, Mickey. *I.E., An Autobiography.* New York: Putnam, 1965.

——. *Life Is Too Short.* New York: Villard Books, 1991.

Ross, Lillian. *Picture.* New York: NYRB Classics, 2019 (originally published in 1952).

Rothman, Howard. *50 Companies that Changed the World.* Franklin Lakes, NJ: Career Press, 2001.

Rowley, Don, and Mary E. MacDonald. *MGM Students Movie Stars*. Independently published, 2020.

Russo, William, and Jan Merlin. *MGM Makes Boys Town*. Bloomington, IN: Xlibris, 2006.

Salzberg, Ana. *Produced by Irving Thalberg: Theory of Studio-Era Filmmaking*. Edinburgh, Scotland: Edinburgh University Press, 2020.

Scarfone, Jay, and William Stillman. *The Road to Oz: The Evolution, Creation, and Legacy of a Motion Picture Masterpiece*. Lanham, MD: Lyons Press, 2018.

Schary, Dore. *Heyday: An Autobiography*. Boston: Little Brown & Company, 1979.

Schwartz, Nancy Lynn, with Sheila Schwartz. *The Hollywood Writers' Wars*. New York: Alfred A. Knopf, 1982.

Selznick, Irene Mayer. *A Private View*. London: Weidenfeld and Nicolson, 1983.

Spada, James. *The Secret Life of a Princess: An Intimate Biography of Grace Kelly*. New York: Doubleday & Company, 1987.

Swanson, Gloria. *Swanson on Swanson*. New York: Random House, 1980.

Temple Black, Shirley. *Child Star: An Autobiography*. New York: McGraw Hill Publishing Company, 1988.

Thomas Bob. *Thalberg: Life and Legend*. New York: Doubleday and Company, 1969.

Thomas, Lawrence B. *The MGM Years*. New York: Columbia House, 1971.

Thomas, Rhys. *The Ruby Slippers of Oz: Thirty Years Later*. Morrisview, NC: Lulu, 2018 (originally published in 1989).

Torgerson, Dial. *Kerkorian: An American Success Story*. New York: Dial Press, 1974.

Tougias, Michael, and Douglas A. Campbell. *Rescue of the Bounty: Disaster and Survival in Superstorm Sandy*. New York: Scribner, 2014.

Turner, Lana. *Lana: The Lady, the Legend, the Truth*. New York: E. P. Dutton, Inc., 1982.

Turner, Ted, and Bill Burke. *Call Me Ted*. New York: Grand Central Publishing, 2008.

Turner, Phillip, *MGM Cinemas: An Outline History*. The Brantwood Outline History Series. St. Paul's Cray, Kent, UK: Outline Publishers, 1998.

Urwand, Ben. *The Collaboration: Hollywood's Pact with Hitler*. Cambridge, MA: Belknap Press, 2013.

Vieira, Mark A. *Hollywood Dreams Made Real: Irving Thalberg and the Rise of M-G-M.* New York: Abrams, 2008.

———. *Irving Thalberg: Boy Wonder to Producer Prince.* Berkeley: University of California Press, 2009.

Watson, John V. *M-G-M Presents in CinemaScope: 1953–1954: The Seven Films Released by the Studio in the New Anamorphic System during 1953 and 1954.* Independently published, 2019.

Wayne, Jane Ellen. *The Golden Girls of MGM: Greta Garbo, Joan Crawford, Lana Turner, Judy Garland, Ava Gardner, Grace Kelly and Others.* New York: Carroll & Graf Publishers, 2004.

———. *The Golden Guys of MGM: Privilege, Power and Pain.* London: Chrysalis Books Group, 2004.

———. *The Leading Men of MGM.* Boston: Da Capo Press, 2006.

Weatherwax, Bob, and Richard Lester. *Four Feet to Fame—A Hollywood Dog Trainer's Journey.* Orlando: BearManor Media, 2017.

Welles, Orson, and Peter Bogdanovich. *This Is Orson Welles.* New York: HarperCollins, 1992.

Wellman, William A. *A Short Time for Insanity: An Autobiography.* New York: Hawthorn Books, Inc., 1974.

Williams, Esther, with Digby Diehl. *The Million Dollar Mermaid.* New York: Simon & Schuster, 1999.

Winkler, Irwin. *A Life in Movies: Stories from 50 Years in Hollywood.* New York: Harry N. Abrams, 2019.

Young, Jordan. *The Crowd: The Making of a Silent Classic (Past Times Film Close-up Series).* Orange, CA: Past Times Publishing Company, 2014.

Ziarko, Charles. *MGM: Saving the Best for Last: Dore Schary and the Death of MGM.* Independently published, 2013.

Zicree, Mark Scott. *The Twilight Zone Companion*, 3rd ed. Los Angeles: Silman-James Press, 2018 (originally published in 1982).

Zinnemann, Fred. *Fred Zinnemann: An Autobiography: A Life in the Movies*. New York: Charles Scribner's Sons, 1992.

BOOKS: NOVELS AND ESSAYS

Alcott, Kate. *A Touch of Stardust*. New York: Doubleday & Company, 2015.

Benedict, Marie. *The Only Woman in the Room*. Naperville, IL: Sourcebooks, 2019.

Benjamin, Melanie. *The Girls in the Picture: A Novel*. New York: Delacorte Press, 2018.

Bolton, Guy. *The Pictures*. Pittsburgh, PA: Point Blank, 2018.

Bond, Shelly, Kristy Miller, and Brian Miller. *Femme Magnifique: 50 Magnificent Women Who Changed the World*. San Diego: IDW Publishing, 2018.

Epstein, Joseph. *Essays in Biography*. Mont Jackson, VA: Axios Press, 2012.

Fitzgerald, F. Scott, *The Last Tycoon*. New York: Charles Scribner's Sons, 1941.

——. *The Pat Hobby Stories*. New York: Scribner, 1995 (originally published in 1940–1941).

Girard, Anne. *Platinum Doll*. Pittsburgh, PA: MIRA, 2016.

Graham, Carrol, and Garrett Graham. *Queer People*. New York: Vanguard Press, 1930.

Griffith, Bill. *Nobody's Fool: The Life and Times of Schlitzie the Pinhead*. New York: Abrams, 2019.

Harding, John W. *The Ben-Hur Murders: Inside the 1925 Hollywood Games*. Maryland: Pulp Hero Press, 2019.

Huxley, Aldous. *Ape and Essence*. New York: Harper & Brothers, 1948.

Kaminsky, Stuart. *Murder on the Yellow Brick Road*. New York: Pocket Books, 1977.

——. *You Bet Your Life*. New York: Pocket Books, 1978.

Kanin, Garson. *Moviola*. New York: Simon & Schuster, 1979.

Koslow, Sally. *Another Side of Paradise*. New York: HarperCollins, 2018.

Letts, Elizabeth. *Finding Dorothy*. New York: Ballantine Books, 2019.

Lewis, Arthur H. *It Was Fun While It Lasted*. New York: Trident Press, 1973.

Meissner, Susan. *Stars over Sunset Boulevard*. New York: New American Library, 2016.

McCoy, Horace. *They Shoot Horses, Don't They?* New York: Simon & Schuster, 1935.

O'Nan, Stewart. *West of Sunset*. New York: Penguin Books, 2015.

Porter, Margaret. *Beautiful Invention: A Novel of Hedy Lamarr*. Concord, NH: Gallica Press, 2018.

Puma, Fernando, ed. *7 Arts Number Three*. Indian Hills, CO: Falcon's Wing Press, 1955.

Robbins, Trina. *Hedy Lamarr and a Secret Communications System*. Mankato, MN: Capstone Press, 2006.

Salinger, J. D. *The Catcher in the Rye*. New York: Little Brown & Company, 1951.

Saroyan, William. *Letters from 74 Rue Taitbout or Don't Go But If You Must Say Hello to Everybody*. New York: World Publishing Company, 1969.

Schulberg, Bud. *What Makes Sammy Run?* New York: Random House, 1941.

Trigiani, Adriana. *All the Stars in the Heavens: A Novel*. New York: HarperCollins, 2015.

Turnbull, Martin. *The Garden on Sunset: A Novel of Golden-Era Hollywood (Hollywood's Garden of Allah Novels, Book 1)*. Los Angeles: Rothesay Press, 2012.

——. *The Trouble with Scarlett: A Novel of Golden-Era Hollywood (Hollywood's Garden of Allah Novels, Book 2)*. Los Angeles: Rothesay Press, 2012.

——. *Citizen Hollywood: A Novel of Golden-Era Hollywood (Hollywood's Garden of Allah Novels, Book 3)*. Los Angeles: Rothesay Press, 2014.

——. *Searchlights and Shadows: A Novel of Golden-Era Hollywood (Hollywood's Garden of Allah Novels, Book 4)*. Los Angeles: Rothesay Press, 2015.

——. *Reds in the Beds: A Novel of Golden-Era Hollywood (Hollywood's Garden of Allah Novels, Book 5)*. Los Angeles: Rothesay Press, 2016.

——. *Twisted Boulevard: A Novel of Golden-Era Hollywood (Hollywood's Garden of Allah Novels, Book 6)*. Los Angeles: Rothesay Press, 2016.

——. *Tinseltown Confidential: A Novel of Golden-Era Hollywood (Hollywood's Garden of Allah Novels, Book 7)*. Los Angeles: Rothesay Press, 2017.

——. *City of Myths: A Novel of Golden-Era Hollywood (Hollywood's Garden of Allah Novels, Book 8)*. Los Angeles: Rothesay Press, 2018.

——. *Closing Credits: A Novel of Golden-Era Hollywood (Hollywood's Garden of Allah Novels, Book 9)*. Los Angeles: Rothesay Press, 2018.

——. *The Heart of the Lion: A Novel of Irving Thalberg's Hollywood*. Los Angeles: Rothesay Press, 2020.

Walker, Woodrow W. *Murder at MGM*. Tucson: Pagan Moon Productions, 2016.

Wallmark, Laurie. *Hedy Lamarr's Double Life: Hollywood Legend and Brilliant Inventor*. New York: Sterling Children's Books, 2019.

West, Nathaniel, *The Day of the Locust*. New York: Random House, 1939.

Zettel, Sarah. *Golden Girl*. New York: Random House, 2013.

ARTICLES

Bart, Peter. "Enigmatic Krikorian and MGM Were Never a Good Fit." *Weekly Variety*. June 22, 2015.

——. "Sometimes a Roaring Silence Is Best." *Weekly Variety*. April 9, 2013.

——. "MGM's Cooper-Kerkorian Conundrum." *Daily Variety*. August 24, 2009.

"Ben Melniker Ranking Metro Exec in N.Y. after Transfer to Coast: Some Staffers Prefer Eastern Smog." *Weekly Variety*. May 6, 1970.

"Blown Away." *High Score*. December 1995.

Brennan, Judy. "MGM out, Sony in at Filmland." *Daily Variety*. November 15, 1992.

——. "CAA Prods Bank to Feed Its Pet Lion." *Weekly Variety*. April 19, 1993.

Burbank, Jeff. "Culver City Planning Panel Asks MGM to Scale Down Historic Sign." *Los Angeles Times*. March 1, 1987.

Burlingame, John. "Lion First to Launch Own Diskery." *Daily Variety*. November 19, 1999.

Canby, Vincent. "Study of William Wyler Includes Documentary." *New York Times*. September 20, 1986.

Cerra, Julie Lugo, "Was the Big MGM Sign Considered Historic and Where Is It Now?" *The Culver City News*. June 20, 2002.

Cox, Gordon, and David Rooney. "B'way Opens Screen Door." *Weekly Variety*. September 12, 2005.

——. "H'wood and Broadway's Love-Hate Relationship." *Weekly Variety*. September 12, 2005.

Cumberbatch, Benedict. "Tom Hiddleston." *Interview*. September 24, 2016.

Dawtrey, Adam. "Lion King's New World View." *Daily Variety*. December 1, 2005.

Delugach, Al. "Lorimar Signs Pact to Acquire MGM Studio." *Los Angeles Times*. September 9, 1986.

Devere, Ed. "MGM Land Use Crucial to Culver." *Los Angeles Times*. May 18, 1967.

Dreyfuss, John. "MGM Buys Tract at Thousand Oaks." *Los Angeles Times*. August 30, 1967.

Faughnder, Ryan, and Wendy Lee. "Why Amazon Buying MGM Is a Watershed Moment for Hollywood and Tech." *Los Angeles Times*. May 26, 2021.

Friendly, David T. "Leo Roars His Last at the Old MGM Stand." *Los Angeles Times*. November 13, 1986.

Fuchs, Andreas. "And Now for Our Feature Presentation . . ." *The Hollywood Reporter*. March 22, 2004.

Gottlieb, Jeff. "Long-Running Engagement Coming to an End at MGM." *Los Angeles Times*. October 9, 1986.

Graham, Sheilah. "Confessions of Leo the Lion." *Photoplay*. June 1949.

Harwood, Jim. "Just What Has Kerkorian Sold? MGM's Not What It Used to Be." *Weekly Variety*. July 19, 1988.

Hlavacek, Peter. "Kerkorian Guarding Leo." *Weekly Variety*. February 7, 1990.

Hofler, Robert. "Lion Goes Legit." *Weekly Variety*. April 9, 2004.

Hogan, David J. "MGM: When the Lion Roars." *Filmfax*. Number 36, December/January 1993/1994.

Hughes, John. "War Among the Lion Tamers." *Fortune*. August 1957.

"I Love *The Women* . . .". *House Beautiful*. November 2004.

Jacobs, Frank, with illustrations by Mort Drucker. "What's Entertainment?" *Mad*, Number 175. June 1975.

Justin, Neal. "Why Jessica Lange Is Minnesota's Greatest Actor." *The (Minneapolis) Star Tribune*. March 2, 2017.

Kael, Pauline. "Trash Art in the Cinema." *Harpers*. February 1969.

"Kerkorian: The Man vs. the Myths." *Weekly Variety*. March 14, 1990.

Kilday, Gregg. "Beyond Nine Lives." *Daily Variety*. February 18, 2000.

Lang, Brent, and Todd Spangler. "Amazon Buys MGM, Studio Behind James Bond, for $8.45 Billion." *Daily Variety*. May 26, 2021.

"The Lion and the Cobra." *Time*. November 12, 1973.

Maloney, Russell, "The Wizard of Hollywood." *The New Yorker*. August 12, 1939.

McClintick, David, with Anne Faircloth. "The Predator, How an Italian Thug Looted MGM, Brought Crèdit Lyonnais to Its Knees, and Made the Pope Cry." *Fortune*. July 8, 1996.

"Metro-Goldwyn-Mayer." *Fortune*. December 1932.

"MGM Lionizes Versatile New Video Tape System." *Sponsor*. October 12, 1964.

"MGM Quietly Conducting Tours of Lot Since May." *The Hollywood Reporter*. September 3, 1964.

Morse, Leon. "MGM Theater of the Air." *Billboard*. October 22, 1949.

Murphy, A. D. "MGM Records in Six Years Lost $21,885,000 Tho Sales $121 Mil." *Daily Variety*. August 28, 1972.

"NY Times' Bosley Crowther Discusses 'What You Don't Know About the Movies.'" *New York Times*. February 6, 1948.

"Paul Mills Last to Go." *Daily Variety*. October 26, 1970.

Phillips, Brandon. "Creating $ in Its Own Image." *Daily Variety*. February 14, 2000.

Picker, David, "All in the Family: A Studio Veteran Waxes Nostalgic About Being Inside the Lion's Den." *Weekly Variety*. April 19, 2004.

"Playboy Interview: Donald Trump." *Playboy*. March 1990.

Potempa, Philip. "Las Vegas MGM Hotel and Casino Losing Trademark 'Live' Lions." *Times of Northwest Indiana*. January 5, 2012.

Richard, Kevin. "It's Official: New Biloxi Ballpark to Be MGM Park." *Ballpark Digest*. September 24, 2014.

Riedel, Michael. "The Lion that Ruled 42nd Street." *Vanity Fair*. September 2020.

"Screen Genius' Death Stuns Industry's Heads." *Los Angeles Times*. September 15, 1936.

Silver, Alain. "Mr. Film Noir Stays at the Table." *Film Comment*. Volume 8, number 1. Spring 1972.

Stalter, Katharine. "MGM Plans Pilots for Net." *Daily Variety*. December 3, 1996.

Stenn, David. "It Happened One Night . . . at MGM." *Vanity Fair*. April 2003.

Svetkey, Benjamin. "'The Tonight Show's Greenroom at 30,000 Feet:' The Last Debauched Flight of the MGM Grand Airline." *The Hollywood Reporter*. October 1, 2015.

Thomas, Rhys. "The Ruby Slippers: A Journey to the Land of Oz." *Los Angeles Times*. March 13, 1988.

Thompson, David. "The House that Mr. Mayer Built: Inside the Union-Busting Birth of the Academy Awards." *Vanity Fair*. February 21, 2014.

"Trust Everyone, but Cut the Cards." *Fortune*. August 1939.

"UA Started with Artists in Lead Role." *The Hollywood Reporter*. November 3, 2006.

Vincent, Roger, and Claudia Eller. "MGM to Move from Luxurious Century City Offices." *Los Angeles Times*. December 30, 2010.

Webb, Michael. "Cedric Gibbons and the MGM Style." *Architectural Digest*. April 1990.

Welkos, Robert W. "The Case of the Missing Mansion: OK, OK, 'Gone with the Wind' Fans, We Know Twelve Oaks Is a Memory, But Tara's in Georgia, in Pieces—We Think." *Los Angeles Times*. February 27, 1994.

BIBLIOGRAPHY

MOVIES AND HOME-VIDEO SPECIAL CONTENT

An American in Paris (PBS-produced documentary on DVD)

Ben-Hur (documentary on DVD)

Buster Keaton Rides Again (1965 documentary)

Echo in the Canyon (2018 documentary)

Girl 27 (2007 documentary)

The Founder (2016 feature film)

Meet Me in Saint Louis (DVD special features include *Hollywood: The Dream Factory*)

MGM: When the Lion Roars (1992 documentary miniseries)

That's Entertainment! The Complete Collection (documentaries on DVD)

WEBSITES

MGM: https://MGM.com.

MGM Resorts: https://www.mgmresorts.com/en.html.

Culver City: https://www.culvercity.org.

Karina Longworth's podcast: www.youmustrememberthispodcast.com.

The Film Colony, with Alicia Mayer: https://hollywoodessays.com/.

MGM Grand Airlines history: https://simpleflying.com/mgm-grand-air/.

MGM Grand Adventure Theme Park history: https://themeparkuniversity.com/extinct-at tractions/mgm-grand-adventures-part-1-lost-in-the- shuffle/.

MGM Grand Adventure Theme Park video: https://www.youtube.com/watch?v=2KrtHut-vdb4.

Site dedicated to Disney parks: https://yesterland.com.

Site dedicated to America's sports stadiums: https://www.stadiumjourney.com.

Article by Bill DeYoung on the fate of the HMS *Bounty*: https://stpetecatalyst.com/vintage-st-pete-behind-the-scenes-at-mgms-good-ship-bounty/.

BIBLIOGRAPHY

Ruby slippers press conference: http://www.youtube.com/watch?v=JB6K1PHb5t-M&sns=em.

John McElwee's definitive classic-age Hollywood site: https://greenbriarpictureshows.blogspot.com.

Scott Brogan's all-encompassing Judy Garland site: https://www.thejudyroom.com.

Sharon Rich's comprehensive Jeanette MacDonald and Nelson Eddy site: https://maceddy.com.

Gary Wayne's all-purpose, all-encompassing Hollywood site: https://www.seeing-stars.com.

Steve Martin's animal actor site: https://workingwildlife.com.

The Viking (Spokane, Washington) with Mickey Rooney's picture in it!: https://spokane-viking.org.

INTERVIEWS

Conducted by the author in person, via conference call, or email.

David Bowen (October 2020)

John Escobar (April 2021)

Rob Feeney (April 2021)

Greg Gormick (July 2020)

Rob Klein (September 2020)

Steve Martin (June 2021)

Richard Adkins-Matukonis (March 2021)

Alicia Mayer (December 2020)

Roger Mayer (2010)

Donnie Norden (February 2021)

Les Perkins (February 2021)

Sharon Rich (May 2021)

Stephen X. Sylvester (May 2021)

Karl Thiede (May 2021)

Nicholas Toth (June 2021)

Martin Turnbull (October 2020)

Charles Ziarko (February 2021)

Index

Page references for figures are italicized.